WOODEN BOATS

John Scarlett

WOODEN BOAT REPAIR MANUAL

 INTERNATIONAL MARINE PUBLISHING COMPANY
CAMDEN, MAINE

Library of Congress Catalog Card Number 81 – 80232
International Standard Book Number 0 – 87742 – 143 – 9
Published simultaneously in Great Britain
by David & Charles (Publishers) Limited

Published by International Marine Publishing Company
21 Elm Street, Camden, Maine 04843

Contents

Introduction

The great increase in interest in sailing over the past two decades has coincided with a decrease in the number of small boatyards where one could find friendly, skilled shipwrights who would repair wooden boats for quite reasonable prices, and who would advise those owners who could not afford even those low prices on how best to tackle the work themselves.

Now the scene has changed, and only the fairly wealthy can afford to pay for major repairs to their wooden boats. Quite repairable boats are being written off because the cost of professional repairs is more than the boat would be worth. At the same time, an increasing number of owners are discovering that a wooden hull does have a lot of advantages over fibreglass or ferrocement, even if only that a tide-table can be attached over the chart table with a drawing pin! Some owners are able to find old-style boatyards where they can get helpful advice, others join clubs or groups and are helped by members who have already tackled similar repair jobs on their own boats. However, there are still many would-be owners of wooden boats who are put off by what they imagine are the difficulties and expense of repair work needed on the boat they would like to own.

Since he and some friends founded the Old Gaffers Association some seventeen years ago, the author has been engaged in what at times seems to be almost continuous correspondence on the subject of boat repairs. A pretty fair sub-title for this book would be 'From Letters to OGA Members and Friends', since much of the material is rewritten from notes made when answering the many queries received on how best repairs to an old boat can be tackled.

No claims are made that this book covers all aspects of work on wooden boats, or that all reasonable methods of making repairs are described; but one claim which can be made is that every technique described has been used on a successful repair job, either by the author, by other owners in the Essex boatyard which for some fifteen or more years was almost his second home, or by members of the Old Gaffers Association.

All the work described has been carried out by amateurs, most of whom have had no more formal training in woodwork than used to be offered at the average secondary or evening school (some did not even have that), and this book is offered to readers in the hope that it may encourage them to undertake for themselves repairs which they may have felt were beyond their capacities.

Apologies are offered for the inconsistencies in the sketches which clarify the text. They are mainly copies of sketches made at various times to illustrate points in the author's correspondence. A few are to scale for a particular boat, some are more or less in proportion, but the majority make no pretence of being to any scale or proportion; they are merely more or less representative sketches. Unless specifically stated, cross-hatching is not intended to show the direction of the grain of a piece of wood. Apologies are also offered for a certain vagueness in dimensions. It is impossible to be precise when the boats covered range from 2 m (6 ft) long to over 18 m (60 ft). Since the work described is repair work, there should be enough original timber around to give adequate guidance on appropriate sizes! Generally, the 'average' boat considered is a sea-going sailing cruiser of about 7 tonnes (tons).

Inevitably in a book of this nature there must be some duplication of what has already been written by authors such as John Leather and others, but as far as possible any such duplication has been kept to the minimum necessary for clarity.

Although financial necessity is often the spur which drives owners to repair or restore old wooden boats, the author has found that such necessity can be outweighed by a very real pleasure in working with one of nature's most prolific and versatile building materials, and in admiring and attempting to copy the true craftsmanship of those who built wooden sailing boats. The reader is left to determine for himself whether the use of the word 'craftsmanship' is intended as a deliberate pun.

Part one

Preparations

Chapter 1

Preliminary considerations

Qualifications

Anybody who can saw a piece of wood to a line and can plane or chisel the piece to make it fit against another piece can do the work involved in repairing an old wooden-hulled boat, but before attempting to start major repairs on an old boat there are two other important qualifications which must be met. One is a genuine interest in boats coupled with at least a basic knowledge of the principles of their construction; the other is the availability of a substantial amount of spare time. A modicum of patience is helpful – the author never had enough of that!

In fact it is probably true to say that the only initial qualifications required are interest, time and patience. Woodworking skills can be acquired in time, and essential tools can be bought, borrowed, or made as and when required. Knowledge of the fundamentals of boat construction can be acquired in any good library. But since the necessary acquisition of skill and knowledge does take time, it requires the driving force of genuine interest coupled with the patience to try, try, and try again.

Without adequate spare time there is little point in attempting any major repairs on a wooden boat. Boats have a nasty habit of deteriorating if they are not properly looked after, and and it is far from unknown for an over-enthusiastic owner to haul a boat ashore and strip off half the deck, only to discover that the proposed repair is going to take very much longer than he had thought, with the result that the repair and restoration work does not even keep pace with general deterioration. The end result of this is usually that a boat which could have been repaired by someone with sufficient spare time ends up as a nice hot bonfire. Alternatively, the unfortunate owner may find he has to sell off his boat at a very much lower price than he could have got for it before he started the repair work. It is quite impossible to quote specific times for any work on boats, but broadly speaking it is inadvisable for anybody who cannot spare the whole of most weekends over a period of months to start on any major repair on a boat of any size.

Experience is the best teacher, and any novice contemplating serious work on wooden boats would be well advised to spend a winter or two helping other more experienced owners with theirs. Any owner who has started a major repair job will probably be delighted to have the free services of an unpaid apprentice and, provided that the mentor's instructions are properly heeded and the learner never overestimates his skill or knowledge, not much can go wrong. In the early stages, the help accepted may well be confined to heavy lifting, hammering etc; to some of the dirtier, more tedious jobs like cleaning out bilges and chipping and painting the various crude lumps of rusty iron which tend to clutter the bilges of older boats (it is left to the reader to decide whether or not this includes the engine!); and to the making of tea and generally attending to the creature comforts of the skilled worker/owner. Relegation to such menial tasks should not deter the learner. If he is willing and able to tackle the more skilled work, any normal owner will soon discover the learner's capabilities and make the best possible use of the skills and efforts available.

At this point one warning must be given. Avoid the temptation of overmuch discussion whilst working. It is very easy for two workers to lose so much time talking about the job that less work is done in a day than one person on his own would have done. There is usually time for a chat about the work over a pint or two in a nearby hostelry after the work has been done. Some owners with several years' experience of large repair projects prefer to work single-handed because they have been caught out too many times by so-called helpers who either spend far too long discussing each job, or who expect to spend most of the day drinking in the nearest pub at the owner's expense.

After a period of helping others at work, the learner can tackle a job on his own boat. Some may suggest that it is best to start with small repairs on dinghies and small boats, and work up to larger craft gradually. There is a measure of sense in this, in that all the pieces of a small boat are that much lighter and cheaper; but against this is the fact that work on larger boats is often very much less precise than that required on dinghies so that in many ways it is considerably easier to learn skills on larger craft.

Tools and stock

Another preliminary which must be settled is the question of a toolkit. Several books on boat ownership and cruising have published lists of toolkits regarded by their authors as being essential for the maintenance of a boat, but in over a quarter of a century of repairing boats of all types and building a carvel-hulled four-tonner with hollow mast, this author has never possessed anything like these 'minimum essential toolkits', so it is not proposed to publish such a list here. Clearly, some tools for sawing wood and metal will be needed, as will a plane, a chisel, some means of drilling holes and a hammer. Screwdrivers, wrenches, spanners and so forth will also be needed, and on carvel-hulled craft a caulking iron or two is necessary. Other more specialised tools can usually be borrowed or even made as required, and a little bit of ingenuity (plus the ever-essential time) will often avoid the need for an expensive tool. Many authors appear to regard mastery of the adze and drawknife as prime essentials for any work on boats. This author has so far managed to avoid ever having to use either of these rather terrifying weapons.

When tools are being bought for work on boats, avoid any which are offered especially for home handymen, particularly the nicely boxed small electrically driven tools. They are seldom man enough for the work required. In the boatyard in which the author did most of his work on boats, the yard's portable drill and electric sander were massive tools, but it was far from unknown for even those gargantuan tools to stall, especially in drilling for keelbolts etc. The circular saw had multiple vee-belt drive from a 5 hp three-phase motor, and if skilled professionals need that amount of power, so will the amateur who is working on a full-sized boat. In fact the skilled man can usually manage with less powerful tools than the amateur.

Another point to be considered is that boats are often found in close proximity to sea water, and sea water is not exactly the best of lubricants for hand-held electric tools. The author found that he could cut seasoned oak 25 mm (1 in) thick with a handsaw in less than a quarter of the time it took on a popular 'home handyman's' tool which was advertised as being capable of such work – and he did not have to pay out for having the handsaw rewound!

Anybody who is contemplating repairing wooden boats is advised to make the earliest possible start on the acquisition of suitable timber and a 'junk box' of handy items such as bronze bolts etc. Some timbers tend to dry out excessively over long periods of time and may become somewhat short-grained and brittle, but pine, cedar, teak, mahogany and the various teak-like timbers such as afrormosia and iroko can be hoarded indefinitely. The stem-facing on the author's four-tonner was cut from a piece of teak known to be over ninety years old, and some of his present stock of pine and larch is from a house built in the 1840s. Oak crooks – corners of thick branches in which the grain makes a well defined bend – and hardwood planks in which the grain pattern follows a fairly regular curve, are especially valuable to the boat repairer.

Economics

Boat repairing should not be attempted by

accountancy-minded types who like to cost out their time with a record of incidental expenses, and expect to see an end product whose value matches the outlay. If one allows for an hour or two driving to and from the boat, and all the costs such as assuaging the thirst which always seem to be associated with matters nautical, plus the costs of tools, materials and time spent, the whole project will inevitably be utterly uneconomic, and the cost-effective solution is to charter a boat for sailing holidays. However, if one looks on boat-repair work as a pleasant task mainly enjoyed in fresh air, offering the benefits of the very real satisfaction of a job well done at the end, plus a small extra bonus of an increase in the value of one's boat and the savings of the costs of paid labour, it can be one of the most rewarding of hobbies.

The words 'mainly enjoyed in fresh air' are worthy of further comment. There will inevitably be times when the would-be worker will be somewhat frustrated by what may be termed over-freshness of the air. An understandable desire to spend spare time on sailing in the summer months tends to concentrate work on boats to late autumn, winter and early spring. Cold weather can be combated by hard work, warm clothing and frequent doses of hot soup, cocoa or strong tea (coffee never seems quite so warming); but whether trying to work huddled under a tarpaulin in a steady, penetrating drizzle, probably wearing boots into which muddy water from an unexpectedly deep pool in the saltings has overflowed, should be classed as enjoying a hobby in the fresh air may be questioned. However, the satisfaction at the completion of the job, and the pleasure of relaxing in the warmth of a local pub in the company of other boat-minded people at the end of the day cannot be questioned.

Site

The choice of site for work on a wooden boat depends on a number of factors, the most critical of which are the size and type of the boat, the nature of the work to be done, the facilities available at the owner's home, travelling requirements, and working facilities needed such as access to heavy duty power saws etc. There can be no doubt whatsoever that the best place to work on any boat is a traditional small boatyard where skilled shipwrights can give advice and be employed to tackle any jobs beyond the skill or strength of the owner, and where heavy sawing etc can be done at short notice and at a fair price. Unfortunately there are now far too few such boatyards, and those owners lucky enough to keep their boats in one of them should have no need for a book such as this.

When considering where to do the work, boats can be divided into three categories: dinghies and small boats which can be carried by two or three adults, small cruisers which can be lifted out of the water and transported by lorry or trailer without undue difficulty, and larger cruisers which must be worked on more or less where they are normally sailed.

Dinghies can be worked on wherever convenient, so require little consideration here. Large cruisers leave few options open, so it is the middle category of small cruisers of up to perhaps 5 or 6 tonnes (tons) weight which requires the most careful consideration. Most recognised sailing centres have some facility available by which a small cruiser can be lifted out of the water and onto a lorry or trailer, and factories, mills, timber merchants etc with waterside premises may be prepared to offer the hire of a suitable mobile or fixed crane for a lift. Usually the owner will have to accept full liability whenever such facilities are used. If the boat can be lifted or floated onto a trailer or lorry, the owner will have a free choice of working site. The most likely choice will be in the owner's garden – but this is where problems may arise. Can the lorry be backed into the chosen site? Is there space to store the boat with free access for working all round? Can adequate facilities be provided to lift, slide or roll the boat off a lorry? If the boat is to be lifted off, can the lorry carrying the boat and a suitable mobile crane both get onto the site and, equally important, can they leave the site when the boat is off-loaded? A lorry can be driven out from beneath the hull when the boat is lifted by a crane, but it could be possible that when the boat is lowered to the ground the crane will be trapped on the site.

If the chosen workplace is in an owner's garden, it may be possible to arrange access for a crane through a neighbour's driveway, probably at the cost of removing some fencing or a well established hedge. It is up to the owner to decide whether he cares more for the boat or the garden in such cases. It is important to get the goodwill of neighbours, and to consider the effects of work in a garden on them. A wooden hull makes a splendid resonant cavity (as anyone who has moored near a boat with a metal mast and unfrapped halliards will know), and any hammering and banging is likely to cause some disturbance to near (and even not so near) neighbours.

The size of site available also requires careful consideration. Not only must it accommodate the boat, with possibly extra room all round for a working staging; it must also allow space for large and heavy pieces of timber to be moved around the boat. A rough rule of thumb is twice the length of the boat and twice the width. The length can be shortened a little, but if any full-length planks or stringers are to be replaced, thought must be given as to how the timber will be moved from one side of the boat to another. Space for such manoeuvring can be obtained by occasional access over a lawn, rosebed or vegetable garden, or even by passing one end of the plank through a lounge window (remembering to open the window first and remove any fragile ornaments likely to be caught by the end of the plank as it waves about). Even with provision of such 'occasional access', the actual length of working site needed will be more than one and a half times the hull length.

Usually considerations of location, size, access and availability will determine the working site, but it may happen that these allow of several possibilities, in which case other determining factors arise. The availability of a building for storage and for working on small parts of the boat would be a worthwhile bonus on any site, as would the availability of a cover over the boat (eg a Dutch barn). The nature of the ground on which the boat will stand should also be considered. Smooth concrete may appear ideal, but it is not. Some concreted yards will not take the weight of a medium sized cruising yacht without cracking but, far worse, whenever the sun shines the concrete will reflect the heat up and will dry out the hull unmercifully. Hard-packed earth is the best standing ground for a boat, and a modicum of vegetation on the site will help to keep the air around the boat humid. Obviously a site which will flood or become waterlogged in wet weather should be avoided if at all possible.

One other point which must, alas, be considered is the security of the site. A boat under repair can be a tempting target for vandalism, and if the general public and especially schoolchildren have access to the chosen site, great care must be taken to avoid any risk of accident.

A boat which is too large to be moved to a convenient site near the owner's home will have to be worked on at or near the normal sailing area. If the work to be done includes major repairs to the hull structure below the waterline, then the best place will undoubtedly be a proper boatyard with a slipway or lifting facilities. The time out of the water (and hence the cost) can be minimised by planning the work very carefully and having everything possible prepared before the boat is taken out of the water. However, it is as well to remember that it is not uncommon to find, when the boat is out of the water, that more work is needed than was anticipated.

If the work below the waterline is all around the turn of the bilge, it may be possible to do it all with the boat careened over in a mud berth or at the head of a beach. In areas which have a good range of tide, extensive work on the hull below the waterline can be done with the boat secured on a hard standing at the highest point which can be reached at the top of a spring tide. This may well allow a week over neap tides when the water will not even reach the hull. Most owners are naturally hesitant about doing major work on the hull of a boat between tides, but many of the worries about such work are groundless. If the work (eg replacing planks) cannot be completed over one lot of neap tides, the boat will come to no harm if she is left with planks out so that she fills with sea water on the spring tides. Many older boats sailing today have spent months or even years submerged in sea water with no adverse effect. Obviously anything in the boat which could be affected by the sea water must be removed, and if the engine cannot be taken out arrangements must be made to ensure that it is not harmed by its immersion.

Not quite so obviously, adequate facilities must be provided to let the water out of the hull as the tide goes down, otherwise the weight of water left in the hull by the receding tide will be trying to force the planks away from the frames. The precautions to be taken to let water out will depend on the hull shape. A 'wineglass' hull with a deep, narrow keel will not hold much weight of water in the keel portion, and the removal of a toilet or engine seacock will suffice, whereas a full-bodied, flat-floored hull will contain a much greater weight for the same depth of flooding and it may well be desirable to remove a plank to let out the water.

A hard sand or shingle beach or harbour bed will provide a better working site than a mud berth in as much as access to the boat will be easier and cleaner, and any dropped tools will be easier to find. On the other hand, if the work is above the water-line, a mud berth will keep the hull of the boat fully supported and free from all risk of falling over.

The choice of working site for a larger boat will be influenced by the area in which the boat sails, the nature of the work to be done, and the owner's finances, and it is seldom possible to consider an ideal working site. Occasionally though, an owner lives aboard his boat and his employment makes it possible for him to sail the boat to what seems to be the best possible working place. But it is advisable to check very thoroughly that the proposed site is as good as it appears. As with many other aspects of life, the grass often looks greener on the other side of the fence, and it can be frustrating to say the least to make a major move to a new area only to discover that whilst the new site makes some aspects of the work easier it makes others substantially more difficult.

Chapter 2

Lightening the boat

If a boat is to be taken ashore for any period of time, the first thing is to take as much weight as possible out of the hull, preferably whilst the boat is still afloat. The removal of the mast and all standing and running rigging will not only eliminate the need to move a quite significant weight, it will also lower the centre of gravity and make handling the hull much easier.

Removing the engine

If the boat has an inboard engine, it may be better to leave this in place. All other items found in the average cruising yacht can be manhandled, but a crane or hoist will usually be needed to lift the engine clear. Also, if the engine is removed, there can be problems in lining it up again when the boat is refitted. Against these arguments for not removing the engine are the facts that it is probably the heaviest removable item in the hull, any work necessary on the engine will be very much easier if it is out of the hull, and if major repairs to the frames or planking are to be undertaken, the engine may have to be removed anyway.

Whilst the removal of a heavy engine is not a task to be undertaken too lightly, it is not at all impossible for the average owner to undertake on his own. As with getting the hull ashore, the task is simplified if all removable bits and pieces are taken off first. Some owners even go so far as to remove the cylinder head and sump casing before lifting out the main body of the engine. Whether this is desirable or necessary will depend on the work contemplated on the engine and also on the lifting facilities possible. If a substantial quayside crane is available, it is usually easiest to remove the entire engine unit in one lift, but if 'do it yourself' facilities are to be used, partial stripping in situ may be better.

On some boats it may be necessary to remove some of the doghouse or cockpit joinery work before the engine can be lifted out, and it may even be necessary to do a partial lift first and to move the engine aft in order to get it into position for a clear lift out. Obviously, when a heavy weight like an engine is to be lifted out of a hull, every care must be taken to ensure that all slings and chains used are properly secured and that all the tackle used is strong enough for the job. It is advisable to take professional advice on these points. The average engine falling into the hull from deck height will add significantly to the number of planks and frames to be replaced.

If no quayside crane is available, the boat's own gear can be used to lift out the engine. A sailing boat has the makings of a first-class derrick in the mast and boom. If the mast is strong enough and well stayed, but the boom is judged to be too flimsy, a more substantial spar might be borrowed from another boat. The topping lift is unlikely to be strong enough to support the weight of the engine, but the halliards should provide adequate strength, especially on gaff-rigged craft where both peak and throat halliards can be used to support the boom at the required height, with the halliards carefully adjusted to take equal strain.

For the actual lift of the engine, the best equipment to use is one of the portable rope or chain controlled geared hoists, which can be shackled on to the end of the boom; but if such a hoist is not available, other items of boats' gear can be used. The mainsheet on most older cruising yachts can provide a very useful purchase, and if this is insufficient, a deck tackle can be clapped onto the fall. On some boats it may be possible to take a clear lead from the boom end forward to the anchor winch.

Before any attempt is made to lift the engine, the boom must be adequately stayed to restrict any sideways movement, and a thorough check must be made to ensure that all gear and fittings used are sound and strong enough for the job. The boom can be side-stayed by securing the middle of a rope around the boom at its outer end with a rolling hitch, and making the ends fast to suitable strong points such as running back-stay chainplates. Fittings such as jib-sheet cleats should not be used, as they are intended to resist a pull from forward, not an upward strain. Obviously, the rolling hitch on the boom is made so that the two ends leave the hitch on the upper side of the boom. Alternatively, a pair of jib sheets can be shackled onto the boom-end fitting and led through suitable chainplates, or even through their normal fairleads (but note that the lead must be from the aft, not foreside, of the fairleads). It is a wise precaution to supplement any shackles or sister hooks used to secure the purchases to the boom end with flexible wire strops passed right round from block to block, bypassing the eyes on the boom-end fitting, the ends of the wire strop being secured with bulldog clips. Such a wire strop does not need to be hauled tight, as it is there to take the strain only if a shackle or the boom-end fitting fails.

The actual lift should be made with the tackle between the boom-end and the engine. If this tackle cannot provide sufficient lift, the purchase from the mast to boom-end can be used once the engine is clear of its bearers. When this is done, the side-stays will have to be eased off to allow the boom to lift, which is best done by having a couple of helpers who can ease off the stays through whatever strong points they have been led to.

A further safety precaution is to have handy a pair of stout wooden struts which can be inserted beneath the engine as it is lifted so as to restrict the distance it can fall in the case of any mishap. Thus the lift would be made in stages, first clear of the bearers and onto struts across the bearers, then to cockpit thwart level, and finally clear of the cockpit coamings and ready for swinging ashore.

Care must be exercised when a weight like an engine is swung ashore from the boom-end. If the boat is afloat or in a soft mud berth, she will heel over as the weight is moved out over the side, and if the person easing off the stay on the side away from the quay is not prepared, the heel can accelerate the sideways movement of the boom and engine, possibly with catastrophic consequences. Two or three willing helpers can make the removal of an engine a fairly simple, pleasant task, but with forethought and care the job can be done by one person without overmuch physical exertion, provided he takes his time over it.

One obvious point which can easily be overlooked when preparing to remove an engine is to ensure that all connections to the engine have been undone before the lift is started. Failure to undo the shaft coupling will be obvious – the engine will not lift. The exhaust flange is usually equally obvious, and will generally include the outlet for the cooling water. The water and fuel inlets to the engine should be flexible enough not to offer obvious interference as the lift is started, but any electrical connections which should have been undone may well not be apparent until there is a momentary pause in the lift followed by a jerk as the connection or the insulator to which it is attached breaks.

If for any reason the boat's mast and boom cannot be used, a pair of sheer-legs can be rigged out of two stout spars. The legs can either be rigged upright over the engine to provide a straight lift onto bearers inserted across the cockpit coamings as the engine is lifted, or the legs can be rigged with their heels resting against and secured to the main chainplates, with a stay from the top of the legs to the forestay fitting (Fig 1). With such an arrangement, the engine can be lifted and then swung forward to rest on the cabin top whilst the legs are transferred to another position ready to swing it ashore. Whenever angled sheer-legs are used to swing a load to a new position, it is preferable to arrange that the load always stays the same side of the base of the legs. A load can be swung right through between the legs, but when this is done the strain of holding the legs up transfers from

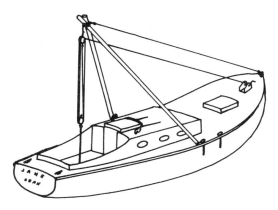

Fig 1   *Sheer-legs rigged to hoist out an engine*

the stay on one side to that on the other side as the legs pass through the vertical position, and if the movement of the legs through the vertical is not very carefully controlled the load can take charge as the need to haul in on one stay is abruptly changed to a need to ease away handsomely on the other which, until the legs reach the vertical position, has been taking no strain. Keeping the load the same side of the legs at all times ensures that the strains in the stays are constant in direction, and eliminates any risk of the heels of the legs kicking back as the load changes sides.

Removing the mast

How easy it will be to remove the mast depends on how the mast is stepped. A tabernacle-stepped mast is easy – it has only to be lowered to horizontal and the bolt taken out. If the owner has never lowered the mast and is not sure of the best way to do it, then the procedure for lowering a keel-stepped mast from vertical to horizontal can be followed. One point which must be watched is that it is not unknown for coachroofs to be added or rebuilt, or for skylights to be fitted so that the mast can no longer be lowered to horizontal. If this is the case, the mast will have to be lowered as far as possible, then a temporary support arranged for the upper end whilst the pivot bolt is removed and the heel raised to clear the obstruction. The temporary support usually takes the form of a pair of sheer-legs with their lower ends wedged in

the corners of the cockpit or lashed securely to suitable deck fittings. Before any attempt is made to remove the pivot bolt, a stout wire should be secured to the gooseneck fitting, led aft to a suitable strong point and made fast as tight as possible. Without such a restraining wire, the mast will kick forward violently as the pivot bolt is knocked out, usually with considerable damage to itself and to whatever part of the superstructure it was which made it impossible to lower the mast in one go. Also, the damage to any operators nearby can be quite nasty.

Deck-stepped masts are uncommon on larger, older boats. If encountered, they can be handled in the same way as a keel-stepped mast, but with only a short lift to clear the heel from the step.

The lifting through some 2 m (5 or 6 ft) and the lowering to horizontal of a massive keel-stepped pine spar adorned with a substantial weight of rigging can appear a daunting prospect. However, if tackled scientifically it is not as bad as all that. The easiest way to do it is to attach a strong sling just below the hounds, find a friendly crane operator, and get him to wind away. Failing this, it may be possible to persuade the master of a cargo vessel to allow the use of a derrick for an hour or so; or there may be a much larger boat around with a boat davit which can be pressed into service. So far, nobody seems to have persuaded a friendly helicopter pilot to lift out a mast!

When, as is usually the case, the boat from which the mast is to be removed is the largest boat in the area, and there is no suitable crane for miles around, other means of handling the spar must be found. It will have to be lifted until the heel comes clear of the deck, and then lowered to horizontal, all without any risk of the heavy spar taking charge. This can all be managed; the only equipment not likely to be on the boat already being a stout pair of legs of sufficient height to lift the heel clear of the deck (plus an allowance for a hoist, winch or tackle) and sundry shores and odd pieces of timber.

Preparations must be made carefully and methodically. During its raising, and lowering to horizontal, the mast will be prevented

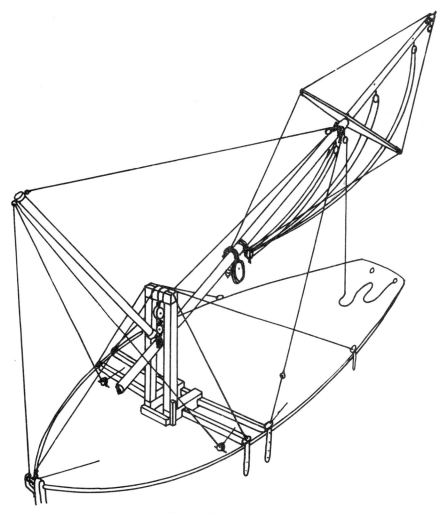

Fig 2 *Mast being lowered: note how the weight is shared between the tackle near the heel and the stay to the stem-head roller via the boom end*

from swinging sideways by a pair of lower shrouds, taken to the aft main chainplates. It will be prevented from falling over forwards by a backstay to its normal fitting, or by a halliard, topping lift or upper shroud taken to a mainsheet fitting. Forward control during the lift will be by the forestay, and control whilst lowering will be by an inner forestay or lower headsail-halliard. If the mast can be climbed, as much as possible of the other rigging should be removed.

When the mast is being lowered, some means of support for the upper end must be provided so that it can be lowered under full control. This is achieved by securing a strut on the foreside of the mast, held at right angles to it by an inner forestay or headsail-halliard, such that as the mast comes down the strut will rise to vertical (Fig 2). The easiest way of rigging such a strut is to use the boat's main boom. Most boats of any size usually have some fitting on the foreside of the mastband to which the end of the boom can be secured. If there is no such fitting, a tight lashing will have to be used, and a pair of short pieces of wood should be lashed either side of the

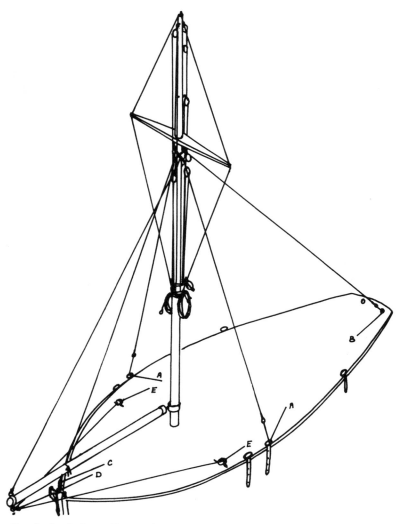

Fig 3   *Preparing the rigging to lower the mast*

boom so that it cannot slip sideways off the mast. On a gaff-rigged boat, the gaff can be used instead of the boom – it already has jaws which will hold it in place. The outer end of the boom (or gaff) is shackled to the stay or headsail-halliard. If a halliard is used, its fall must be made fast to the mast-band or to a cleat on the mast.

   Side control over the outer end of the boom can be by a pair of jib sheets shackled to the boom-end and led through their normal fairleads (E on Fig 3). If the stem-head roller will withstand an upward pull,

then a wire can be led from the boom-end under the roller and back along the deck to the anchor winch or to a deck tackle (D on Fig 3). If the stem-head roller is unsuitable for an upward pull, then the wire will have to be led through a sheave shackled to the forestay fitting. Suitable arrangements must be made so that the forestay, lower shrouds and whatever is used as a backstay can be surged out under control as the mast is raised. If the rigging is secured by lanyards, these can be undone to the last turn. If rigging screws are used, these will have to be removed and replaced by lengths of the stoutest rope that can be led through the eyes on the chainplates (unless the eyes are very large). If the chainplates have only small holes to accept a clevis pin, blocks through which the rope extensions to the stays can be surged will have to be shackled to the chainplates. If a halliard or the topping lift is used as a makeshift backstay, its fall must be made fast to the mastband or to a cleat on the mast. All other standing and running rigging which cannot easily be removed should be coiled and tied in to the mast as high up as possible. The rigging situation is now as sketched in Fig 3 with two shrouds A, backstay B, and forestay C prepared for surging out as the mast is raised.

Arrangements can now be made for the actual lifting mechanism. First, a pair of blocks of timber about 150 mm (6 in) high should be secured in place on deck, either side of the mast, with their aft ends against the cabin front or some other suitable structure. These baulks serve to spread the weight of the lift over two or more deckbeams, but they also prevent the heel of the mast from moving sideways as it is lifted clear of the hole in the deck, so they must be adequately braced in position to resist any movement. Wooden struts wedged out to the bulwarks or chainplates will provide the simplest bracing (Fig 4).

The gallows used to lift the mast consists of two stout uprights just under a metre (2–3 ft) higher than the lift actually needed

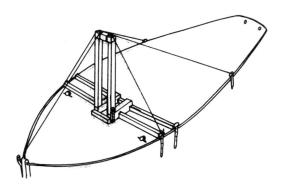

Fig 4   *Legs rigged on deck preparatory to lifting the mast; for clarity all details not directly associated with the legs are omitted*

and a strong cross member. The uprights are secured in position in front of the mast, far enough apart so the mast can be swung between them, as shown in Fig 4. It should be noted that, for simplicity, the mast and all its rigging is omitted from this sketch. The gallows must be securely stayed so that it will remain upright and will withstand the not inconsiderable fore and aft loadings placed on it as the mast is lowered to horizontal (Fig 2). Suitable staying comprises a pair of side guys to the forward main chainplates, a pair of backstays which can be taken to running backstay fittings or to the mainsheet fittings, and a forestay to the stem head. These stays must be set up really tight. Arrangements must be made to support the mast after it has been lowered to horizontal. Larger, older cruising yachts may be equipped with substantial boom gallows, or the normal boom crutch may be adequate. If the boat has no suitable facilities, then a pair of sheer-legs can be used, with their lower ends lashed to the mainsheet fittings or some other suitable strongpoints on the aft deck. Some form of trestle or blocks will also be needed to support the heel of the mast, but until the mast is horizontal this is best left ashore or below in the cabin until it is needed.

The next stage in the preparatory work is to rig the lifting tackle from the head of the gallows to the mast. If the boat has a halliard winch mounted on the mast, a wire can be run from the head of the gallows onto the winch drum. The easiest way to secure the wire to the gallows is by using a wire with an eye-splice on one end, passing the fall of the wire through the eye. The mast can then be lifted by winding up on the winch. When no suitable winch is to hand, the most powerful tackle available should be rigged between the head of the gallows and a strop round the mast below the gooseneck (Fig 5). It is as well to note that if the gooseneck fitting is fairly high above the deck it should be ignored, and the forward strut and the lifting sling secured to the mast as near the deck as possible. The fall of the hoisting tackle can be taken to the anchor winch, or to a deck tackle rigged to suitable strongpoints.

Finally, a supply of baulks of wood

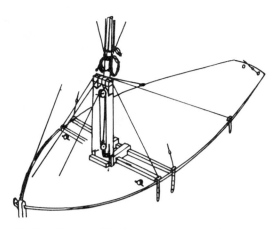

Fig 5 *Lifting tackle rigged between the legs and the mast*

should be laid out below, ready to be placed below the heel as the mast is lifted so that if the lifting tackle fails the heel cannot fall back. If a deck tackle is being used to gain sufficient power, it is highly likely that it will have to be re-rigged and overhauled at least once during the lift, and whilst this is being done the heel of the mast will have to be adequately supported down to the keel of the boat.

All this preparatory work can be done by one person, but a team of three or four helpers will be needed for the lifting and lowering. It is absolutely essential that everyone knows exactly what is going to happen, and what he must do. One person will be operating the tackle to lift the mast – on a bigger boat this might need more than one. A helper below deck will have to place suitable shores below the heel of the mast as it rises, and once the heel is clear of the step this helper may be able to aid in the lifting by putting a stout lever below the heel. The key people are those who will control easing off the shrouds, forestay and backstay as the mast rises. It is essential that they work in unison with the lifting, ensuring that the mast remains substantially vertical all the time, but with minimal tension in the stays. Clearly if they are pulling hard on their stays, the person or persons trying to raise the mast will have to overcome their pulling as well as the weight of the mast.

If the number of available helpers is limited, the lift can be made in very slow stages by only one or two people. The four stays are slackened a little (a few inches), the mast is raised until the stays are tight, then a wedge or block is slid under the heel. Pause to check all is well; ease off the stays another inch or two; lift, shore, wedge or block; repeat *ad nauseam*. Provided the operations are carried out in strict sequence and the stays are never slackened far enough to allow the mast to move far out of vertical, it is a perfectly safe exercise, but very slow and tedious. During the lifting, the side-stays and lowering wire to the boom-end are left slack.

Even with few or no helpers, the heel of the mast will ultimately rise clear of the deck (Fig 6), and as it does so, the weight of the boom on the foreside will make it swing aft as far as the drift on the hoisting tackle will allow. If a halliard winch on the mast is being used to power the lift, it is as well to rig a preventer line round the mast and back to a suitable foredeck fitting to limit this swing, which might otherwise jerk the wire off the drum of the winch. Once the heel of the mast is clear of the deck, a wedge or chock should be placed over the hole to make sure that the heel cannot slip back again!

If a halliard winch on the mast was used for the hoist, it must now be relieved of the strain by a rope lashing from the top of the gallows, round the mast immediately below the winch. Several turns of moderate-thickness rope should be used rather than one turn of wire or thick rope, and the piece of rope used should be long enough to allow it to be surged out to lower the heel once the mast is horizontal. As soon as the strop is secured, the lifting wire should be slackened off and removed. If a tackle was used, the parts of the tackle should be seized tightly together with a lashing, and the fall of the tackle can then be taken off the anchor winch or deck tackle and made fast to a suitable cleat, ringbolt or belaying pin.

The heel of the mast will now be swinging fairly freely in a fore and aft direction, hanging from the top of the gallows. Whilst the mast is vertical it cannot swing forward because of the top of the gallows, but as

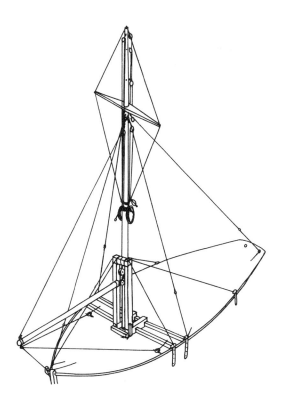

Fig 6 *The mast lifted with its heel clear of the deck and ready for lowering to horizontal*

the mast is lowered it can (and will) swing in an alarming manner. If the gallows was well-built and securely stayed, this tendency to swing can be countered by keeping a good, equal tension in the two shrouds so that their pull is forcing the heel forward. If the swing worries the operators, it can be restricted by passing a figure-of-eight lashing round the uprights of the gallows and the mast at the point at which the lifting tackle (or strop if a halliard winch was used for the lift) is made fast to the mast.

The side-stays to the boom-end must now be tightened, and the fall of the wire from the boom-end is taken to the anchor winch or a deck tackle. The geometry of the system results in the stress on this lowering wire being substantially greater than the weight of the mast, and the stress increases as the mast is lowered. Because of this increase in stress during lowering, it is essential that the means used to surge out

this wire during the lowering are adequate for the job. Any helper with some mathematical knowledge can estimate the probable load on the system. If there is any doubt whatsoever about whether it will be possible to use a given deck tackle or winch drum to control the lowering, then it is as well to provide some means of snubbing off and holding the wire whilst a stronger tackle is applied to its fall. If an ordinary deck tackle is being used, it is possible that the tackle will have to be undone, hauled up, and re-applied to the fall of the wire at least once during the lowering operation. A considerable length of wire (roughly one and a half times the length of the boom) will have to be paid out. If the boat is rigged with a powerful purchase on the mainsheet, and it is known that when sailing well squared-off there is a fair length of sheet in hand, then it is probable that the mainsheet will make an ideal tackle of just about the right length for lowering the mast. Whatever tackle is used, a stopper knot (figure-of-eight knot) must be put on the end of its fall before it is used. Then if it is found that the rope is not long enough, it can at least be allowed to run right out before the tackle is re-applied. Make sure that the knot is large enough to provide a thorough stop before relying on it.

One obvious point which is nevertheless surprisingly easy to overlook is that since this is a lowering operation, the tackle must be hauled up closed, with its blocks as near touching as possible, before it is applied to the tail of the wire. It is distinctly annoying to discover on starting to lower that the tackle has been applied fully extended ready for a haul-in.

Anything which will make control of the lowering wire easier is usually worth doing. If the boat has large-diameter sheet winches, a rope fall on the wire with three turns round a winch drum will give very good control.

Once the lowering wire has been secured ready for easing out, a final check is made that all is in order, the forestay is taken off its stem-head fitting and lowering is started by a gentle tug on the backstay. Tension must be maintained on the shrouds both to ensure that the mast comes down lying fore

23

and aft and also to minimise any swing at the heel. The side guys to the boom-end will have to be adjusted as the mast is lowered, but if rope with a bit of 'bounce' is used for these they can be taken to suitable cleats and merely adjusted once or twice during the operation – continuous control should not be necessary. It is best if whoever was looking after the shrouds during the lowering abandons the shrouds when the mast is within reach of the deck and guides the mast down gently until it rests on the boom gallows or whatever support has been provided. As already mentioned, the loading on the wire to the boom-end is considerable, and at least one mast has been broken when it was lowered too abruptly onto a support.

Once the upper end of the mast is secure on its support, whatever support has been arranged for the heel can be placed in position and the heel lowered down onto it, either by surging out the rope strop holding it to the gallows or by releasing the hoist tackle. As the mast is lowered, the side-stays to the end of the boom must be shortened to keep the boom safely upright. When the heel of the mast has been lowered, the boom can be taken down.

If a halliard was used to connect the outer end of the boom to the mast, the halliard can be slackened off to lower the boom forward, but if an inner forestay was used then the job is not quite so simple, as the stay cannot be lengthened and the gallows prevent the boom from being lowered over the mast. In this case the best solution is to undo the lower end of the boom from the mast and take the lower end forward, whilst helpers control the upper end with the side-stays, by pulling the forestay in to the mast, and by easing away on the wire under the stem-head roller, so that the boom can be kept resting against the head of the gallows as its end is carried forward.

If the boom is lowered by slacking away on a halliard so that its upper end falls forward, care should be taken to see the boom does not swing sideways away from the fore and aft centre-line of the boat. As the boom comes down, the halliard will drop onto the head of the gallows which will keep open the angle between the halliard

and the boom so that the loading on the halliard will not become excessive.

With the boom safely out of the way, the final stage in the operation is to move the mast forward so that the rigging can be removed without having to reach out far over the stern. If there are sufficient helpers to lift the mast, this is simple (apart from when one of the helpers stands on the bight of a shroud or halliard, or when a loop in some piece of rigging finds its way under the end of a jib sheet or mooring cleat). If the mast is too heavy to be carried forward in a clean lift, then the lifting tackle from the gallows head can be used again. The lower end of the tackle is made fast to the mast a metre or so (3–4 ft) aft of the gallows, and the heel of the mast is hauled up some 500 mm (1–2 ft). When the upper (aft) end of the mast is lifted clear of the boom gallows or whatever support was arranged, gravity will swing the mast forward. If the upper end of the mast is resting on some temporary support, the support and mast will all swing forward as the heel is lifted off its support. If such movement cannot be tolerated, then either helpers should hold the mast clear of its aft support before the heel is lifted (being ready to accommodate the inevitable forward swing), or the swing should be prevented by a restraining line which can be released when all is set for the mast to be allowed to swing forward. Two or three such lifts and swings should suffice to move the mast far enough for all the rigging to be removed without risk of falling overboard.

This is usually the point at which any volunteer helpers depart, leaving the owner with the horizontal mast blocking access to his cabin (in which, naturally, he has left pipe, cigarettes, chewing gum, brandy flask or what-have-you) and a pretty fine tangle of rigging to sort out!

At fitting-out time, the mast can be raised and stepped by reversing the lowering procedures. It should not be necessary to state that before the mast is raised to vertical a very thorough check should be made that all the rigging is correctly fitted and that all shackles and rigging screws up the mast are securely wired so that they cannot possibly come undone whilst sailing. It is well worth-while writing out a full checklist for all mast rigging, encapsulating the list between two sheets of adhesive-backed clear plastic, and methodically checking off each item before the mast is raised. Masts are usually rigged only once a year (or once every two, three or more years) and it is very easy to forget something in the excitement of being nearly ready to sail, or in the misery of trying to do the work in pouring rain and a near-freezing wind. Under such poor (but alas all too often prevailing) conditions, a waterproofed checklist can be a great comfort and help.

In any heavy lifting such as the removal of an engine or mast, the basic laws of physics must never be overlooked. It must be borne in mind that the stress in a guy wire etc increases as it makes a finer angle to the strut it is supporting, and that a spar which is more than strong enough in pure compression can be woefully inadequate if it has to withstand any bending stresses. Also, if the boat's own gear is used to rig any necessary tackles, due allowance must be made for aging of ropes etc. It must be remembered that no knot or splice is ever as strong as the rope or wire in which it is made, and in all such lifting operations the motto must be 'better safe than sorry', even if this does mean the job takes longer. So long as heavy weights are kept under control and never allowed to swing free, all these lifting operations are perfectly safe, but it is most important that everybody concerned knows what is going to happen and what he or she must do.

Once the mast is lowered and moved forward, all rigging should be stored away carefully. All ropes should be washed out thoroughly in fresh water, and dried before they are coiled for storage. All the wire rigging should be wiped clean, coiled and oiled. Wire rigging is usually tied into coils, but much neater storage is possible if each piece of rigging (or pair of pieces such as shrouds) is coiled into a suitably labelled container. Old 35 mm film drums are ideal for smaller boats' halliards and shrouds, and worn out tyres are excellent for holding the heavier rigging from larger boats. Port-side rigging can be identified by blobs of red paint. One great advantage of using old tyres to hold coils of rigging is the ease with which they can be rolled around – coils of steel wire-rigging are surprisingly heavy.

Removal of internal ballast

The third major item to be removed from the hull is any internal ballast. When ballast is taken out of a boat, a clear record should be kept of the correct stowage.

Some older boats have specially shaped cast-iron ballast, with all individual pieces numbered or otherwise marked, but the author does not know of many such boats which still have a copy of the original stowage plan. Looking at the bilges with all the shaped pigs in place, it can appear that the stowage is straightforward and obvious, and that the making of a plan will be a waste of time. However, it is a different story when the hull has been re-launched and the time comes to re-stow the ballast. Then the job will appear far from obvious. It is like a curved jigsaw puzzle – but the pieces are not little bits of cardboard, they are pigs of iron weighing anything up to 25 kg ($\frac{1}{2}$ cwt). And like any jigsaw puzzle there is often only one correct place for each piece.

The normal form for such ballast is blocks which fit between pairs of frames, supported by a generous lip at each end resting on the frames and holding the weight of the iron clear of the hull planking. The thickness of the top lips varies, becoming thinner near the turn of the bilges as the space below the cabin sole becomes less. Thus any misplaced pig could either be resting on the hull planking instead of on the frames, or it could prevent the cabin sole from resting properly on its bearers. It is not unknown for an owner to get most of the ballast apparently correctly stowed, only to discover that the last half-dozen pigs are all very slightly wider than the space between the frames into which they have to be fitted. A couple of hours spent with a paintbrush, tin of old enamel, notebook and pencil before the ballast is disturbed will usually prove to have been time well spent when the time comes to fit out again.

In fact it is very good policy to label every item taken out of the boat as it is removed. The author always used a very simple technique of putting red-paint numbers on anything removed from the port side of a boat and green paint for the starboard side.

As much as possible of the interior joinery work on the boat should be removed before the hull is hauled ashore. Many locker doors are on simple lift-off hinges, and others may be drop-in-place doors. Bunk boards, cabin sole, and often cabin-sole bearers can all be taken out. Other than the ballast or perhaps a stove, none of the removable items in the average cruising yacht appear very heavy, but the total removable weight is far from insignificant – as any owner who has ever offloaded all the bits and pieces onto a hand-hauled trolley or bogie will be only too well aware. One rather obvious point which is very easily overlooked is to ensure that all water and fuel tanks are emptied.

Chapter 3
Moving the hull

Lifting

When all possible weight has been removed from the hull, it can be brought ashore and moved to the chosen working site. If the boat is to be moved any distance by road, it must be properly supported and secured on the lorry or trailer, and if the boat is lifted out of the water by a crane or hoist and lowered onto the lorry, it is as well to ensure that adequate provisions are made for offloading at the end of the journey.

Whenever a boat is lifted by a crane or hoist, it is essential to see that the slings used are properly secured, that they support the hull adequately, and that arrangements are made to ensure that the slings cannot cut into the hull at deck level. Early in 1979 a wooden-hulled boat was damaged beyond economic repair when a lifting sling slid up the sloping keel and the sling cut into the hull planking between two deck beams. Any competent boatyard should take good care of such matters; it is when some other facility such as a hired mobile crane or a waterside industrial crane is used that the boat will be most at risk. Nipping of the hull can be avoided by passing the slings over the ends of stout beams secured to the deck of the boat (Fig 7). The lengths of the slings should be adjusted to ensure that the lifting point is as nearly as possible over the centre of gravity of the hull, the position of which can be calculated roughly from the known hull shape. If a hired crane is used, it is as well to check on the lifting capacity of the crane at varying radii of swing. One very specialised and not very heavy racing yacht was destroyed when a mobile crane overbalanced as it was trying to lift the yacht on to a quay, and the crane fell some twelve feet down on to the boat.

If a crane can be used to unload the boat from the lorry or trailer, the preparations

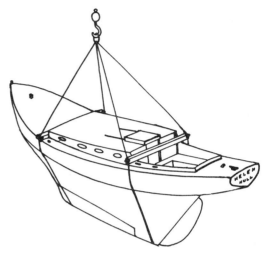

Fig 7 *Lifting slings with transverse baulks to prevent the slings nipping the deck and topsides*

for the journey can be limited to ensuring that the boat cannot fall over if it is balanced on its keel, or in the case of shoal-draft boats that it is secured down on one bilge, with some padding between the hull planking and the bed of the lorry. A deeper hull should be centred on the bed of the lorry, with chocks to prevent the keel from slipping sideways and blocks to support the bilges in the way of the mast and at the forward end of the cockpit. Struts can be wedged in place from the chainplates down to the bed of the lorry and, as a further security, wires can be run from each chainplate across the deck and through the opposite chainplate and down to turn-buckles secured to the frame of the lorry. This crossing of the wires ensures that the pull on the chainplates is inwards, and not downwards and outwards as it would be if the wires were run straight down. The main deck beam is well able to take the loading of crossed securing wires.

If the boat is to be slid or rolled off the lorry at the end of the journey, the hull should either be raised above the bed of the lorry on transverse baulks of timber so that rollers or the main members of a cradle can be inserted beneath the hull, or a pre-made transport cradle should be used.

Rolling

A small or medium sized, flat-floored, shoal-draft hull with a good length of straight keel is most easily moved off the lorry end-wise, with stout wooden rollers or lengths of heavy-gauge iron or steel tubing beneath the keel. Some form of ways along which the boat can be rolled will have to be built, up to the height of the platform of the lorry. Large baulks of timber such as old railway sleepers can be piled up to build a suitable unloading platform or ramp. Clearly the job is easiest if the unloading ways are level, but there is no need to be frightened of unloading a boat down sloping ways. A stout wire or chain from the mooring point on the foredeck of the boat, through a large sheave secured to the front of the lorry and back over the stem head roller to the anchor winch, can be used to control the boat as it slides or rolls down the ramp. It must be remembered that if the boat is lowered down sloping ways as it is offloaded, it will have to be hauled up again when the time comes to reload it, and moving heavy boats uphill is not so easy as moving them downhill. The ways need to be built up with a main-strength member along the line of the keel, and side-ways to support the ends of the rollers.

The built-up ways must be secured so that there can be no risk of any of the baulks moving as the weight of the boat comes onto them. The easiest way of securing large baulks is by nailing scrap pieces of wood across the piles of baulks, with at least two nails into each baulk.

Rolling is easiest if the boat can be balanced on its keel, but it can be heeled over if a stout plank is inserted under the bilge on which the boat is lying. The length of the plank should be equal to the length of the straight portion of the keel of the boat. Rolling off is simplified if the rollers are placed in position on the lorry before the boat is loaded, but if this has not been done, it is not too difficult to transfer the weight of the boat to rollers provided the boat was laid on transverse baulks. The rollers are pushed through beneath the keel of the boat, adjacent to the baulks on which the boat is resting, and each roller should lie on the side of the baulk away from the direction in which the boat is to be moved. The rollers should be slightly smaller in diameter than the baulks – in practice, the latter are usually selected after suitable stout rollers have been found. Pairs of hard-wood wedges with a slope of about one in eight are then inserted beneath the rollers, one under the keel of the boat and one under the bilge on which the hull is resting. If the boat is upright with a support under each bilge, then three wedges should be used under each roller. All the wedges are then hammered home until the rollers are jammed firmly under the hull, starting with the wedges under the keel. A long-handled maul is the ideal tool for this job, but the author has seen an ordinary pickaxe used with its point covered with a hardwood block. It is possible to hammer the wedges in hard enough for sufficient weight to be transferred to the rollers to enable all but one of the transverse baulks to be removed from under the boat. The last baulk cannot be removed in this way, because as soon as all the weight is transferred to the rollers they will start to roll down the wedges and the weight will come back onto the solid baulk.

The easiest way to prevent this from happening is to insert a stout lever between the bed of the lorry and the outer end of the boat, and then lever the boat onto the lorry, thus pushing the rollers further up the wedges. The last baulk is then easily removed, and the boat is allowed to roll down off the wedges and along the bed of the lorry. If the boat does not roll easily, the lever can be used to persuade it along. Extra rollers must be inserted as the boat moves forward, so that the boat is never in any danger of overbalancing off the leading one. As each roller approaches within a foot or so of the end of the lorry, another should be placed on the end of the built-up ways

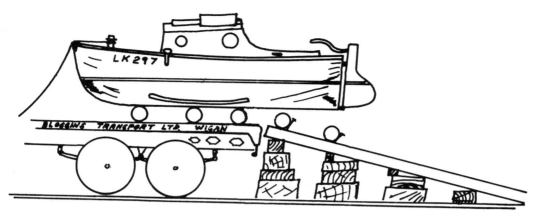

Fig 8 *Rolling a small cruiser off a lorry: note the rollers resting against stout nails in the sloping ways*

and held ready to take over as the boat moves past the lorry's end. If the built-up ways slope down, the boat will have to tilt down to match the slope of the ways as its centre of gravity passes off the roller then nearest to the end of the lorry (Fig 8).

This is the trickiest part of the whole operation. The boat must not be allowed to crash down heavily as it passes the point of balance, therefore as many helpers as possible should be mustered. Depending on the size of the boat, two or four of the strongest helpers should be positioned at the ends of the hull and the remainder should hold at least two rollers in place on the sloping ways ready to take the weight of the boat as it tilts down. The helpers at the ends of the boat must be alert to sense any tendency of the boat to overbalance, and as the boat reaches its point of balance on the rollers it should be held down at the end on the lorry and up at the outer end, moved slowly and gently along until the out-of-balance can be clearly felt, and then allowed to tilt down slowly on to the rollers held ready on the ways. If the helpers are limited in number or the boat is heavier than it is felt they can handle in this way, a lever under the overhanging end can be used to lower the end gently as the boat passes beyond the point of balance. If helpers are really limited, rollers can be held in place on the ways by driving stout nails into the ways ahead of the rollers. One nail in each outer

way will suffice. The nails must be really stout, and they must be hammered in at such an angle that they can be removed with a claw-hammer or similar implement once the weight of the boat is on the rollers.

Rollers cannot be used to move heavy boats unless a really strong cradle is built with very broad-base timbers, because the weight of the boat will be concentrated on limited areas of the rollers and if there is any tendency for this concentrated weight to crush them, it will be extremely difficult to persuade them to roll.

Skidding

Heavy boats are better moved in a cradle whose main base members can slide in greased ways. These main base members must be planed smooth, and should be stout enough to spread the weight they will be carrying over their whole length. Their ends should be cut with a slope on the lower face. The ways in which the base members will slide are also made of substantial baulks of timber, about 13 mm ($\frac{1}{2}$ in) wider than the base members, planed smooth on their upper faces, and with planks about 25 mm (1 in) thick nailed to their sides to form shallow troughs (Fig 9). Four such ways are needed if a boat is to be moved any appreciable distance. Before use, the ways must be liberally spread with thick grease.

Greased ways are easiest to use when the

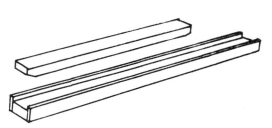

Fig 9 *Slider and skidway*

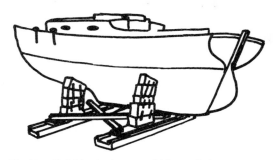

Fig 10 *Hull blocked up on skids ready for moving sideways*

boat is to be moved sideways. A base must first be built up of piles of timber or clean flat paving slabs, on which the ways can be laid. If the boat is to be offloaded from a lorry, then the base must be built up to the height of the bed of the lorry. One of the ways should be positioned roughly under the mast, the other roughly under the cockpit and, with the base members of the cradle placed in them, these greased ways are slid under the boat as it lies on baulks on the lorry. Obviously, the baulks on the lorry will have been selected to be just slightly higher than the height of the ways plus the cradle base members. The two ways must be laid exactly parallel. It is advisable to nail planks across the tops of the two cradle base members at each end, and at least one diagonal member so that the cradle cannot distort as the boat is moved. Piles of baulks of timber, or stoutly made box members are then built up on the ends of the base members to support the bilges of the boat (Fig 10). If baulks of timber are used, they should be secured by nailing planks over the side or end of the pile. A pair of struts can be run from the ends of the forward cross member up to the chainplates.

The second pair of greased ways are placed on the prepared base beside the lorry, and lined up carefully with the pair below the boat, to which they should be lightly attached by scrap pieces of timber nailed over the sides of the ways (Fig 11).

When all is prepared, the weight of the boat must be transferred from the solid baulks on which it was transported to the base of the built-up cradle. This operation requires at least two people. Fine-angled

hardwood wedges are placed between the base member of the cradle and the keel of the boat, one wedge from each side, so that the two opposed wedges lie side by side. The two people, one on each side of the boat, then hammer home the opposed wedges, both striking simultaneously, until the weight of the boat is transferred from the baulks to the cross member of the cradle.

The shores under the bilges are then checked and if necessary wedged firm to the hull; the process is then repeated for the other base member of the cradle.

When the weight of the boat is on the movable cradle and the transverse baulks have been removed, the boat can be slid over. This can be done by pushing against the hull of the boat, but is not really advisable other than on smaller boats, as the effort is being applied fairly high up whereas the resistance to the movement is at the base of the pile. If the two sets of shores under the bilge are not well secured, there is a possibility of the owner learning more about the replacing of planks and frames than he had intended.

The correct way to skid over a cradle is to nail some wooden dogs down to the base members so that the keel of the boat cannot slip sideways on them, then to pass a wire sling round over the cross members and under the keel to run along behind the keel. The ends of the sling are joined between the bilge shores on the hauling side. Then a steady pull applied to the sling will drag the cradle along the ways. The simplest way of applying this pull if the ground is fairly hard is to dig a row of holes about 152 mm (6 in) deep between the ways, and

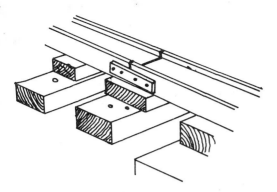

Fig 11 *Sections of skidway joined with piece of scrap timber nailed on*

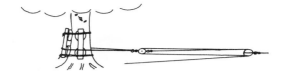

Fig 12 *Hauling-line rigged to a stout tree: note the padding to prevent damage to the bark*

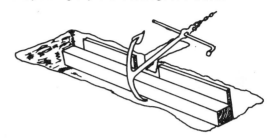

Fig 13 *Anchor pulling against planks in a trench dug in soft ground*

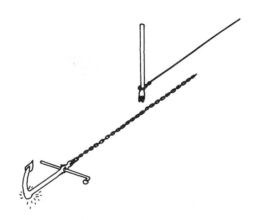

Fig 14 *Use of an anchor, chain, and forked lever to pull boat on skids*

to use a stout lever with its lower end in the hole and a strong lashing from the sling to the appropriate height on the lever. This method has the advantage of being adjustable to suit the strength of the operator and, as it moves the boat only a short distance for each pull, it gives ample opportunities to check that all is well: that the cradle is moving fairly down the ways, that the bilge supports are remaining in place, and that the supports for the greased ways are not in danger of collapsing under the load.

If the ground is too soft to use a lever (even in quite hard ground, some of the effort applied to the lever will be wasted in moving the edge of the hole), some form of fixed anchor-point beyond the end of the ways will be needed. Strops round brick-built outhouses, sheds etc should not be used. Such buildings may have a surprisingly low resistance to shearing stresses, and the object of the exercise is to offload the boat, not to transport the outhouse. A sturdy, well-rooted tree can be used, but it must be really well protected from any sling passed round it. The trunk of the tree should be well padded, then stout boards placed round outside the padding, with the sling passed outside the boards. Old motor-scooter tyres make ideal padding, which must extend round three sides of the tree (Fig 12). It is advisable to lash all the padding fairly securely in place so that if adjustments have to be made whilst the boat is being moved, and the strain on the slings is released, the padding cannot slip. Obviously the sling will

be passed round the tree as near ground level as possible.

If no suitable tree or other fixed point is available, one will have to be provided. Probably the most effective is to dig a T shaped trench beyond the end of the ways, and bury the boat's anchor in the trench with a stout baulk of timber hooked under a fluke (Fig 13). It is the timber baulk which does most of the work, so the larger this can be the better. If the boat has only CQR or Danforth anchors, which will not hook over such a wide piece of timber in the same way as a good fisherman's anchor, vertical pieces of wood either side of the anchor can be used to spread the load over an adequate area of the side of the trench.

Power to move the boat can be applied in a variety of ways. If the anchor chain is left shackled to the anchor, or is used as a fixed sling round a tree etc, then a lever with a forked end can be dogged over the links of the chain and used in the same way as a lever into the ground (Fig 14). The pivot and the point of application of the load can be very close together so tremendous power can be applied, and the closeness of the chain-links makes stepping along very easy indeed. On lighter boats, a hauling tackle can be rigged up from various bits of the boat's gear, such as the mainsheet and throat halliard. A Spanish windlass (a loop of rope joining the two slings, with a lever inserted in the loop so that the two sides of the loop can be twisted together) can be used, but this is not easy because the pull required is too near the ground to make twisting the windlass easy.

Only four skidways will be needed because as the boat moves off one pair onto the other, the pair it has just left can be relaid ahead ready for the next move.

A sideways move on skids is the easiest to organise, because the skids form the base of the cradle, and are passed directly beneath the keel of the boat. If the boat is to be moved endwise on skids, the ways are laid on either side under the bilges of the boat, and a multiplicity of stout cross members beneath the keel should be used. For an endwise skid, the bilge supports on the cradle should be built beneath the main transverse floor-timbers of the boat, and these bilge supports should be wedged up so that they are taking a substantial percentage of the weight of the hull. The bilge supports transfer the weight of the hull directly to the base of the cradle over the greased ways, instead of almost all the weight being on the centres of the transverse members.

One point to be watched when unloading a boat from a road vehicle with rollers or skids is that, as the boat moves off the vehicle, the springs of the vehicle will relax and the floor of the vehicle will rise. The best type of road vehicle to use is one of the low loaders with removable rear axles, in which the bed of the lorry rests on the ground during unloading (or loading). If an ordinary platform lorry is used, great care must be taken to see that if the boat is being rolled off there will not be an abrupt drop as the boat leaves the last roller on the lorry. It may be necessary to use a pair of stout levers to ease the boat down onto the rollers on the built-up ways. If the boat is being moved on greased skids, offcuts of plywood or thin planks can be slid under the ways beside the lorry as the lorry rises on its springs. Provided the operation is taken slowly and steadily, and a check is made that the hull is adequately supported at all stages, there is no need to be afraid of moving a boat on rollers or skids.

With good greased skids, and a well planned layout, two men can move 15 or 20 tonnes (tons) of boat without undue physical exertion. In fact the hardest part of the job is moving the skids and supporting baulks of timber about. The actual moving of the boat can be a welcome light relief.

If a boat is too large to be moved by road, or if a waterside working site is the only one available, the boat can be moved up clear of the water on greased skids. Moving a heavy boat up a sloping beach on skids can be very hard work indeed, and the use of a powerful motorised winch can be desirable. If there is road access to the site, a local garage may be prepared to hire a breakdown truck equipped with a suitable one. If the move up the ways cannot be completed in one pull, either mechanised or with a powerful tackle etc, do not forget to provide adequate means of preventing the boat from slipping back whilst the pull is readjusted, or whilst a set of skids is being relaid ahead of the boat.

The intelligent use of levers, wedges, skids, rollers, sheer-legs and tackles can bring most of the heavy tasks associated with work on boats within the physical capacity of a small team of keen people.

Chapter 4

The working area

Supporting the hull

Once the boat has been moved on to the working site, it can be properly supported. It can be left sitting on the greased skidways, but if this is done wooden dogs should be nailed into the ways so that the boat cannot slip along them, and then stout wooden boxes should be built over the exposed ends of the ways. It is impossible to remove all the grease, and one foot inadvertently placed on the exposed end of a greased way can result in repairs to human ribs delaying those to wooden ribs! If the work on the boat is to be at all extensive, it is better to remove the wooden ways and store them away until they are required to move the boat back to the water.

How the boat should be supported depends on the work to be done, and on the nature of the ground. If the ground is at all soft, then the broadest possible base should be provided to all supports so as to spread the load. If the hull planking or frames adjacent to the keel are to be replaced, the keel should be supported on blocks very slightly narrower than the keel itself, to allow adequate access for the work. At least three supports under the keel should be used, and it is as well to place such supports so as to allow access to keel-bolts. It is advisable to use built-up supports rather than single blocks, so that if it is found necessary to move a support for access to a bolt head etc the support in question can be knocked out from under the boat. Supports consisting of piles of blocks can be built up with an opposed pair of wedges incorporated so that the load carried by the support can be adjusted by hammering in the wedges (Fig 15). Whenever this is done, a wooden dog should be nailed to the block on which the wedges rest, hard against the heel of the wedge, so there can be no risk

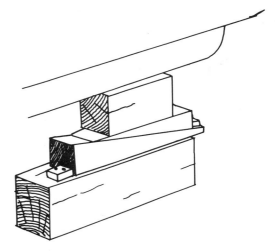

Fig 15 *Keel-blocks with opposed wedges: note wooden dogs to prevent the wedges from slipping back*

of the wedge slipping back. The lower wedge of such an opposed pair should be blunt ended, and it should be placed with its thin end overhanging the end of the block below it so that it can be knocked back to release the pile of blocks.

If the boat has an overhanging counter stern, some support should be provided about half-way along the overhang. The best support here is a stout pole cut to suitable length, with a softwood plate between the top of the pole and the hull, and a hardwood wedge driven between the base of the pole and the ground. The stem head can be supported with a pole either side placed beneath the stem-head roller fitting and with a wedge driven under the foot of each pole (Fig 16).

At least three pairs of bilge supports should be provided, all placed under suitable transverse floors in the hull. The supports can be wedged poles (Fig 17), piles of blocks, or built up box structures (Fig 18).

Fig 16 *Heavy shoal-draft hull supported on bilge blocks, with struts to the stem-head fitting*

Fig 17 *Deep-draft hull supported with shores under the bilge*

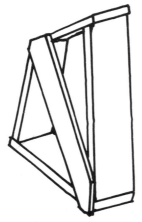

Fig 18 *Built-up bilge shore for small cruising boat*

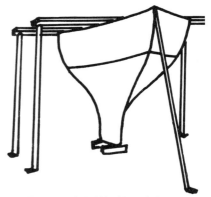

Fig 19 *Deep-draft hull held upright by beams over the deck with outboard shores, leaving clear access to the hull planking*

If a substantial amount of work is to be done on the hull planking, it may be necessary to provide further means of holding the hull upright when all bilge supports on one side are removed. Such support can be achieved by securing a pair of stout beams across the deck of the boat so that they project about two feet each side, then wedging pole-supports under the ends of the beams (Fig 19). The beams can be secured by lashing them with wire to the chainplates, then wedging them up from the deck or bulwarks so that they are firm; or by removing suitable deck fittings and then through-bolting, with suitable packing to accommodate any deck camber.

Before the job of supporting the hull can be regarded as finished, a final check must be made that it is sitting upright and that as far as possible all the various supports are carrying equal loads. If the hull is known to be out of shape, some of the supports under the bilge can be 'hardened up' a little so that they tend to push back towards the correct shape as the hull dries out.

It is advisable to check on all supports at intervals whilst the boat is ashore. Wood can swell or shrink as the weather changes, and the ground under the boat may settle under the load. Pole-shores under the bilges can sink slightly into the ground, and if they do they can easily be dislodged. Blocks beneath the bilges or specially built box frames are not likely to fall away and leave the boat liable to fall over, but if they are not all carrying their fair share of the load there can be a risk of the hull distorting as work is done on it.

Cover

With the hull safely propped up ashore, the next item to be dealt with is a cover under which the work can be done. All well equipped cruising yachts should have their own tailor-made winter cover and, if nothing better can be found, this can be used as a working cover. But usually it is too small to be satisfactory. It makes for easier work on the hull if the cover can be mounted much higher than would be normal for winter storage – about 1.2 m (4 ft) at the deck edge is a fair height to aim for – and if work such as replacing planks is to be done regardless of weather conditions, the cover will need to extend well beyond the sides of the boat. If a substantial amount of work is contemplated on the hull, a really good cover will be a good investment. It needs to be totally waterproof, and strong enough to withstand the weight of a moderate fall of snow and the buffeting of a strong wind. Early morning visits to the boat on one's way to work to clear overnight snow from an inadequate cover are not conducive to giving one's best to the task of earning enough money to continue to own a boat, and restless nights spent worrying whether a strong wind will tear the cover are similarly unpleasant and unnecessary. Work on the boat is simplified if the cover can be supported by sheer-legs standing beyond each end of the hull, all held up with suitable guy wires. If a large enough cover can be bought or borrowed, the edges can be guyed straight down to the ground like the fly-sheet of a tent.

After too many years struggling with a variety of inadequate cover supports, the author bought two long lengths of British Columbian pine about 50 mm (2 in) square, and used up a collection of offcuts of timber about 600 mm (2 ft) long to nail the two pieces of pine into a deep girder which was more than amply strong to support a cover plus a load of snow and yet was light enough for one person to handle. When not in use over a boat, this girder proved quite handy as a long ladder for work on a house. Equally, an old ladder will make an excellent ridge support for a cover.

Workbench

Some form of workbench will have to be provided. Obviously a nice solid carpenter's workbench, complete with planing stop, vice and all trimmings would be very nice, but normally something much less grand has to suffice. If the building site allows sufficient space, a very satisfactory bench can be made up from an old kitchen table with reasonably stout legs. Almost any table top is likely to be strong enough, but the joints between the legs and the top will be unable to stand the stresses imposed by sawing and planing, so the table should be strengthened by nailing crossed diagonals between the legs all round. Since most tables are a trifle high for comfortable working, the legs can be sunk into the ground.

A normal 1 m (3 ft) table is too short to be able to cut and plane long planks on, so extra length can be made up by hammering pairs of posts into the ground and nailing or screwing on cross members at the top. When planks are being marked out and cut, the spare pieces of timber can be used as a makeshift top for such a long bench. When the author built his four-tonner, a semi-permanent top for such a long bench was gradually built up from all the offcuts from the hull planking; later when all the long timbers had been dealt with, the bench top was gradually dismantled and made into bunk boards and similar items of cabin furniture. Fig 20 shows the basis of such a bench. For ease of drawing the illustration shows fairly regular shaped pieces of timber; in practice, a somewhat motley collection of pieces of whatever is available will usually be used. It should be noted that the supports for long planks should extend about three-quarters of the length of the longest timbers to be handled beyond each end of the actual working table, so that any sawing etc can always be done over the table, with the workpiece being moved along to suit.

If the work is being done in a location in which some form of semi-permanent bench cannot be erected, a couple of suitable wooden boxes can be used, or even in

35

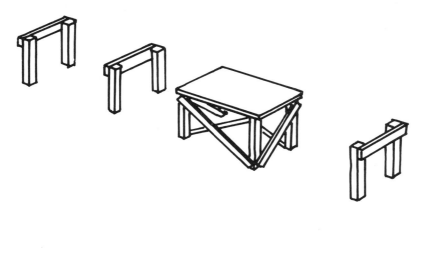

Fig 20 *Old kitchen table stiffened up as a*
workbench, with frame supports for long planks

extremis the side deck or cabin top of the
boat. Some owners of cruising yachts carry
a workbench as part of the boat's
normal gear – usually on boats of less than
20 tonnes (tons) a moderately stout plank
fitted with suitable lugs so that it can be
clamped either across the main hatch slides
or across the aft end of the cockpit
coamings.

A portable engineer's vice which can be
clamped to the strengthened table when
required can be an asset, but is by no
means essential. A permanently fixed vice
is usually a liability unless the bench is long
enough for the longest piece of timber to be
worked on to be laid with its end at least
600 mm (2 ft) clear of the vice. All woodwork for which a vice might be used can
be accommodated either by clamping the
workpiece to the uprights of the bench by
G cramps (with suitable softwood packing
pieces) or by screwing blocks to the table
top either side of the workpiece and driving
in oak wedges to hold the work. One advantage of using a makeshift workbench is that
one need not think twice before nailing or
screwing packing blocks to it as required
for any particular job.

Two or three bench-hooks for small sawing or chiselling jobs can be handy, but are
not essential, as blocks can be nailed to the
bench top at whatever is the most convenient point for any given work.

Another non-essential which will be
found very handy to have around is some
sawing trestles, or horses. The author made
a set of three trestles out of 152 × 13 mm
(6 in × ½ in) planks, built up in box form
rather like a gymnasium vaulting horse,
with a single top plank nailed to sloping
side timbers and fitted with L section
splayed legs. These three trestles can be
stacked, all three can be carried under one
arm; being somewhat larger than the usual
solid baulk trestle they are easier to work
on, and they have innumerable other uses
such as forming convenient side-tables for
garden picnics. Despite their light construction, they have been in constant use for
almost twenty years. Three trestles are
needed so that, when long planks are being
cut, there can be a trestle at each end and
one just behind the point of work. When
sawing medium-sized pieces of timber on a
single trestle, always make certain the
trestle is standing firmly on all four legs,
and insert packing wedges under the legs if
necessary. The author very nearly lost a
thumb when one leg of a trestle sank into
a patch of soft earth just after a cut had
been started in a piece of well-seasoned
oak, and all the power which should have
gone into driving a freshly sharpened saw
through the wood was dissipated in mangling the adjacent thumbnail onto which the
saw jumped as the trestle shifted. After this

Fig 21 *A pair of high trestles and a couple of stout planks is the safest working platform*

he decided to make the lightweight trestles, whose L section legs have a much larger bearing area on the ground than the more conventional square-post legs.

Recollection of this painful incident prompts a reminder to make sure there is a first-aid kit handy on the working site.

Staging

Another question which is best settled early on in the work is the provision of some form of working staging. Out of the water even a small cruising yacht stands quite high, and it is almost inevitable that some form of working platform will be needed. At the start of the job it may seem that the provision of a sawing trestle and a plank or two will suffice, or that old boxes can be stood on to reach the higher points on the hull. Having suffered sundry abrupt descents from a variety of 'lash-up' stagings, once holding a freshly opened quart of paint, the author is now firmly convinced that the minimum requirement is a pair of really stout builders' high trestles and the maximum width of stout planking that can be laid between them (Fig 21). Any time saved in the early stages of the job by makeshift bodges is likely to be lost many times over later on, not to mention the risk of injury when (not if) an inadequate staging collapses. If high trestles are used it is most important to see that both trestles are sitting firmly on all four feet and that both are upright, so that there can be no tendency for the planks to rock.

Work under the hull

Collision damage may be confined to the topsides where the work is easy to get at, but a shoal-draft boat which has grounded on an anchor or stake will need repairs to the bottom of the hull. This usually entails the owner working on his back or side right under the boat. If the boat is ashore on a good flat surface, a garage mechanic's wheeled working trolley will facilitate access to the working area; possibly Junior's skateboard could be borrowed. But the usual working site is seldom smooth enough for a small wheeled trolley to be of much help, so the worker must inch his or her way beneath the boat, taking care not to dislodge any of the blocks or shores which support the hull. Having at last wriggled into position it is distinctly annoying to discover that one has left the hammer – or drill, clamp, pipe, cigarettes, matches, nails – out of reach and one must wriggle all the way out again. This is where a patient, unskilled helper can be of great help, passing tools etc as required. But since such helpers are apt to wander off leaving the fuming owner stranded without tools, the best solution to this problem is to put all essentials into an old seed box with a length of string roughly equal to the length of the boat tied on each end. With the ends of the strings tied at each end of the boat, the improvised tool-box can be hauled along to the working area once the worker has got himself settled comfortably (or rather with the minimum of acute discomfort).

Whenever work is being done under a boat, some form of eye protection is advisable. The amount of dust, dirt and other debris which can become dislodged during any hammering operations needs to be experienced to be believed, and drilling and sawing generate fine chips which seem to have a special affinity for the corners of eyes. Industrial safety goggles are probably best, but possibly a motor cyclist's crash helmet with visor would be excellent for work beneath the hull. Another point to watch is that on a centreboarder the centre-plate is well and truly secured, so that there can be no risk whatsoever of it descending and decapitating the owner. Some form of internal clamp or bolt, plus at least one keel block beneath the business end of the plate should be regarded as the absolute minimum, and if there is any doubt about the strength of the pivot bolt, a keel block should be placed under each end of the slot.

Rolling a hull on its side

Shoal-draft cruisers of up to about 8 m (25 ft) in length can be rolled over to facilitate work on bottom planking. Two people can roll a hull over without undue effort provided they take it slowly and steadily, in small steps, trying all the time to keep the height of the centre of gravity of the hull constant or rising slightly. Initially, the supports under one bilge are lowered by about 25 mm (1 in) and the rolling is started. Once the hull has tipped to the point at which it can no longer balance on its keel blocks, then the rolling is continued by wedging up the keel supports. Care must be taken to ensure that the supporting blocks under the lower bilge coincide with the main transverse floor timbers, and that the ends of the hull are adequately supported. The broadest possible piles of blocks should be used to support a hull which is being rolled over, as the load on a pile may not be truly vertical, and a tall pile of small blocks will abruptly fly out of position if the effective load on the pile passes outside the area of contact between any of the blocks in the pile.

Part two

General techniques

Work on wooden boats is in many ways much the same as any other form of woodwork, but it does involve other disciplines such as blacksmiths' work, rigging and sailmaking. Some processes such as caulking are unique to boatwork and a number of others, whilst not confined solely to working on boats, are seldom met with elsewhere. There are also tools whose major use is in the boatbuilding trade. Adzes and drawknives are typical. No attempt is going to be made here to describe the actual technique of using tools – especially such splendid generators of hospital patients as adzes and drawknives in inexperienced hands. Much can be learnt from the written word, but craft skills must be acquired by personal tuition and supervised practice.

Once skill in handling basic woodworking tools has been obtained, the amateur can extend his repertoire, and people who have never met a skilled shipwright or seen an adze used have taught themselves to master the use of this very versatile tool; nevertheless an hour's tuition is worth many, many hours of trial and error work.

Some of the 'specialised' techniques are described in the sections where they would most commonly be applied (eg the fitting of trenails in grown frames); but a number which are likely to be used on more than one type of work have been collected together to form this 'general' section which can be referred to when appropriate in the subsequent sections on 'itemised' repairs.

Chapter 5

Fastenings

Plugging holes left by old fastenings

Wooden boats are held together with a very large number of fastenings of varying types and sizes, and any repair work will involve removing and refitting a far from insignificant number of fastenings. Occasionally it will be possible to refit a fastening into an old hole, but more usually this will have to be plugged and a fresh hole drilled for the new fastening. If the hole in the wood is clean, it can be plugged without further work, but care must be taken to see that the hole is really clean. If a screw has been run into the hole, and the screw was greased before it was fitted, it is most unlikely that it will be possible to bond in a plug with resin glue; the hole will have to be opened out to expose clean wood to which the resin will bond.

If only small holes in thick pieces of wood are to be plugged, and it is certain that it will not be necessary to fit a new fastening near the old hole, the plugging can be done with a dowel bedded in with a soft mastic. However, this is seldom the case. Far more usually the old hole must be plugged to maintain as far as possible the strength of the timber and to provide a sound site for fitting a new fastening. This can be achieved by gluing in a properly fitting dowel with a really good synthetic resin glue such as resorcinol resin. Formaldehyde or phenolic adhesives may seem easier to use, but they do not bond nearly so well to hardwoods and they are not so durable (as many home builders of plywood dinghies have found as the dinghy ages). Casein or animal glues are quite unsuitable for use on boat hulls. Epoxide resins can be used for bonding wood, but their best use on boats is as fillers for small cracks, into which the liquid resin can be poured and allowed to set. Liquid epoxies can be loaded with clean sawdust to make a (very messy) plastic wood which can be used in a variety of places on a boat.

Blind holes in frames etc can be plugged with straight parallel-sided dowels, and some through holes can be closed with a straight plug, but there are places where any stress on the plugged area will always be from one side, and a tapered plug (naturally fitted so the stress tightens the plug in the hole) should be fitted.

Dowels should always be cut from timber similar to that into which they are to be fitted, but not necessarily exactly the same type of timber. It must be remembered that it is probable that a new fastening will have to be fitted through, or partially through, the dowel, and the grain in the dowel will be running along the direction of the fastening and not across it. Thus the more open-grained softwoods and some of the softer mahoganies are unsuitable for use as plugs.

Preparing and fitting parallel dowels is a simple operation; tapered plugs require a little more thought. Usually, some form of tapered cutter will have to be improvised. A very suitable one is the tang of an old round file which has been broken off short (and most amateur workers' toolkits contain a broken end of a rat-tail file). But if a broken-off end of a file is used it must be with care, remembering that files are hard and brittle and if mishandled they can shatter, possibly causing serious damage to eyes or skin. An alternative to the tang of an old file is an old thick knife-blade suitably ground down to an appropriate taper.

If the worker has access to a lathe and is conversant with basic metalworking, it is a simple hour's work to knock up a tapered hole cutter in the form of a cruciform reamer, and also to make a tapered cutter (rather like a pencil sharpener) to produce the necessary tapered wooden plugs. The non-metalworker who opts to use the tang of a file to make the tapered holes will have to resort to good old-fashioned whittling to produce plugs. This is a nice relaxing job which can be done almost anywhere, anytime, and the boat repairer likely to use tapered plugs is well advised to make sure that suit-pockets, briefcase etc are suitably equipped with sharp knife and supply of offcuts of wood. It is surprising how many plugs can be whittled during a train journey on a business trip. Whittling whilst flying on business is probably better not attempted: the security guards might look askance at a well sharpened knife or chisel!

The plugs should be coated with resin glue and hammered into the holes firmly enough to ensure that they fill the hole properly, but not so hard as to risk splitting the rib or plank. Once the glue has set firmly, the ends of the plugs can be cleaned off flush with a sharp chisel.

Drilling and riveting

General

Many amateur workers are reluctant to undertake riveting on boats, regarding it as a magic art acquirable only by time-served shipwrights. Whilst it does require some practice to make a well-rounded riveted head, it is by no means as difficult as people seem to think. The process is described at length in John Leather's book *Clinker Boatbuilding* and any reader who has no experience of riveting is advised to read that book and to practise on some scrap timber. Basically the process is simple.

On clinker-built hulls, the nails are normally left with their heads flush with the surface of the planking, but on carvel hulls and other general riveting, the holes are usually counter-bored to sink the head below the surface of the timber so that it can be stopped over later.

The timbers to be riveted must be in their final position relative to one another before the hole for the rivet is drilled, but they do not have to be absolutely hard together, as closing down the rivets will put a tremendous pull on the joint and draw together any timbers which are capable of movement. The pull of the rivets can be sufficient to crack a carvel plank whose inner face has not been correctly hollowed to match the curve of the frames. To obtain the neatest possible appearance, the positions for all rivets should be marked out in pencil or chalk. Rivets placed at irregular intervals along a line which is not quite straight look very slovenly. For clinker hulls a simple gauge can be made up to ensure that all rivets are the same distance in from the edges of the planks.

Before considering the process of riveting, some thought must be given to the means of making the holes themselves.

Drills and drilling

The author used to find that drills were an expensive item, especially the smaller ones necessary for riveting on small boats, until one of the shipwrights in the local yard demonstrated their method of obtaining drills. A not too rusty bicycle wheel is acquired from a scrap dump or rubbish tip, and all the spokes are removed. The threaded and headed ends of the spokes are then cut off with a large pair of snips or toggle-linked end-cutters. One end of a spoke is heated in a bogie stove or by a blowlamp until it is bright red; it is then placed on a suitable flat iron or steel block, given a single good clout with a hammer, and plunged into cold water. This spreads and flattens the end. This end is next ground off to give two cutting edges, each at an angle of about 60 degrees to the axis of the drill, making sure that the cutting edges have been ground back to the maximum width of the swelled end of the spoke (Fig 22). The finished drill is then cropped off to a suitable length. Different sizes of drills are made by varying the strength of the hammer blow.

These 'spade' drills are remarkably free cutting, and have many, many times the potential life of an ordinary high-speed steel twist-drill when used on hardwood. The only point to be watched is that when deep holes are being drilled (eg through ribs), the drill should be withdrawn and cleared of chips once or twice for each hole. In theory,

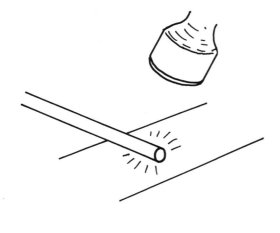

such drills should be properly hardened and tempered, but the local shipwrights never bothered. The cooling after hammering gives adequate hardness, and the author is still using one of the dozen drills he made from one of their spokes well over twenty years ago. Drill-bending in use can be minimised by cutting the drill off just long enough to do the job it was made for. The most common cause of failure is that after prolonged use the drills shear off at the point where they leave the chuck, so it is as well to allow about 13 mm ($\frac{1}{2}$ in) over-length.

One great advantage of these home-made drills is that very deep holes can be drilled, using progressively longer drills. If attempts are made to use one very long drill, it is almost certain to bend before the hole gets to any great depth, and the use of a series of drills of stepped lengths does enforce regular clearing of the hole!

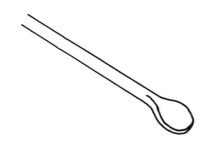

Riveting

Holes for the nails are drilled, using a drill very slightly smaller than the across-flats dimension of the square copper nail. On carvel hulls the hole will be counterbored to a diameter slightly larger than the head of the nail, to a depth of about 6 mm ($\frac{1}{4}$ in). On hardwood clinker planks the hole should be countersunk so that the nail head can sit flush with the surface of the wood, but on softer woods such as cedar or spruce only a very light countersink should be made as the closing of the rivet will pull the head down into the wood. The nail, which should be about 13 mm ($\frac{1}{2}$ in) longer than the thickness of wood to be riveted, is driven through the drilled hole until its head is flush with the wood, taking great care not to bend the fairly soft copper nail. A pin-punch is used to sink the head of the nail into a counterbore. If the nail bends at all, it should be withdrawn and discarded, and a new straight nail used. If more than about 3 per cent of the nails used bend, then the drilled holes should be fractionally (a few $\frac{1}{1000}$ in) larger (assuming a basic ability to hit straight with a hammer). If no nails ever show any sign of bending, it can be assumed that the drilled hole could be a shade

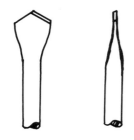

Drill Making:
Fig 22A   *Hammering the end of the heated rod*
Fig 22B   *The flattened end*
Fig 22C   *The drill ground to two cutting edges*

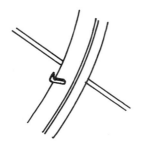

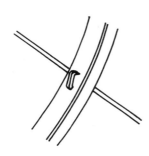

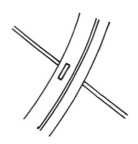

Clenching:
Fig 23A *The tip of the nail is bent*
Fig 23B *The projecting end of the nail is bent*
Fig 23C *The nail end is hammered into the*
timber

smaller, but that is only a guide for the very amateur – a skilled professional shipwright would hammer in nails all day without bending any. If the hull is on the light side, it may be desirable to have a helper inside the boat to hold a heavy block of wood against the plank or frame immediately beside where the nail is expected to emerge. A large mallet head is ideal; even better is a piece of metal of about 2–3 kg (4–6 lb) weight, faced with 25 mm (1 in) of softwood.

On small dinghies, the nail may be clenched over. This is done by turning over the point of the nail at a right angle, then bending over the nail where it leaves the surface of the wood so that the end of the nail forms a staple lying along the grain of the wood, into which it will sink to give a smooth, flush finish (Fig 23). Whilst the nail is being clenched over, it is prevented from moving back through the wood by the helper holding a heavy block of metal against its head. Professional shipwrights usually have their own special riveting 'dollies', which may be quite well turned with a taper at each end, one end finishing in a slightly domed surface about 13 mm ($\frac{1}{2}$ in) in diameter for flush nails, and the other end turned to leave a 'pip' about 6 mm ($\frac{1}{4}$ in) in diameter and about 10 mm ($\frac{3}{8}$ in) long for 'holding up' against nails which are counterbored into the wood. Some shipwrights fit transverse steel pegs into the sides of the dolly like small handles, which prevent it from slipping out of the helper's hand (Fig 24). Dollies vary in size from about 300 mm (1 ft) long and 75-100 mm (3-4 in) in diameter for use on large boats, down to perhaps a quarter of these dimensions for smaller cruisers and dinghies. When selecting a piece of metal to be used as a dolly, one must bear in mind that it must not be so big or heavy as to be awkward or tiring to hold against the nail head, but on the other hand it is the weight (or more precisely the inertia, which is directly related to the weight) of the dolly which does the work of resisting the force of the hammer blows and causes the nail to rivet or clench over tightly instead of slipping back through the wood. The helper must be careful to hold the dolly against the head of

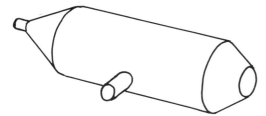

Fig 24 *Riveting 'dolly' with pip on one end and cross pin*

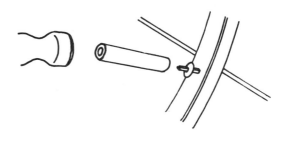

the nail and not the wood beside it, as otherwise the wood will be bruised.

On larger dinghies and cruising yachts the nail will be riveted over a copper roove – a large, slightly domed copper washer. Rooves of the correct size must be bought with the nails. If the roove is too small, it will not be possible to drive it over the nail; if it is too large, it will not be possible to rivet the nail over it, and it will not stay in place on the nail. The roove has a circular hole which is just slightly larger than the size of the nail measured across the flats, so it has to be driven down over the end of the square nail, the corners of which 'bite' into the metal of the roove. Either a hollow-ended punch or a piece of thick-walled steel tubing about 50 mm (2 in) long is held over the roove, and lightly tapped down with a small 200 g (½ lb) hammer. The roove is put on with its dome outwards, and care must be taken not to hit so hard that the roove is flattened against the wood or even in extreme cases turned inside out. It is tapped down until its outer edge rests against the wood (Fig 25).

The end of the nail is then cut off as square as possible, leaving about 3 mm (⅛ in) or just under projecting through the roove. Toggle-linked end cutters are the best tool for this job. Heavy duty, direct-action pliers or side cutters can be used, but they are a real strain on the fingers, and most workers would be able to use them for only perhaps a dozen nails of reasonable size. The roove should stay firmly in place on the nail, held by its grip on the nail's corners. If it shows any sign of slipping, it is best replaced.

The next operation is to rivet the end of the nail over the top of the roove, by tapping fairly gently with a 200 g (½ lb)

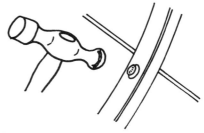

Riveting:
Fig 25A *The roove is hammered over the end of the nail*
Fig 25B *The nail is cut off to length*
Fig 25C *The end of the nail is riveted over the roove*

hammer. For best results, the ball end of the hammer should be used to spread the end of the nail evenly and smoothly over the roove, leaving the roove still conical so that it is partly acting as a metal spring keeping the wood really tightly held. People with no experience of riveting may be surprised at the drawing power of a well-closed rivet. A plank which cannot be clamped or pushed hard home (by a small amount) will be gently but firmly drawn into place by a few taps on the rivet. The helper must ensure that the riveting dolly is held firmly against the head of the nail during the closing of the rivet. Most amateurs' first two or three attempts at riveting tend to look somewhat of a mess – although they are probably quite sound; but once the knack has been gained, it is a soothing, relaxing and very satisfying job. Neatness of work possible may be gauged by the oft-told story of an Essex master shipwright who would draw his silk handkerchief over the inside of a new hull, and woe betide the shipwright or apprentice concerned if the handkerchief snagged on an imperfectly closed rivet! Having sailed in the products of that yard, the author can vouch for the fact that it was hardly possible to feel where the riveted-over nail end merged into the dome of the roove.

Fitting screws and bolts

Woodscrews must always be properly fitted if they are to do their job effectively. The outer piece of wood being screwed should be drilled with a clearance hole which is a tight but not binding fit on the shank of the screw, and the hole should just enter the inner piece of wood. A pilot hole should be drilled into the inner piece to a depth which is just shorter than the length of the screw (Fig 26). Tables of 'correct' drill sizes to be used have been published, but the author is not aware of any such tables which make full allowances for different types of timber, different materials from which the screws are made, and different lengths of screws. Smaller holes are needed in fir or pine than in well-seasoned oak, and a longer screw can be fitted safely into a larger pilot hole than a short screw. Common sense and experience offer the best guide on the right size drill to use, and if the worker is making up his own drills it is easy enough to make a new one slightly larger (or smaller). A full set of twist-drills

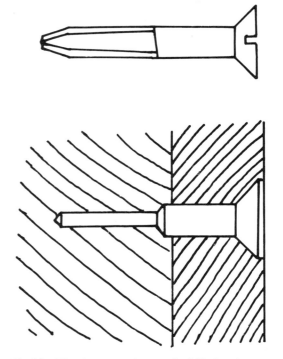

Fig 26 *Woodscrew and properly drilled and countersunk hole*

is an expensive (and likely to be short-lived) luxury for the average boat owner. Another point in favour of using home-made drills for boat work is that, when drilling for woodscrews, the smaller diameter drill is required for the deeper hole whereas bought drills are made shorter as the diameter decreases.

Screws (bronze or gunmetal) should be lightly greased before fitting. A good quality screwdriver with a blade which is properly ground to fit the slot of the screw should always be used. Some workers like to use the ratchet-action 'pump' type screwdrivers. These certainly run the screws in rapidly, but if the blade slips out of the slot in the screw it will leave a nasty gouge in the wood beside the screw head. These high-speed screwdrivers are ideal for use with cross-head screws, but they cannot be recommended for use on plain slotted screws on boatwork, where more often than not the screw will have to go in at an awkward angle. The author always preferred to use a screwdriver bit in a carpenter's brace rather than a screwdriver, but if this is done the brace should not be turned with anything like the full power possible on the handle if the screw is at all tight. Full power on the handle of a normal brace can wring the head right off a No 14 gunmetal screw being driven into well-seasoned oak.

There can be few things more frustrating than to get a screw stuck immovably into an old oak frame or stem about a turn or two before it is fully home. This may occur if the pilot hole drilled for the screw is either too tight or too short, but it can occur simply because the wood is very tough and hard. One way of avoiding a stuck or sheared-off bronze or gunmetal screw is to run a steel screw in first, to within about a turn and a half of tight, then to fit the final screw in the hole prepared by the steel screw. Fifty to a hundred years old oak can be very hard indeed and sometimes metal-working techniques yield a better result than normal woodworking methods. Through-bolts should be put in with a grommet of caulking cotton under their head, and nuts should be well greased before they are fitted. Large, fairly thick washers should be used under the nuts.

One vital rule when selecting screws or bolts for work on a boat is to guard against galvanic (electrochemical) action. This is a very complex subject. An owner who is fully familiar with all the principles involved can make the best possible use of the wide range of metals available, but the average amateur can best play safe by following simple rules:

Never mix ferrous (iron based) and cuprous (copper based, eg bronze, gun-metal or copper) metals

Use stainless steel screws or bolts on aluminium fittings (better to use bronze fittings and bolts though)

Avoid the use of brass under any circumstances

If ferrous fittings or fastenings are required, try and use wrought iron. If this is not possible, use mild steel

Have all iron or steel parts and fastenings hot-dip galvanised; never use electro-tinned fastenings on boatwork

Often the type of keel will dictate what metal must be used for strap floors and for their fastenings. A cast-iron keel will require iron keel-bolts, which means galvanised-iron floors and bolts must be used; whereas if the keel is lead with bronze bolts, the floors and their bolts must also be bronze or gunmetal.

Chapter 6

Scarph joints

Broadly speaking, woodwork on boats does not involve any great skill in making complex joints, and anybody who can make a simple halving or dovetail joint can do most of the work on a boat. Indeed one can see on display at the Boat Show dovetail joints which are far from well-made. However, one joint with which the would-be boat repairer will almost certainly have to gain familiarity is the scarph joint in its various forms. These are used whenever it is necessary to join timbers end to end with the maximum possible strength and the minimum increase in size or weight.

The manufacturers of modern synthetic resin glues point out with justifiable pride that their products, if used according to the instructions, will result in joints which are much stronger than the wood they join. This is absolutely true, but what is not so often pointed out is that this does not mean that two pieces of wood can be glued to have the same (or better) physical properties as a single piece. The strength of the glued joint can make the final structure weaker in some respects, because the change in strength at the glue-line can cause distortions in the stress patterns within the structure, and these distortions can lead to premature failure of the wood adjacent to the joint. A perfect adhesive should have exactly the same strength and other physical properties as the materials it is to join. Since this is impossible to achieve on wood, whose properties can be quite variable, joints must be designed to minimise the effects of the discontinuity in strength.

It must be noted that it is possible to take advantage of the superior strength of resin glues and to design laminated structures which are much stronger than could be made from a single piece of wood. A solid mast made from a baulk which has been split lengthwise and glued up with one half

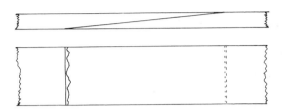

Fig 27   Plain scarph joint

reversed is a simple example of such a structure.

Scarph joints minimise the risk of breakage near the joint by spreading the discontinuity over a considerable length, so that at any cross section taken along the joint there is a substantial area of timber carrying a normal, undistorted stress.

The simplest and easiest to cut of the scarph joints is the plain scarph (Fig 27) in which the ends of the two pieces to be joined are cut off at a long fine angle. The joint is usually cut across the thickness of the timber, and the slope used should be long. Various authorities quote different figures from 1 in 8 upwards for the minimum length of a plain scarph; but 1 in 12 is a good figure to aim for. Often the length achievable is dictated by other factors, such as the spacing of the frames in a hull. The plain scarph is usually cut with a plane. It has two main drawbacks. One is that it can be very difficult to locate the two pieces accurately for gluing; the second is the long feather edges at the ends which often break away to leave unsightly joint faces. It is best to restrict the use of this joint to joining sawn pieces of timber which will later be trimmed to final size, and preferably to pieces which will in turn form part of a larger glued structure such as a built-up mast or a laminated beam or frame.

The first variant of the plain scarph is the keyed scarph in which a thin key is set into

(upper left) *Deck replacement: covering board fitted and dowels being fitted over screw heads*

(upper right) *Mast repair: cutter's mast broken at upper peak halliard eyebolt. Broken top and scarph joint cut on sound portion;* (lower left) *new top scarphed on to mast. Note clamps used and Spanish Windlass;* (lower right) *mast bands on and repaired spar ready for varnishing*
(M. D. Millar)

*Some of the boats in the first (1963) East Coast
Old Gaffers Race hoping for a breeze*

Fig 28   *Keyed scarph joint*

each half of the joint (Fig 28). This joint can still be cut with a plane, with just the keyways having to be chiselled out. This joint is positive in location, and before the days of strong waterproof glues it enabled scarph joints to withstand greater compressive or tensile loads. Modern adhesives, properly used, eliminate any need for a key to achieve strength. The keyed scarph has the objectionable feather edges of the plain scarph.

The stopped scarph is similar to the plain scarph, but has the fine feather edges cut off at a thickness at which the wood will not break away, but which does not significantly affect the strength of the joint (Fig 29). The joint is self-locating provided the

Fig 29   *Stopped scarph joint*

two pieces are pushed together, and the stops can be cut deep enough to offer the same resistance to compressive loading as a keyed scarph. All resistance to tensile stresses must be provided by the adhesive or by fastenings. A stopped scarph is slightly harder to cut than a plain scarph, since it cannot be cut with a try-plane, but must be chiselled or cut with a small rebate or block plane used across the grain. This is seldom a disadvantage on boat-repair work since it is rarely possible to use a plane at the end of the original piece to which a new length is to be joined. Also a stopped scarph can be cut with a saw (with extreme care!), which gives a better face for gluing than a planed plain scarph.

A stopped scarph can be keyed to withstand tensile stresses as shown in Fig 30, but such a joint would normally be used only in the absence of any good resin glues.

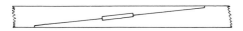

Fig 30   *Stopped keyed scarph joint*

This does not imply that the joint is obsolete. It is quite possible to have to repair a wooden boat in places where resin glues are not available, or where conditions of temperature or humidity make their use impracticable. On large joints, two or more keys may be used.

Fig 31   *Stepped scarph joint*

The next joint to be considered is the stepped scarph (Fig 31). This is ideal for joining plywood, as each step can be cut to coincide with a glue-line in the ply. It can also be easily cut in plain timber on a circular saw, using a broad cutter and making many cuts, altering the depth setting for perhaps every five alterations of the fence setting. Equally, the joint is easily cut with a rebate plane. It would normally be used where the width of the timbers to be joined is greater than the total length of the joint, and can be regarded as having the same strength and general properties as a stopped scarph. An equivalent to a keyed version of the joint can be made by making the middle step three times the width of the others and undercutting it as shown in Fig 32 but, like the stopped keyed scarph, this is a joint for use only when a good resin glue cannot be used.

Fig 32   *Keyed stepped scarph joint in five-ply*

The last of the family of scarph joints to be mentioned here goes under various names, such as hooked scarph, dovetail scarph or (worst of all) wedged double dovetail scarph.

Normally, all the joints so far considered are cut across the thickness of the timber. The hooked scarph is cut across the width and is most commonly found joining covering-board pieces, where continuity of strength is important. Unlike all the above joints, the hooked scarph is self-locking, and does not depend on any adhesive or fastenings for its strength. A glued hooked

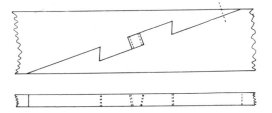

Fig 33 *Hooked scarph joint*

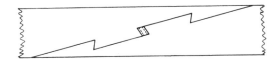

Fig 34 *Hooked scarph with angled wedge*

scarph is, of course, stronger than one left unglued.

As can be seen in Fig 33, it consists of two parallel-angled faces which alternate along the joint, the outer pair of alternations forming the dovetails or hooks which give the joint its name and also give it the self-locking property and continuity of strength. The inner pair of alternations are cut parallel in plan, but with a slope to their faces so that a wedge can be driven between them to lock the hooks firmly together. The slope of a hooked scarph is usually less than that of other scarph joints, at between 1 in 4 and 1 in 6. Long hooked scarph joints can have the central wedge cut thinner than shown in Fig 33 and angled so that the wedge faces form a third dovetail locking the centre of the joint (Fig 34).

On an unglued hooked scarph, pins, dumps, or screws are usually put through the ends of the joint (dotted lines on Fig 33) to prevent the two pieces from twisting relative to one another. When laying out hooked scarph joints, care must be taken not to set the tails or hooks too near the edges. Some amateurs regard these joints as difficult to make, but in fact the wedge in the centre means that the only factors which must be watched are that the angled faces on both pieces are the same distance apart throughout, and that the two faces of the outer tails will mate simultaneously.

A variant of the hooked scarph which is sometimes seen is the keyed scarph, in which the key takes the form of two dovetails back to back so that it locks the joint as it is driven in. Such a dovetail key can be used with a plain or a stopped scarph.

Chapter 7

Measuring

Taking measurements on boats under repair

When a new boat is being built it is usually set up level, with its waterline horizontal so that all verticals can be established with a plumb-line; but when repair work is being done the boat may not be level either fore and aft or athwartships. Most of the measurements required will be made with reference to other points on the hull and not to any pre-set levels, but there can be occasions when it is handy to have a reference back to the true waterline datum. One way in which this can be achieved is to insert into the inner faces of the stem and aft deadwood or sternpost, light screw-eyes at waterline level on the centre-line of the hull. A string stretched between the eyes will give the required working datum. The positions for the eyes can be determined by measuring the freeboard fore and aft whilst the boat is afloat, then measuring inside the hull from the underside of the deck. If the boat has a centreboard-case or a permanently fitted mast support-pillar, pairs of eyes equally spaced either side of the centre-line can be fitted so that the lines pass clear of the obstructions.

A lightweight, large set square will often be found helpful, and can be made up from three laths tacked together in the form of a 3,4,5 triangle. A really long, flexible straight-edge is another very useful item. The easiest and cheapest to make is a length of thin hardboard, which can be made up from three 1.8–2.4 m (6–8 ft) lengths with long scarph joints glued and riveted together. The strips need to be about 100–150 mm (4–6 in) wide. The straightness of the edge is easily verified by using the edge to draw a line down a long plank, then turning the straight-edge over and making sure it still touches the drawn line along its whole length. A set of flexible straight-edges cut from hardboard in lengths from about 0.6 m–4.5 m (2 ft–15 ft) can be used to lay off comparative measurements for new planks, frames, beams etc. It is always preferable to work to marks carefully made on a plain edge rather than to actual rule measurements, because when measurements are being read off a rule and then laid out on the workpiece there are two chances of making a mistake, whereas a single pencil or chalk mark on a plain edge is quite unambiguous. One wonders how many pieces of wood have been cut too short because a worker has not realised that in taking off a measurement he was working from the 'wrong end' of a rule, and (on a two foot rule) what he thought was eleven inches was in fact thirteen. This is so easily done, especially when working in awkward, confined spaces, that it is better to use a method which does not involve any such risks.

Some form of adjustable angle-gauge is almost certain to be needed. These can be bought at any good tool merchants; or a couple of laths or offcuts of metal strip known to be straight can be joined with a bolt and wingnut.

One measuring problem which causes some workers considerable worry is how to determine the exact length of a timber which must be bent into place and fitted into a recess at each end. A very simple way is to use a flexible straight-edge which is shorter than the required timber to measure from each end back to a common datum point or line near the middle of the required piece. For example, the exact length for a new plank on a double-ended hull can be determined by laying off the length from each end to the fore side of a midships frame. If simple hardboard straight-edges are being used, the ends can be cut to the appropriate angles to fit the recesses into which the plank must be fitted. Such shaping and re-shaping of the ends of the straight-edges gradually reduces their length, but a set of three strips should outlast work on at least half a dozen boats.

One point to watch when taking measurements on an old (or even not so old) boat, is never to assume that any measurement taken on one side of the hull can be applied on the opposite side. Some boats are symmetrical to very fine limits indeed – especially the older class-racing dinghies, for some of which the measurement rules were extremely strict – but some cruising yachts and old working boats are far from symmetrical, with appreciable differences of some centimetres (inches) between the lengths of such items as side deck beams.

A working knowledge of geometry and trigonometry can be a help in determining accurate measurements within a boat's hull. Anybody who can navigate a cruising yacht will certainly have more than adequate mathematical ability to solve any triangulation problems involved in working out hull dimensions. However, lack of any mathematical ability is no bar to repair work provided one can work a piece of wood down until it does fit!

Spiling

Spiling is a method of transferring curves or other irregular shapes from one surface to another. It can be used to mark out the shapes of replacement planks, bulkheads, or any other features which must fit against curved or angled surfaces where simple measurements of lengths and widths are inadequate. The first requirement is some form of datum baseline – which can be straight or curved. If the width of a plank, or the curvature on the edge of a clinker plank, is being set out, the datum would usually be a straight-edged batten or long piece of hardboard or plywood bent around the hull. For cutting out a bulkhead or cupboard side which must fit against the curved inside of the hull, the baseline could be a suitable curve drawn on a piece of scrap plywood or hardboard which vaguely fits against the hull's side.

Fig 35 *Spiling to take off the shape of a plank using a long straight batten*

The datum baseline is divided into segments, which may be uniform, or in areas of sharp curvature may be closed up. The distance from the datum line to the curved surface to be matched is measured at each division-point with a pair of dividers, taking care to measure square to the datum line. If the datum line is straight, the dividers can be used to prick off the distance measured straight onto the timber to be cut, taking care to make the mark squarely to the datum edge (Fig 35). When a curved datum line is being used on a thin piece of plywood, eg to measure for a bulkhead, the distance measured can be pricked off on the plywood inside the datum line (Fig 36). When all the distances have been pricked off, the plywood is laid on the material to be cut, and the dividers are used to transfer the measured distances from the points pricked off inside the datum line to the material. When all the points have been pricked off, they are joined into a fair curve. The proper way (really the only way) to do this is to bend a flexible batten round so it touches all the pricked-off points, and then to run a pencil along the batten.

This is a very easy process for those whose work involves frequent use of such techniques, but those who are not accustomed to the drawing of fair curves may not find it quite so easy. If helpers are

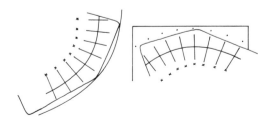

Fig 36 *Spiling to take off the shape of a bulkhead using a piece of hardboard or plywood*

available, then it is not too difficult for two people to hold a long batten whilst a third person runs the pencil along. The single-handed worker may have to tack the batten down to the workpiece with wire nails, or use odd weights (ballast pigs are handy for this) to hold the batten in place. Usually the amateur will find that his (or her) fair curve does not pass through all the points pricked off. If the pricked-off point lies inside the drawn line, it is not worth worrying – if the line is wrong at that point the excess wood can be planed off; but any

pricked-off points which lie outside the line should be checked – the curve required might not be as fair as the batten, or the batten might not be perfectly uniform. In fact really good pieces of uniform timber which will bend to fair curves are not all that common, and an amateur boatworker is well advised to keep carefully any really good battens he finds. Wood may look quite uniformly grained and knot free, but on bending it substantial variations in stiffness may be found.

Chapter 8

Steaming

Boatwork often involves bending pieces of wood to a curved shape, or twisting planks etc. Seasoned new wood will bend quite well dry, but there is a limit to the amount of bend which can be put into any given timber. Wood can be persuaded to bend by heating it on one side (the inner side of the bend) and soaking the other side – some canoes are made by this technique. But this way of changing the shape by altering the moisture content is effective mainly across the grain of the wood.

Wood which will almost take a required bend dry can sometimes be given extra flexibility by a thorough soaking – a couple of weeks' immersion. But soaked, bent wood will straighten again as it dries out. The classic method of putting small radius, permanent bends in hardwoods is by steaming the wood. This is a job which is feared by many quite competent amateur woodworkers, but their fears are quite without foundation. Provided a reasonably efficient steaming system is set up, and the right timber is used (see also page 99), steaming and bending is a very pleasant and rewarding task. In fact, it is not unknown for amateurs who have finished all the work on their boat to take up making traditional bentwood chairs, or supplying mast hoops to their friends.

Some form of steam-chest and boiler will have to be rigged up, their elaborateness depending on the amount of steaming to be done. The simplest system is a length of old galvanised-iron drainpipe with a bend at one end. The pipe should be the thin-walled variety rolled up from sheet metal, not the heavy cast-iron type which would take far too long to heat up. If a length with a bend cannot be found, then one end can be flattened and folded over. The bent end is securely closed with a wooden plug, and the pipe is supported with the closed end on a

Fig 37 *Old drainpipe rigged up for steaming ribs*

pile of two or three bricks and the open end resting in a suitable forked stick driven into the ground (Fig 37). The pipe must slope, and the steeper the slope the better, but the open end should not be more than about 1.2 m (4 ft) above the ground. Whilst a forked stick is the simplest and easiest form of support for the open end, many suitable alternatives are possible, such as resting the pipe on a convenient low wall or fence, or wiring it to hang from the roof of an open shed.

The length of the pipe should be such that when the lower end of the pipe is filled with water to above the highest point that will be heated by the fire or whatever other means is provided to boil the water, the longest timber to be steamed can be contained in the pipe with its end clear of the water.

Suitable means of heating the pipe to boil the water fairly rapidly must be provided. A 2.8 l (5 pt) blowlamp or large propane gas-torch can be used, but the usual method is a wood fire. By the time one gets round to steaming ribs, there will probably be a fair selection of old planks and other scraps of timber waiting to be burnt. Primus stoves, or camping gas-burners can be used to heat the water, but only on a small pipe. It needs several such 'domestic' stoves to boil water at a rate sufficient to steam ribs of any reasonable size – over about 19 mm × 13 mm ($\frac{3}{4}$ in × $\frac{1}{2}$ in); and a multiplicity of small stoves takes up too great a length of pipe for the system to work effectively.

Such an iron-pipe system has the advantage of cheapness and simplicity – it can be rigged up in half an hour from scrap material – but it has several disadvantages. First, it will usually discolour the ribs steamed in it. This does not matter if the inside of the boat is to be painted, but it can mar the appearance of a varnished or oiled dinghy hull. Secondly, both the water level and the source of heat must be carefully and continuously controlled. The ribs should be kept clear of the water, but the source of heat must be kept to below the water level. Put the other way round, the water level must be maintained above the highest point at which any flame touches the metal pipe. If the flames are allowed to spread too high, or the water level gets too low, then the part of the pipe in the flame which is not filled with water will heat up very rapidly and the result can be charred or burnt timber (which does not bend well). The third disadvantage is that the upper, steam-filled length of pipe loses heat quite rapidly, and it can be difficult to steam a long rib (such as a midships rib for a 2.4 m/8 ft dinghy). The upper end of the pipe can be lagged by putting a length of asbestos pipe round it, but it is inadvisable to try lagging it with old blankets or other combustible materials; the usual result is that the lagging catches fire and the whole pipe gets somewhat hotter than it should.

However, provided the operator is well aware of all the possible snags, iron-pipe steaming-tubes can be used with great success. One helpful precaution is to keep a large kettle boiling on a stove beside the system, so that the water level can be kept topped up regularly, and also so that the

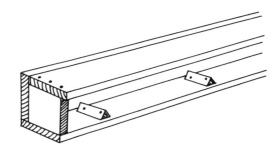

Fig 38 *Partially built steam-chest with one side still to be fitted*

operator can enjoy a cup of tea or coffee whilst waiting for the wood to stew. When in use, the open end of the pipe should be lightly plugged with a screwed-up rag, sufficient to keep the steam in the pipe but not to make a high pressure system.

Better results can be obtained from a proper steam-chest, and the amateur who is doing the job as much for the pleasure and experience of doing the work as for the end result will certainly find it more rewarding to do the job properly. The steam-chest itself comprises a simple wooden box slightly longer than the longest rib to be steamed. Four 102 mm × 25 mm (4 in x 1 in) planks nailed or screwed together to leave 76 mm (3 in) square inside is about the smallest reasonably practical size for steaming a rib or two. Triangular pieces of wood about 25 mm (1 in) high are nailed across inside the base of the chest, about 229 – 305 mm (9 – 12 in) apart. These triangular pieces are cut short about 13 mm ($\frac{1}{2}$ in) from the sides of the chest. One end of the box is closed by an end-piece nailed in (Fig 38). The finished

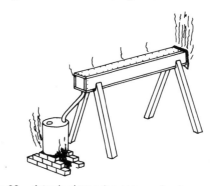

Fig 39 *A typical wooden steam-chest*

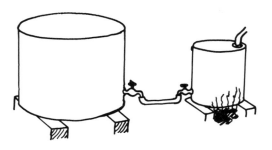

Fig 40 *Self-feeding boiler for a low-pressure steam-chest*

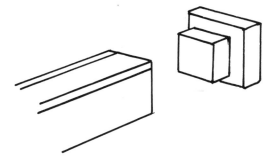

Fig 41 *End-plug for a low pressure steam-chest*

chest is mounted on four woden legs, which can be notched and nailed to the sides (Fig 39) so that it stands with a slight slope down to the closed end and also with a slight slope across so that all condensation will drain down to one corner. A length of metal pipe is pushed tightly into a hole drilled in this lower corner and taken down to the boiler, which will normally stand below the end of the steam-chest, just far enough away so that if an open fire is used as the source of heat there can be no risk of setting fire to the chest itself. Almost any form of boiler can be used. A large kettle whose spout comes out of the top of the body is ideal, or a small empty oil drum can be used (make sure *all* the oil is out of it before starting steaming). The boiler can be stood on two short walls of bricks, between which the fire can be lit. Since the object of the exercise is to generate as much steam as possible, the boiler should have a fairly large-diameter base and should not be too deep. Also it must have some access which can be opened whilst the system is in use so that the water supply can be kept topped up.

A very superior system can be built if two different sized drums, both with taps near the bottom, are available. The two drums are joined tap to tap with a short length of metal pipe. The smaller drum, which must be a closed one, and which acts as a boiler, has the steam-outlet pipe

fitted into the normal top filler plug, and is mounted on bricks; the larger drum, which is better open-topped, is stood on wooden blocks beside the boiler (Fig 40). The level of water in the two drums will be equal, and the system can be kept topped up by pouring cold water into the large open drum to maintain the level. Such a two-drum system offers the great advantage that it can be run safely with much less water in the boiler than would be possible with a single-drum boiler, so less heat is required and the system steams up faster. Also, it can be run safely as a (low!) pressure steamer. Any excessive build-up of pressure in the system will result in the steam blowing the water back from the boiler into the large drum until the steam escapes through the pipe linking the drums. If the water level is kept to about 51 mm (2 in) above the taps such a system cannot explode, but it is liable to make some peculiar noises if the steam does blow back. However, with a wooden steam-chest this is most unlikely to occur as the boiler is kept fully occupied supplying steam to escape through the many inevitable small leaks in the box.

The steam-chest should be provided with a loose fitting end-plug made of a couple of pieces of wood (Fig 41) to ensure that all the steam generated does not simply escape.

Part three

Repairs to the hull structure

On all but small dinghies, most repairs to the hull structure of a boat will involve some removal of internal and external fittings etc. Outside the hull, items such as chainplates, various beadings, bilge keels etc will possibly have to be removed. Inside, anything from a crude makeshift bulkhead to a full ceiling (lining of planks inside the frames) and some very beautiful Victorian mahogany furniture may have to be taken out. Obviously the less the interior of a fully fitted hull has to be disturbed the better, but it is always safer to err on the side of having taken out too much rather than too little. One essential when stripping out a hull is to keep a very clear record of where and how each piece was fitted, and to label everything. Just like ballast, most of the pieces of wood inside a boat will fit in one place, and in one place only. All the following sections are written assuming that the hull has been stripped down to expose the parts requiring repair.

Chapter 9

The outer skin

Repairs to the outer skin of a boat may be necessary because the boat has suffered mechanical damage (eg in a collision); because it has been attacked by worm or rot; or because although the timber is sound, the hull leaks. The first two reasons require that part of the skin of the boat be replaced.

In the case of collision damage, the area to be repaired is usually obvious but rot and worm attacks may spread considerably further through the skin than was originally appreciated, and often the full extent of the area to be repaired may become clear only after the work has been started. It is obviously vital to ensure that all the afflicted material is removed or burnt. What is left is best soaked in a proprietary wood preservative such as Cuprinol.

Types of hull

Before considering the actual repairs, it is as well to have an understanding of the major differences between the various types of wooden hull. Basically, five types need to be considered: (a) sheet-plywood; (b) moulded-plywood (which can be assumed to include double-diagonal planking and various other 'special' types of construction such as the Ashcroft system); (c) clinker-planked; (d) carvel-planked and (e) strip-planked.

A sheet-plywood hull is built up on frames covered with sheets of plywood, and the hull form is almost invariably hard chine. Some people have been misled, because the hull has clearly defined angles and the skin starts life as a flat sheet of plywood, into believing that cross sections of the hull will reveal straight edges to the frames. This is far from being the case, as the ply skin is usually rolled into portions of surfaces of (very large) cones, and hence

all cross sections taken square to the centre-line of the boat will show some curvature – possibly slight, but nevertheless not straight. The shape of such sheet-ply hulls is dictated by the framework over which the ply skin is attached.

Moulded plywood hulls retain their shape because the ply skin was built up as a compound curved surface, so any repairs must retain the curvature within the skin. Any framing or bulkheads are there to add strength to the hull at appropriate points, but usually they are cut to fit the already moulded hull.

Similarly, the shape of a clinker-planked hull is determined by the shaping and fastening of the individual planks. The ribs, which are usually of steam-bent timber, serve only to supply 'across the grain' strength which would be lacking if the hull had only riveted planks. It is worth noting that clinker-ply hulls are usually built without any ribs, as the plywood strakes have the same strength across as they do along.

Carvel hulls, on the other hand, depend on their ribs and framing both to hold them together and to keep them in shape. The width of the planking and the caulking between the planks can contain any compressive stresses on the hull, but all tensile stresses are taken by the framing.

Strip-planked or clinker hulls hold their shape in the same way as a moulded-ply hull, but because of their weakness across the grain of the strips they require internal framing similar to that of clinker hulls.

Most repairs to the skin of a boat, whether necessitated by damage, rot or worms, will usually be associated with repairs to the framing as well. To avoid excessive complications, this text will be written as if the repairs are to be treated totally separately. In almost all practical cases, both planks and frames will be replaced together.

On sheet-plywood hulls, it is clear that any new framing necessary should be provided before the new plywood skin is replaced. On moulded-ply, clinker- and strip-planked hulls the skin or planking is repaired first and then any new ribs are fitted. Carvel hulls, however, require that most of the frames and ribs are in place before any new planks are replaced. On boats with alternate sawn and bent frames, the sawn frames should be replaced before the planking, but the bent frames can be done after the planking.

One general point to be borne in mind is that on hulls in which the shape is controlled by the skin, ie clinker or moulded-ply, all replacement strakes must be cut to the correct curvature and fitted without any edgewise bending. On carvel hulls, a certain amount of edgewise bending of the planks can be tolerated, and on strip-planked hulls the edge-bending is a fundamental part of the construction method.

Plywood hulls

Not many older cruising yachts were built of plywood, but many dinghies were, and some plywood dinghies survive to a remarkably old age. Both the two main classes of plywood hulls – those moulded to shape and those built from sheet plywood on frames – may suffer from mechanical damage, and those built from sheet plywood may suffer from delamination. The first step on any repair is to assess the area of damage. If this is small, it can usually be corrected very easily on either type of hull; but if a large area is affected, special precautions may have to be taken to retain the hull's correct shape.

Small repairs with liquid adhesive

Both sheet-ply and moulded-plywood hulls can suffer from small areas of delamination. Often the first evidence of this is that paint refuses to stay on the hull, and cracks and blisters may appear in the paint. The extent of the damage is easily assessed by tapping the hull, with either a knuckle, bowl of a pipe, knife handle, or any other suitable implement. The resonant 'bong' of sound

plywood is very different from the diffuse sound in a delaminated area. When delamination is suspected, any exposed edges of plywood should be given particular attention (eg where the skin of the hull overlaps the transom and no beading is fitted).

Once all the delamination has been found, all paint should be removed from the affected areas. The outer skin of the plywood is usually found to be wrinkled, and may exhibit a few open cracks (Fig 42).

Fig 42 *Signs of delamination on plywood*

All fastenings should be removed from the area, and the wood should be allowed to dry out thoroughly. If the delamination is only small in area and is confined to the outer layer, a cure can be effected by easing the outer veneer up with the blade of a screwdriver (Fig 43) and filling the cavity with a liquid adhesive. The two-part liquid

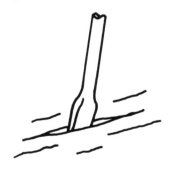

Fig 43 *Opening a split in delaminated plywood*

epoxide resins (eg Araldite D with hardener 951) are excellent for this purpose. Once it is certain that the cavity is full of resin and there are no trapped air pockets, the screwdriver is withdrawn and cleaned. It is advisable to wash all tools used (and the

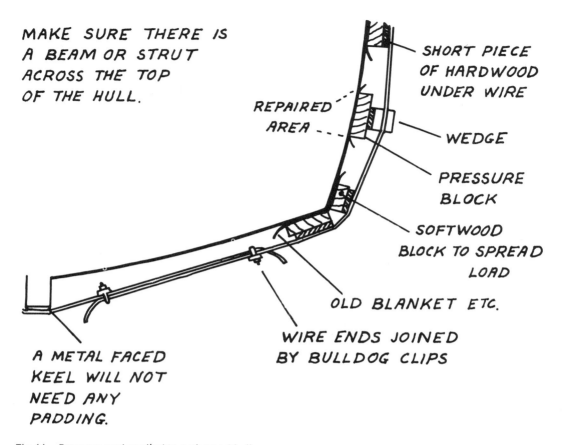

MAKE SURE THERE IS
A BEAM OR STRUT
ACROSS THE TOP
OF THE HULL.

REPAIRED
AREA

SHORT PIECE
OF HARDWOOD
UNDER WIRE

WEDGE

PRESSURE
BLOCK

SOFTWOOD
BLOCK TO SPREAD
LOAD

OLD BLANKET ETC.

WIRE ENDS JOINED
BY BULLDOG CLIPS

A METAL FACED
KEEL WILL NOT
NEED ANY
PADDING.

Fig 44   *Pressure-pad applied to a plywood hull
with a wire passed round the hull*

operator's hands) in warm soapy water. After allowing about ten minutes for the resin to soak in, a thin sheet of polythene is laid over the treated area, and a block of wood pressed down over the polythene sheet to press the outer veneer back into place. Pressure can be applied to the wooden block by wedging it to some convenient strong point, or by a tourniquet run right round the hull of the boat. For small areas, a very broad webbing strap can be passed round the hull, with suitable padding at all corners. On open boats it is usually necessary to cut a wooden strut to fit inside the hull at the top so that the tourniquet cannot close up the top of the hull. For larger areas, where a higher pressure will be required, a pair of wires round the hull should be used. All corners of the hull should be protected with some soft padding such as a couple of layers of cloth cut from an old blanket, then pieces of softwood to spread the load, and finally strips of hardwood such as oak or beech, so that the wire will not bite into the softwood. The wires are passed right round the hull, drawn hand-tight, and the overlapping ends secured with two bulldog grips. Wedges can then be driven between the wires and the pressure block to hold the repair firm until the resin sets, which is usually in about twenty-four hours (Fig 44).

Patching

If the delamination is too extensive for local filling with resin, or if more than one layer is affected, then the plywood will have to be patched. An old screwdriver or similar blunt tool can be used to peel away the veneers in the damaged area until sound wood is reached (Fig 45). There is no point in being gentle over this operation, or in trying to limit the amount of veneer removed. If the wood will not stand up to attack by a blunt old screwdriver, it is not fit to be left in the boat. The only thing that needs to be watched is the number of layers of veneer removed. If the repair needs to go more than half-way through the plywood, then precautions must be taken to preserve the shape of the hull (see section on larger repairs to plywood hulls, page 69).

Fig 45 *Peeling off the outer veneer of an area of delaminated plywood*

Provided the damage is confined to the outer three or four veneers of the plywood, the end result of all the digging will be as Fig 46: a fairly large irregular-shaped area of the outer veneer torn off, with progressively smaller areas of inner veneers missing, and with all edges jagged and odd splinters of veneers left glued to lower layers. This is where the careful work starts. The hole in each veneer must be opened out to a regular shape. This does not need to be square, or even rectangular, but it is advisable to make at least one corner a right angle. The exposed faces of all inner veneers must be cleaned free of all splinters and lumps of old glue (Fig 47). The finished hole in each layer needs to be about 38 mm (1½ in) on each side larger than the hole in the layer below. It is at this stage that what started as a small repair can get rapidly larger if the inner veneers of the plywood tend to break up as attempts are made to get a clean flat surface, and it may be decided that it will be better to replace an entire panel of the plywood rather than make a large-area repair. Whether this is so depends on the quality of the plywood used originally. If it was poor plywood, then replacement of the whole panel will probably save further repair work the next season (and the next again). If the plywood was of reasonably good quality, it should be possible to make a satisfactory repair without too much trouble. The highest quality marine-ply and moulded hulls built up from sawn veneers should present no problems at all.

Fig 46 *All delaminated veneers removed from an area of plywood*

Once the hole has been cut with clean edges and flat faces, the patching can start.

Fig 47 *Cutting straight edges on each layer of veneer*

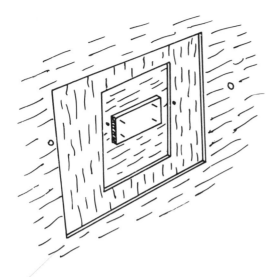

Fig 48   *Patch glued into first veneer and held in place with wire staples*

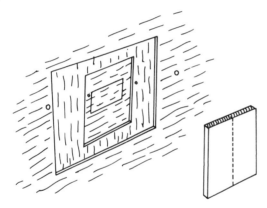

Fig 49   *Patch in the first veneer cleaned off, and patch for the next layer ready to fit*

Incidentally, it must be noted that the flatness of the faces refers to their cleanliness and suitability to accept a layer of veneer glued over them. Sheet-plywood hulls are designed on conic sections, and moulded hulls are usually designed with very lovely and complex curves, so unless the area of the repair is very small indeed the faces of the veneers will not appear flat when measured against a straight edge.

A piece of thin mahogany (between 6.4 and 3.2 mm/$\frac{1}{4}$–$\frac{1}{8}$ in thick) is carefully cut to shape to fit the hole in the innermost veneer to be replaced, taking care to see

that the grain runs the right way to match the veneer it is being set into. The patch is then set into the hole using a pure resorcinol adhesive. The patch can be held in place by a pressure block or, if the patch is thin and there is not much curvature, it can be held by driving in about half a dozen staples from a large office stapler used with its base swung back (Fig 48). As soon as the patch is securely held in place it is as well to clean all surplus resin from its edges. If any dribbles are left to harden they will make the next operation more difficult.

If resorcinol resin is being used, care must be taken to do the work when the temperature is right. The resin will not set properly if it is too cold. In the United Kingdom there is little need to worry about it being too hot, although in a really hot summer it may possibly get so hot that the glue sets too quickly. Anybody working on a boat under such conditions should have taken a day off and gone out to crew for another owner!

When the resin has set completely, the patch in the first layer can be cleaned off flush with the rest of the layer, using a small block plane (after any staples used have been removed), and the patch for the next layer prepared and fitted (Fig 49). If this is a large patch, it can be made up out of two or more strips. The process is repeated until the outer veneer has been patched and cleaned off, then any fastenings in the area can be replaced, and the repair painted over.

Small areas of mechanical damage which go right through the skin of the boat, such as those caused when a boat sits on a stake or an anchor fluke (Fig 50), can be repaired by a similar technique. Successive veneers are cut out, working from the outside, until the centre veneer is reached. The centre veneer must be cut out with the smallest aperture which will expose sound wood all round. The cut-outs in the outer layers need to be larger than would be used to repair delamination of only one side of the skin; a minimum of 51–64 mm (2–2$\frac{1}{2}$ in) each side larger than the hole in the next veneer below should be left (Fig 51). The patch for the centre veneer must be cut to size, and then planed or sanded down to its correct

Fig 50 *Hole punched through plywood hull: note that this and the following three sketches are not to scale*

Fig 51 *Veneers down to the centre layer cut back*

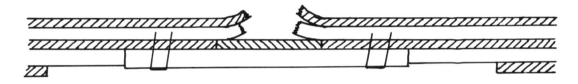

Fig 52 *Patch laid but not glued in the centre layer, with patch in the next layer glued and stapled*

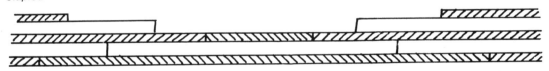

Fig 53 *Outer veneer patched, and inner veneers cut back ready for gluing in patches. Note that the edges of the patches in the inner layers are midway between those in the outer layers*

thickness before it is fitted. This centre-layer patch is laid in place without any glue, then the patch for the next veneer out is glued in place, and stapled to the original wood (Fig 52).

When all layers on the outside of the hull have been patched, the veneers on the inner side of the plywood are cut out, taking care to cut the edges midway between the edges of the patches in the outer layers (Fig 53). Patches are then glued in these inner layers to complete the repair.

This technique can be used to repair small holes in sheet-plywood and in moulded hulls. Since only the smallest hole practicable is cut in the centre veneer,

and at all other points less than half the thickness of the plywood is removed, the original curved shape of the hull cannot be lost. Done with care, a repair of this nature is almost invisible, and if good quality mahogany and resorcinol resin are used it will be every bit as strong as the original hull.

It should be noted that all repairs of this type to ply hulls can take quite a long time if the work is being done out of doors or in an unheated building. Other than on very hot days, it is probable that temperature conditions will allow only one layer to be patched in any one day's work. By the time the first lot of glue used has set solid

Band of Hope: *42ft x 38ft x 13ft 4in x 4ft 11in*
Essex Bawley: *built by Cann of Harwich in 1881.*
Her rig is as the original rig except that a boom
has been fitted to the mainsail. Owned by
Maurice Bailey of Slough

Sea Fever: *28ft x 9ft x 3ft 3in: ship's lifeboat
converted to a comfortable small cruiser. Owned
for many years by Robert Simper of Ramsholt*

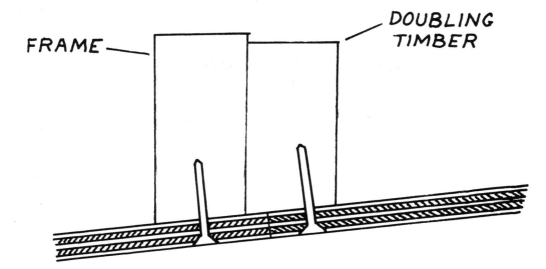

FRAME ——

DOUBLING TIMBER

Fig 54 *Plywood panels butt-jointed over a doubling timber beside a frame*

and the veneer has been cleaned off, it may well be too late to glue in a second patch that day, so a patch on a 7-ply hull may have to be spread over six working days.

Large areas of damage on sheet-ply hulls

On hulls built with sheet plywood on frames, large areas of damage are best repaired by replacing an entire panel of plywood. This causes no problems in maintaining the hull shape, and there will be frame members present to which the replacement panel can be fitted. Matters may not be quite so simple if only a portion of a panel is to be replaced. The frames in plywood-hulled boats are not usually very thick, and to get a secure butt joint between the old skin and the replacement panel it may be necessary to glue a doubling timber beside the frame where the joint is to be made (Fig 54). Alternatively, it may be decided to make the joint in the panels between frames instead of on a frame. The latter approach may sometimes be slightly easier but, whichever method is adopted, the work necessary is not quite so simple as it may seem because of the curvature of the plywood skin. Care has to be taken to see that the hull shape is not

distorted by the repair. Risk of any such distortion is minimised if joints are made either over doubled frames or within a few millimetres (inches) of a frame.

If it is decided to replace part of a panel, making the joint at a frame, then unless the frame is unusually heavy, the first step will be to prepare a doubling timber to sit alongside the existing frame and to support the new plywood skin. This doubling timber should be made of the same kind of wood as the existing frames, and of similar cross section. It is first cut to length to fit well between the chine timber and keel, or chine timber and beam shelf, as appropriate, then the face against which the ply will fit must be worked to the correct curvature and angle so that the new plywood will lie smoothly over it. This is best done and checked with fine feeler-gauges before the old plywood is removed, but once made, the doubling timber will not be fitted until the plywood has been taken out (when it will be much easier to glue and screw it alongside the existing frame). If the worker does not own or have access to feeler-gauges, a very good check for correct fitting can be made by placing cigarette papers along the joint face to be checked and seeing if the new piece of wood will hold them trapped along its entire length

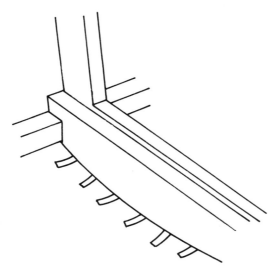

Fig 56 *Checking the hidden angle with a folded cigarette paper under the back. If the angle is not correct (left) a single thickness of paper can be trapped under the front edge, whereas it will be free if the angle is correct (right)*

Fig 55 *Checking the fit of a doubling timber with cigarette papers. If the timber is a good fit, all the papers will be trapped*

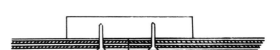

Fig 57 *Plywood panels butt-jointed over a butt strap*

(Fig 55). The fit at an inaccessible edge can be checked by placing a cigarette paper folded double under the back edge of the joint and checking that the exposed front edge will not hold a single thickness trapped (Fig 56).

Joints between panels can be made either as butt joints (Fig 57), in which the edges of the two panels are butted together and the joint is made by a butt strap on the inside, or as stepped scarph joints (Fig 58). If a butt joint is to be made, the butt strap fitted on the inside can be a strip of plywood of the same thickness as the skin, or a thicker piece of solid timber can be used. The risk of distorting the hull shape is minimised if a solid butt strap is used and it is planed to the correct curvature on its outer face (which is no easier than making a doubling timber for a frame). A stepped scarph joint involves more work in preparing the join, but the internal strap fitted over the joint can be fairly thin so the risk of distorting the hull is very much less.

Which type of joint to be used must be chosen by the worker himself, determined by the location of the panel to be replaced and the worker's skill at woodwork. The author would either replace an entire panel of plywood back to an original joint, or use a stepped scarph joint near to a frame.

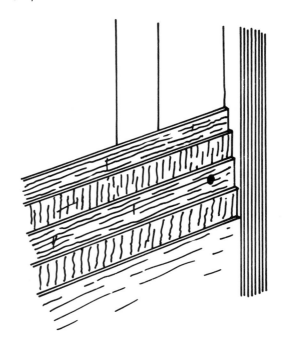

Fig 58 *Stepped scarph joint cut on plywood panel*

Having decided on how large an area to replace, and made any necessary internal-framing doubling pieces, all beadings and any fittings such as chainplates must be removed. Short rows of holes between 6 and 13 mm ($\frac{1}{4}$ and $\frac{1}{2}$ in) in diameter are drilled

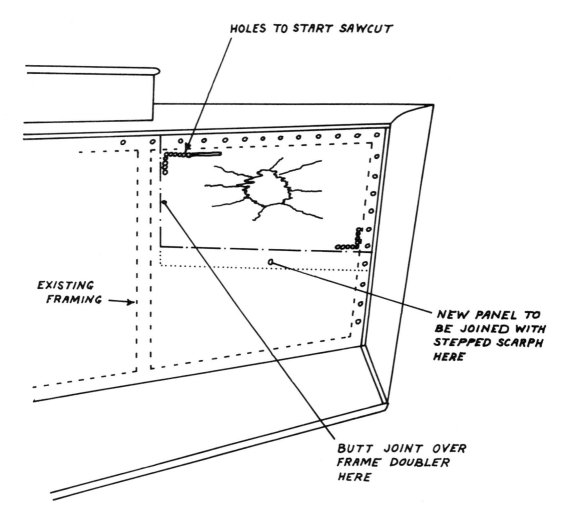

HOLES TO START SAWCUT

EXISTING FRAMING →

NEW PANEL TO BE JOINED WITH STEPPED SCARPH HERE

BUTT JOINT OVER FRAME DOUBLER HERE

Fig 59 *Typical part-panel replacement on a plywood hull: note that the stepped scarph is shown only as an example of the use of such a joint. A repair in this area would probably be re-panelled down to the chine*

in diagonally opposite corners of the area to be replaced, as close to any framing as is possible without risking damage to the frames, apart from frames where the plywood is to be butt jointed over a doubling timber, when the cut should be made about 13 mm ($\frac{1}{2}$ in) away from the frame. A padsaw or keyhole saw is then used to cut from the row of holes alongside the frame timber or along a marked line defining the area to be removed until the cut is long enough to insert a handsaw (Fig 59). All four edges of the area to be repaired are cut, and the bulk of the panel is removed. Edges which are to be jointed are cleaned up straight with a block plane and chisel, leaving an edge which is to be butt jointed over a doubling timber projecting beyond the edge of the frame by about one-third of the thickness of the doubler.

The remaining edges of the area to be replaced which lie over frame timbers must be removed with care so as not to damage the frames. First the ends of such pieces should be cut down to the frame with a sharp chisel (Fig 60), then after all nails

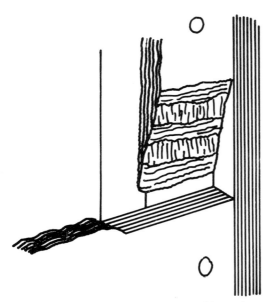

Fig 60 *Straightening the edge of the old panel and removing the plywood from the face of the transom frame*

and screws have been taken out the plywood strips can be pulled away from the frame. If, as is usually the case, the plywood was glued to the frames, it is best to try and split the ply at the second veneer out from the frame and then clean up the face of the frame with a chisel and rebate or block plane (noting that the glue used will probably be hard and brittle, and chips of it can fly into an eye, as well as blunting the plane-iron very quickly). During this work, care must be taken not to damage any overlapping panels, such as the transom in the example shown. Especial care is needed when working into the chine of a hull, as the overlap between side and bottom panels usually changes as the angle between the panels varies along the hull.

When all edges have been cut straight, any stepped scarph joints required are cut. At first glance this may appear a formidable task, but in practice it is quite simple and does not take all that long. First, it is advisable to wedge packing pieces inside the hull to support the inner veneer as the joint is cut. Then the edge for each step is marked on the outer face of the panel. An allowance of 13–19 mm ($\frac{1}{2}$–$\frac{3}{4}$ in) per step should be allowed. Stepped scarph joints in plywood are easy to cut if a straight

piece of hardwood can be clamped or wedged securely against the outer face of the wood to form a cutting guide. The veneers are cut through for each step with a tenon or dovetail saw run along the guide timber, then the individual veneers are peeled off with a chisel and cleaned down to the appropriate glue line (Fig 58).

If the joint in the plywood is to be a butt joint over a doubled frame, the prepared doubler can be fitted in place. If possible, all traces of paint should be cleaned off the side of the existing frame and the doubling timber glued and screwed to it, taking care to see that it is fitted hard up against the projecting lip of the plywood skin. If the frame timber cannot be cleaned well enough to make a good glued joint, a soft bedding mastic should be used. After trying a wide variety of traditional bedding materials mainly based on putty and tallow, and most proprietary marine bedding materials, the author finally found that a proprietary material in common use in the building industry gave excellent results, and was not found to set, even in joints over ten years old. It has the disadvantage of being rather filthy to handle, difficult to remove from fingers, and almost impossible to get off clothes – especially favourite thick woollen sweaters. In fact, it seems that any bedding or stopping materials which can be easily removed from hands etc will not be very effective when used on a boat.

When a doubling timber is bedded in a soft mastic, great care must be taken to keep the mastic off the face to which the new plywood panel will be glued. All old screw-holes in the exposed frame timbers should be plugged with small slivers of wood coated with glue and hammered into the holes. These are cleaned off flush when the glue has set.

The replacement plywood panel can now be cut to shape and any stepped scarph joints required cut. If there is much curvature in the hull, it is advisable to make a template from either a piece of scrap hardboard or stout corrugated cardboard, and it is also advisable to cut the new panel slightly oversize and trim it down to the correct fit. It is always easy to reduce the size of a panel that is too big, whereas if it is too small it will have to be put by for another job and a new sheet of plywood bought.

Once the fit has been checked, the replacement panel can be glued and screwed in place. Stepped scarph joints should always be glued with pure resorcinol resin, but if there are no scarphs, a urea-formaldehyde glue can be used between the panel and the frame timbers and for butt joints. Whichever glue is used, the maker's instructions should be followed carefully, particularly in any mixing needed, and in the temperature at which the glue is used.

A stepped scarph joint can be left with only the resin bonding it, provided sufficient pressure can be applied to both sides of the panel to hold it firm whilst the resin hardens, but it is better to fit a reinforcing strap inside the hull. This strap should be glued in as the joint itself is glued, and the joint can be held firm with two rows of fine screws into the strap, with pins to hold down the outer veneer if it shows any signs of lifting (Fig 61).

Butt joints between plywood panels can be improved by setting in a facing veneer strip over the joint. When the glue holding the new panel to the framing has set, all fastenings either side of the joint are removed and the outer veneer is cut away for 25–38 mm (1–1½ in) either side of the joint line. The fastenings are then replaced securely, and any slight gaps in the butt joint filled with slivers of veneer glued in. If the grain of the outer veneer runs across the joint, the strip to be inset should be cut to match the run of the grain; but if the grain runs along the line of the joint, the inset should be cut at a slight angle to the run of the grain so that there is no risk of it splitting over the joint line (Fig 62). The inset is glued in as already described for making small patches.

Large areas of damage on moulded hulls

Large-area repairs on moulded hulls are not so simple. The entire affected area must be rebuilt, and first of all a partial mould must be made to support the area during

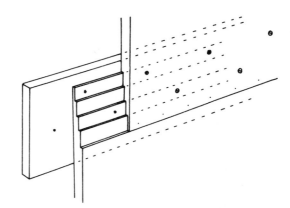

Fig 61   *Cut-away view of stepped scarph joint*

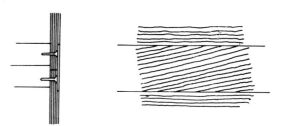

Fig 62   *Facing veneer set in over a butt joint: note that the grain should run at a slight angle across the facing strip so that it cannot split over the joint*

the rebuilding. This is best made up from pieces of about 25 mm (1 in) thick softwood which can be cut to the appropriate curvature and nailed together to form a suitable plug (Fig 63). The spaces left between individual pieces of the mould should not exceed 51 mm (2 in). It may be possible to cut all pieces of the mould and get them to a good fit inside the portion to be repaired; but if the damage is too extensive for this, the pieces of the mould will have to be cut to fit the opposite side of the hull, remembering that all shaping in towards the bow or stern must be cut on the opposite side of the frame pieces to that which shows when the frame is tried against the undamaged side of the hull. These framing pieces must be a fairly good fit to the shape of the inside of the hull, but they do not need to be perfectly finished. When all the mould pieces are prepared, the damaged area of the hull is cut away with a suitable saw, and the mould is assembled in contact with the surrounding good area

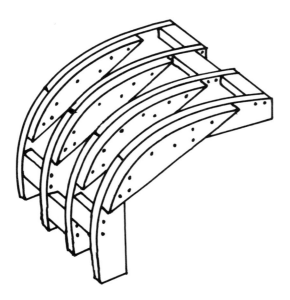

Fig 63 *Re-moulding jig for repairs to moulded-plywood hull*

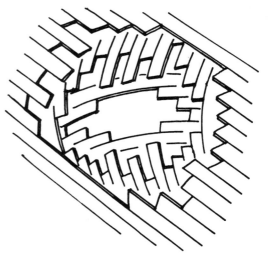

Fig 64 *Veneers in a moulded hull cut back: note that this sketch is not in proportion or to scale*

of the hull. The outer faces of the mould must be covered with thin polythene sheet so that it will not get bonded into the hull structure as new veneers are glued in place. The partial mould can be supported by struts to the beam shelves, cockpit coamings, deckbeams etc.

The separate layers of the hull are cut back over the partial mould to expose the veneer strips from which the hull was built up, and the ends of the individual strips in each layer are cut off square (Fig 64). The usual construction for moulded-ply hulls is two diagonal layers and an outer layer laid fore and aft. At least 51 mm (2 in), and preferably more than 102 mm (4 in) should be allowed between the end-cuts in adjacent veneers, and it can be seen that quite a small area to be repaired can involve the replacement of a very large area of the outer veneer.

Strips of veneer of the correct thickness are prepared. These veneers are usually of mahogany, about 50 mm (2 in) wide. Every effort should be made to match the original hull material. Parallel-sided strips of veneer are cut to length to replace alternate strips of the innermost layer, and checked carefully to ensure that they are the right length, width and thickness. Their ends are

coated with glue and they are laid in place and held to the correct curvature by staples into the mould timbers, or by very fine pins which have first been hammered through thin pieces of scrap plywood or hardboard to facilitate their later removal (Fig 65). If the repair covers an area with any significant curvature, it will be found that the gaps between these first-laid parallel-sided veneers will vary in width. Veneers are cut to size and shape to fill these gaps, laid in with all sides and edges coated with glue, and held to the mould with staples or pins. All surplus glue should be wiped off the face of the veneers before it can harden.

The first set of alternate parallel-sided strips for the second layer are cut to size. All staples or pins holding the first-layer veneers to the mould in the areas in which these second-layer veneers will lie must be removed and a check made that the surface of the inner layer is fair to accept the second layer, then the veneers can be glued in place and pinned down to the first layer and the mould timbers (Fig 66). The first set of alternate veneers in the second layer can be cut and fitted before the glue used on the first layer strips has set, but it is advisable to allow this first set of veneers on the second layer to set thoroughly before starting

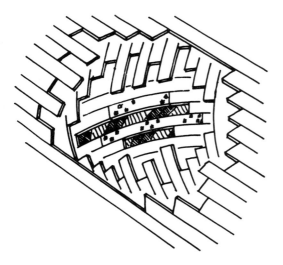

Fig 65 *Alternate veneer strips set in the first layer and pinned to the internal jig*

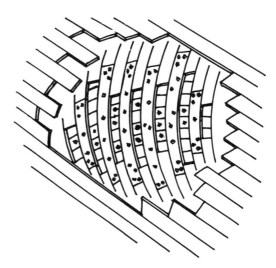

Fig 66 *First layer completed and alternate veneers of second layer glued and pinned in place*

to cut the intermediate strips, which are glued in the same way, remembering to remove any staples or pins from the innermost layer first. When all the second-layer strips have set, the outer layer is completed in the same way.

In areas of sharp curvature, it may be found that staples or fine pins are inadequate to hold down the ends of the strips of veneer. If this happens, then weights, shores and wedges, or a tourniquet round the hull must be used depending on the location of the repair. In all such areas it is reasonably certain that the outer face of each layer will have to be sanded to give a fair surface onto which the next layer of veneers can be glued, so no work can be done on any layer until all the glue used on the previous layer has set.

The repair of a moulded hull is a lengthy operation, and requires great care in ensuring that each piece of veneer fits almost perfectly and that the layer to which it is to be bonded is flat and fair, to yield a glued joint with the minimum thickness of glue. However, it is probably one of the most rewarding types of boat-repair work, and the amateur who tries it may be very surprised to find that, provided care is taken at each stage, pleasure in the end result can

be quite disproportionate to the actual amount of time and effort involved.

Clinker-planked hulls

Anybody contemplating repairs to a small clinker-built boat should first read *Clinker Boatbuilding* by John Leather (published by Adlard Coles Ltd). This book will give the best possible idea of how a clinker hull is built and, armed with this knowledge, any necessary repairs will be found reasonably straightforward.

It is not uncommon to find on old clinker-built hulls that the lands of some of the planks are splitting away, especially around the turn of the bilge amidships and in the run aft (Fig 67). Accidental damage can occur anywhere over the hull. If the problem is split lands on the turn of the bilge, then the shape of the hull should be checked very carefully, and all the ribs in the affected area should be examined to make certain they are not cracked or broken. A few cracked ribs at the sharpest point of the turn of the bilge can result in a hull becoming very badly 'squared' on the turn, and the damage to the lands of the clinker planks may be but a symptom of this far more serious ailment. If so, all the affected ribs will have to be replaced, and the repairs to the planking will have to be made after all the misshapen and cracked or broken ribs have been removed from the area (see page 97) and temporary moulds have been built into the hull to hold it in its correct shape.

For the purposes of this chapter, it will be assumed that the hull has not been distorted – the ribs are found to be sound and in good condition, but some planks must be replaced.

The lengths of planking to be replaced must be decided. A typical average extent of damage on an old clinker hull would be three or four planks each side, over about a quarter of the boat's length amidships. However, if just the actual damaged lengths of planking were replaced, all the joints in the planks would be concentrated in the same areas, which would seriously weaken the hull. The joints in the planks must be staggered with at least two, and preferably three, ribs between joints in adjacent planks; and also at least two unjoined runs of planking separating joints between any given pair of ribs. Here again, three planks between joints is a more desirable figure. This spacing out of the joints means that repairs to a roughly square area of damage to four planks will extend six frame pitches beyond the damaged area at each end (Fig 68). If the damage is to the garboards (the planks next to the keel) only, it must be noted that they can be replaced (or partially replaced) only if a greater length of the next plank out is also replaced (Fig 69).

The type of joint to be made must be considered. The alternatives are a butt joint (Fig 70) in which the ends of the two portions of the plank are butted together over an internal butt strap or plate, and a long scarph joint in which the ends of the planks are tapered in thickness and glued and riveted together (Fig 71). The butt joint is very much easier to make, but it suffers from two disadvantages. First, it is difficult to make a joint which will not leak ultimately, because the butt plate can back the joint only down to the upper edge of the plank below that being joined and, as the hull works, the butt plate will inevitably move slightly away from the plank edge,

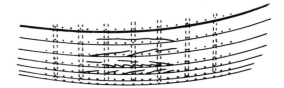

Fig 67 *Typical damage to a clinker hull, with lands along the turn of the bilge splitting off*

Fig 68 *Minimum desirable spacing between joints in adjacent planks*

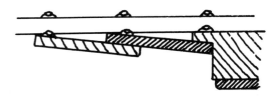

Fig 69 *The garboards in a clinker hull can be replaced only if the next plank is taken out first*

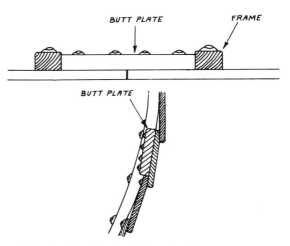

Fig 70 *Butt joint in clinker planking*

Fig 71 *Scarph joint in clinker planking*

leaving only the butted ends of the planks to keep the water out. Such a leak will be small, but nevertheless it is a leak and, as such, something to be avoided if at all possible. (Despite what the vendors of fibre-glass boats would have people believe, it is quite possible to have wooden-hulled boats which do not leak and whose bilges are dusted out, not pumped out.) The second disadvantage of the butt joint is that it robs the hull of some of its inherent flexibility, and by decreasing the flexibility locally, it increases the stresses in surrounding timbers and fastenings.

A well-made scarph joint will not leak, it keeps the strength of the plank as uniform as possible, and it does not rob the hull of so much flexibility. It has been suggested that when scarph joints are used, the spacing between adjacent joints can be reduced to two planks or two frame pitches, but since any form of joint represents a discontinuity in strength, the author does not advise any such closing up of the joints. The disadvantage of the scarph joint is that it requires much more work and care than a butt joint, and whilst a well-made scarph is very much better than a butt joint, a badly made scarph will be a perpetual source of trouble. If an owner has never made a scarph joint, he should make a few practice attempts on scrap timber before deciding to try it on a boat.

Once such decisions have been taken, the damaged planks are removed. First all the fastenings must be taken out. Copper nails which have been clenched (folded twice on the inside of the hull) are carefully prised up with a sharp spike, taking care not to bruise the wood excessively. The turned-over tip of the nail is straightened with a stout pair of pliers, and the nail is tapped out until its head is clear of the planking on the outside. It may be found that instead of moving out through the wood, the end of the nail simply bends every time it is hit. If this happens, the nail-end can be gripped really securely by a stout pair of pliers or by a toggle-action self-grip wrench such as the Mole, with the face of the jaws of the wrench away from the face of the wood by the thickness of the nail. The outer face of the wrench is then given a smart tap with

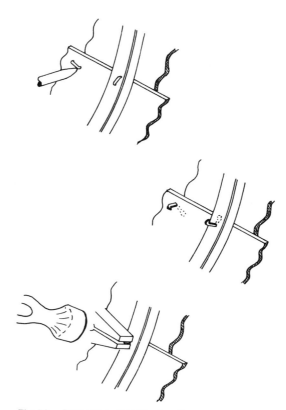

Fig 72   *Removing clenched nails*

a hammer, and either the wrench will slip back on the nail or (more usually) the nail will move in the wood (Fig 72). Once a nail has been started like this it is usually possible to tap it back without further use of the wrench or pliers. If anything more than a light tap is needed to move the nails, the hull should be supported outside by an assistant holding a flat-ended heavy bar of metal, a large mallet or a large hammer against the wood adjacent to the nail. An obvious point which is nevertheless sometimes overlooked is that it is very difficult to move a nail whose head is over a shore or bilge block supporting the hull, or is trapped behind a chainplate!

Once the heads of the nails have been moved clear of the planking, they can be pulled out from outside the hull with a pair of pincers or a claw hammer.

Nails which are riveted over copper rooves are a trifle harder to remove. First of all, the position of the centre of each

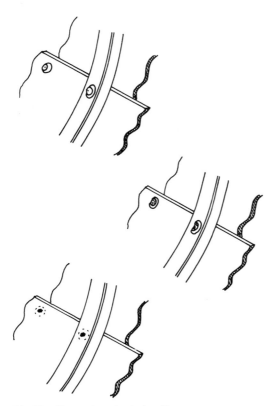

Fig 73   *Removing riveted nails*

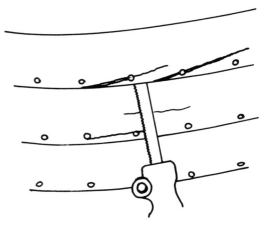

Fig 74   *Sawing through nails in a clinker hull*

nail must be estimated, and an indentation made with a sharp centre punch (Fig 73). Then a really sharp metal-cutting drill about 6 mm ($\frac{1}{4}$ in) in diameter is used to drill away the riveted end of the nail, and into the roove, which will usually then fall clear of the nail. This drilling must be done slowly and carefully to avoid any risk of damage to the wood beside the roove. Copper is a very soft metal; the drill can catch on it and swing off the riveted end very quickly and, if a high-speed electric drill is used, the result can be an unwanted hole right through the planking or well into a rib. Once the roove has been cut clear, the exposed end of the nail can be squared up by a couple of hefty nips from a stout pair of pliers, and it is then tapped back in the same way as a clenched nail. If insufficient length of nail is left to tap back directly, a fine, flat-ended pin-punch must be used to drive the nail back.

In awkward corners of the boat where access to the riveted-over end of the nail may be difficult, the countersunk head of the nail on the outside can be drilled away and the nail pushed through into the hull.

It is sometimes found on old clinker hulls that a previous owner has tried to stop the hull leaking by forcing a hard-setting putty up between the lands of the planks. This practice is one of the common causes of split lands on planks, and the only good thing that can be said about it is that it can make repairing the damage it causes slightly easier. If the lands have been packed, the easiest way of getting the fastenings out is to rake out the packing material, which will probably be fairly brittle and will come out quite easily when the planks dry out, and then to cut through the rivets with a hacksaw blade poked between the lands (Fig 74). Where a plank is to be removed, the blade can be allowed to cut into the wood. The hacksaw blade should be held in a suitable pad-saw handle, and the operator is advised to wear a stout leather gauntlet; one's knuckles can come into repeated painful contact with the land of the next plank down.

If butt joints are to be used, the rivets need be taken out only to the next rib beyond the joint; but for scarph joints the rivets must be removed for at least 450 mm (18 in) beyond the limit of the joint. If the lands have been packed with hard putty, it is advisable to clean out and re-fasten the entire length which has been packed. But

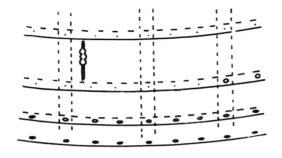

Fig 75   *Holes drilled and plank cut across with
a keyhole saw*

unless the planks are well spread apart,
those rivets between planks which will
remain after the repair should be drilled
out and not sawn through, as it is important not to damage the faces of the lands.

When all the fastenings have been taken
out, the next job is to cut through the
planks which are to be repaired. If butt
joints are to be used, the cutting line should
be midway between a pair of frames, but
for scarph joints the cut should be just clear
of the frame nearer the portion to be removed. The cut is started as a short row of
closely spaced holes, and then opened with
a keyhole saw or pad saw to just clear of
the lands of the planks above and below
(Fig 75). Where an adjacent plank is also
going to be removed, the cut can be continued into the edge of this plank; but
clearly the lands of portions of planks
which are not going to be replaced must
not be touched by the saw.

The best way of avoiding damage to an
adjacent plank whilst the overlapping land
is being cut is to spring the planks apart
and to slide a thin piece of plywood or hard
plastic sheet such as Formica up into the
gap so that it protects the plank not being
replaced. The outside overlapping lands are
then fairly easy to cut through with any
small saw, but the inside (upper) lands pose
a bit of a problem since being on the inside
of a curve it is almost impossible to get at
them with a saw of any reasonable size. An
ideal tool for this job is the curved-ended
handsaw with teeth on both edges used by
electricians and house carpenters to start a
cut into laid floorboarding. In the absence
of such a saw, the best substitute is a short

length of broken hacksaw blade and a lot
of patience. Alternatively, the overlapping
land can be cut through with a chisel in the
manner described for cutting through the
edges of a plywood panel which lie over
frame timbers (page 71).

Once both edges of the damaged portion
of the plank are cut through, the portion is
removed by sliding it towards the keel of
the boat, out from beneath the edge of the
plank above it. The shape of a clinker-built
hull is determined by the shape of the individual planks rather than by the framing,
so it is important to get the old planks out
in one piece with the minimum of (further)
damage to their edges so that they can be
used as templates to mark out the replacement planks. If more than a couple of
planks are being replaced it is a good idea
to paint an identifying number onto each
plank, so that when the replacement planks
are cut they can be fitted in their correct
location. Most important of all is to identify
the side from which the plank was taken if
planks are being replaced on both sides. A
wander around a boatyard in winter
examining the painted waterlines on laid-
up boats can reveal that some boats have
distinctly asymmetrical hulls (or that the
waterline is some 50 mm/2 in higher on
one side than on the other). Most good
quality boats were built with the two sides
as virtually perfect mirror images, and most
class boats had their planks cut from a
single set of templates, but some 'one-offs'
appear to have been built from whatever
suitable timber was available, and plank
widths may be distinctly irregular.

With the damaged portions of the planks
out of the way, the ends of the good
portions are cleaned up flat and square with
a sharp chisel, taking care always to cut
towards the centre of the plank so that
neither land can be inadvertently split off.
It should be noted that the ends of the
planks should be trimmed square to the line
of the keel of the boat, not square to the
edge of the plank. If butt joints are being
used, the next operation is to cut the
butt plates from suitable timber, either
mahogany or a close-grained softwood,
about 20 mm ($\frac{3}{4}$ in) thick. The plates should
be cut to a good fit between the pair of

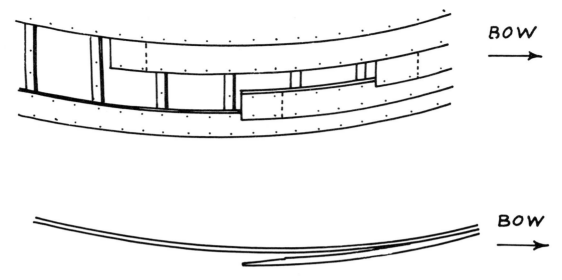

Fig 76   *Marking scarph joints on ends of original planks*

frames concerned, and the edge nearer the keel must be cut to fit the edge of the next plank. If the next plank in is one that is being replaced, then naturally the final trimming of this inner edge of the butt plate will have to be left until the new plank is fitted.

Scarph joints (if these are to be used) are next marked on the ends of the old planks, noting that at the forward end of the repaired section the new portion of the plank lies on the inside of the joint whilst at the aft end the new portion lies on the outside – that is, both joints 'face aft' (Fig 76). The joints should be marked out with a step of 1.6–0.8 mm ($\frac{1}{16}$–$\frac{1}{32}$ in) at each end of a uniform taper, and the length of the joint should be such as to allow the taper to be on a slope of about 1 in 12, which is usually between 89 and 114 mm ($3\frac{1}{2}$–$4\frac{1}{2}$ in) for most smaller cruisers. To mark the joint all round the plank, the plank will have to be carefully sprung away from its neighbours (which is why the fastenings must be removed beyond the area actually to be replaced). This springing of the planks should be done by sliding a broad hardwood wedge between the lands of the planks beyond the joint. Only on very thick planking should it be necessary to use a light mallet to drive the wedge; on most small boats up to about

5 tonnes (tons) it should be possible to push the wedge in by hand. Obviously this springing of the planks must be done very gently to avoid any risk of damage to the plank.

Once marked out, the joints can be cut, using a long-bladed broad chisel to cut the tapered flat, and a thin chisel to cut across the step at the end of the joint. Both chisels used must be really sharp so that they will not be deflected by any irregularities in the grain of the wood. The joints are awkward to get at and attempts to cut them with the average amateur's chisel – which appears to double as screwdriver, scraper, tin-opener and general purpose lever – are doomed to failure. Part of the cutting of the joint faces will have to be done from inside the hull, and part from outside, and it is now that the owner will realise that a useful apprenticeship for boat-repair work would be a period as a circus contortionist! Ambidexterity is a great help in boat-repair work, and those who are normally only right- or left-handed must be prepared to learn to work 'wrong-handed'.

It is a wise precautionary policy for the amateur to mark scarph joints fairly close to the rib on the side of the joint where the new portion of the plank is to be fitted, rather than mark them neatly midway between the ribs. Then if the first cut is not exactly successful, the joint can be re-marked a bit further along the plank. Cutting good scarph joints in clinker planking is probably one of the most tricky operations in boat-repair work, but it is also one of the most rewarding, and provided care and time are taken over the job there is nothing to be afraid of.

As the joint is cut, the thin end of the plank will tend to whip away from the chisel, so some form of support must be provided for it. Where the joint is on the inner face of the plank (ie at the forward end of the section to be repaired) a block of wood the width of the exposed portion of the plank can be laid against the plank and held in place either by a shore and a wedge, or by a rope tourniquet round the hull. The pressure applied to hold this block in place should not extend beyond the wedge which was inserted to spring out the end of the plank – if pressure is applied beyond this wedge the pressure will close the plank into the hull as the taper is cut.

At the aft end of the section to be re-placed, where the joint has to be cut on the outside of the end of the old plank, the sup-porting piece of timber can be shored across to any convenient point inside the hull, such as a carline, beam shelf, centreplate case etc. Since Sod's Law applies in boat-repair work the same way as it does else-where, there will probably not be a con-venient back-up point inside the hull for a shore, so one will have to be provided, per-haps by wedging a piece of timber between the keel and the gunwhale, and shoring onto it (Fig 77).

When all the joints have been cut on the ends of the old planks, the new portions of planks are marked out on timber of appro-priate thickness, using the removed portions of the old planks as templates, and remem-bering to allow extra length on the ends for scarph joints if these are being used. When-ever possible, timber should be used on which the natural curve of the grain matches the curve of the planks to be cut. The easiest way to cut the planks is on a large bandsaw. If this is not available, the best tool to use is a plain handsaw. Hand-held portable electric saws seldom give a

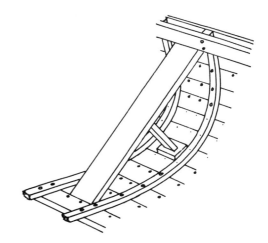

Fig 77　Shore to strut between keel and beam shelf or gunwhale

good result on the curved edges of clinker planks. After cutting, the edges of the plank are planed smooth and to size, and if the ends were not cut off properly when the plank was first cut out, they should now be trimmed carefully to length.

At this stage, the replacement portion of the plank can be tried in place against the hull to check that it is the correct length, and that the curvature of the edges appears right. It is not necessary to push the plank right home into its final position; it can be left low by the width of its overlap with the plank above. If scarph joints are being used, the new portion cannot be properly fitted in until the joints have been cut on it, but the opportunity can be taken to mark the length of the overlap on the new portion. The joints are cut next, and the amateur worker will find this is easy light relief after cutting the scarphs on the ends of the old planks, as the new portion of plank can be securely clamped down on a bench or other suitable surface. Care must be taken to cut both joints on the right sides of the plank – a shaped clinker plank with one joint cut on the wrong face is unlikely to come in handy anywhere else, and unless it is an unusually wide plank there is seldom much chance of cutting it down to replace one of the shorter portions to be repaired because the curvature of the edges will probably not fit.

After the joints have been cut, the next

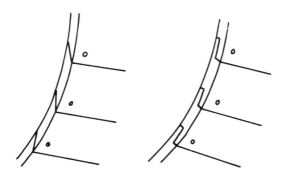

Fig 78 *Alternative shaping of the lands of clinker planks over the transom. The lands at the stem will be shaped similarly*

operation is to put on the slight land chamfer where the plank fits behind the next plank above it (Fig 70). The garboard and possibly the next plank out may not require a chamfer under the flat run aft of a dinghy.

If the next plank out from the one being worked on is to be replaced over a greater length at each end than that being made, the chamfer can be cut after the plank has been fitted. But clearly if the plank under consideration is overlapped by a portion of the original planking at either end, the chamfer must be cut beforehand. It should be noted that, if a plank is being replaced right to the end of the boat, the land chamfer will change at the end of the plank either to a rebate or to a chamfer right across the plank (Fig 78) so that the planks can lie flat to the stem or transom, and a corresponding chamfer or rebate will have to be cut on the inner face of the plank on the edge nearer the keel for the end foot or so. It is easier to cut the chamfers before the plank is fitted, working with a small plane with the plank clamped down to a bench.

One point which must be considered before the replacement planks are fitted to the hull is the condition of the holes left by the old fastenings. If these holes are clean and do not appear to have been pulled oversize, they can be used again for the new fastenings, using nails a size larger than those originally fitted; but if they are at all ragged, they will have to be plugged. Since the new fastenings will have to be in sub-

stantially the same places as the originals, plain parallel-sided plugs cannot be used. Tapered plugs glued with resin glue into tapered holes must be used, care being taken to insert the plugs from the side which the fastenings will be pulling; that is, from the inside on ribs and the upper edges of planks and from the outside on lower edges.

Replacement planks can be fitted as they are cut, or all the planks can be cut and then fitted in one session. The author has always preferred to fit each plank as it is cut, before the next plank above is cut out, partly because it gives a chance to correct any slight errors in the shaping of the planks, but also because it means there will be a variety of different types of work available on any working day, and the old adage 'a change is as good as a rest' applies to work on boats in full force. If all the planks are cut before any are fitted, a small error in the shaping of each can have a cumulative effect to the point at which the last plank to be replaced may not fit at all well to the plank below it.

If butt joints are being used, the butt plates are first fitted to the ends of the original planking. The butt plates are cut from timber slightly thicker than that of the planking, usually (on small boats) between 13 and 19 mm ($\frac{1}{2}$–$\frac{3}{4}$ in) thick. The ends of the plate are cut to be a good (but not binding) fit between the ribs; the lower edge is cut to fit well against the edge of the plank below that being joined, and the upper edge is trimmed off to match the upper edge of the plank. A non-hardening bedding mastic is used between the butt plate and the planks and ribs. The least messy way of applying the bedding material is with a special gun but, in the absence of a gun, a putty knife can be used. The mastic should be applied to the back face of the portion of the original plank and to the upper edge of the plank below, and to the two ends of the prepared butt plate. Sufficient must be applied to ensure that the joint is filled, but care must be taken not to use too much so that the butt plate cannot close up to the planking. The butt plate is pressed into position, and is then riveted to the end of the original plank.

Before starting to rivet, it is as well to wipe away any surplus mastic which has squeezed out, especially from the ends of the butt plate. After the butt plates for both ends of the lowest plank to be replaced have been fitted to the ends of the original planking, the exposed outer faces of the butt plates and the ends of the old planks are coated with mastic and the new portion of the planking is fitted into place.

If more than one plank is being replaced, the first planks fitted can be held in place by G cramps onto the ribs. A single plank (or the last plank to be fitted) must be slid up under the lower edge of the next plank above it, where it can be held in place with shores and wedges or by a couple of tourniquets around the hull. Care must be taken to ensure that the plank is lying correctly in position before any rivets are put in, as a very small angular error in the position of the plank when the first two or three rivets are inserted can result in the aft end of the new portion of the plank being centimetres (inches) out of position, and it is not possible to bend clinker planks edgewise to correct such an error.

Riveting is almost always done working back from the forward end of the plank in question. The forward butt joint is completed first, with four rivets in staggered rows, then the plank is riveted to the plank below it (and to that above if it is the last or only plank of the repair). If some of the bent ribs are to be replaced, then naturally the new plank will not be riveted to the old ribs. If the ribs are sound, the new plank can be riveted to the plank below it and to the ribs as they come, working aft until finally the aft butt joint is completed.

Scarph-jointed planks are treated similarly, except that a resin glue (usually resorcinol) is used on the joints, which are further secured with four small rivets. If the weather is at all hot, scarph-jointed planks must be fitted quickly as the aft joint must be closed home before the resin glue starts to set, and it may be better to fit only alternate rivets to the next plank down initially. These will ensure that the plank is well and truly home in its correct position, so the aft joint can be finally riveted, then the rivets which were omitted on the first

run down the plank can be put in.

If a substantial length of any clinker plank is damaged, it may well be considered easier to replace the entire plank to avoid having to make joints between the original and the new length of planking. Full-length planks will involve the added complication of full-width chamfers or rebates to adjacent planks at the ends, but other than this there are no major difficulties, and on transom-sterned boats it is not necessary to cut the plank accurately to length before fitting it. Usually it is best to copy the original style of fastening at the stem and transom, plugging any old screw-holes with small dowels before the new planks are fitted.

When the first replacement plank has been fitted, the land chamfer on its upper edge should be planed on (if this was not done before the plank was fitted), and the chamfer should be checked along its whole length to ensure that the next plank up can fit fairly against it.

Carvel-planked hulls

Replacement of carvel planking

Besides collision damage, rot, and attack by worm, common to all wooden-hulled boats (page 61), carvel-planked hulls may suffer from decay of the wood around the fastenings (nail sickness), or decay of the edges of the planks to the point at which the caulking between the planks will no longer hold in place. Nail sickness may be general, in which case substantial re-planking will be necessary; but it may be confined to local areas such as around bolts through metal floors, in which case local repairs (graving pieces) may be easier and very much cheaper.

If the edges of the planks are defective, and the caulking will not hold well, it may be possible to glue new edging strips onto the afflicted planks, or the hull may be splined instead of caulked. However, re-edging planks (page 90) is quite a tricky job, and splining may not be desirable for a variety of reasons, so complete replacement of the affected lengths of the planks may be the easiest solution.

Generally the processes are similar to those involved in the replacement of clinker planks, but there are some fundamental differences, the chief of which is that on a clinker hull the planking is usually replaced before any ribs or frames are replaced, whereas on a carvel hull the ribs or frames may have to be replaced first so that there is something to which to fasten the new planks. In the instructions which follow, we assume that all ribs and frames are sound.

First, once the area to be replaced has been decided, the stopping and caulking in the seams between the planks must be removed. Although the repairs may be being done because some (or even most) of the caulking is loose and ineffective, it is highly likely that what remains will prove quite difficult to shift! Some form of stout hook with a good man-sized handle is the best tool for its removal. The tang of an old file with about 6 mm ($\frac{1}{4}$ in) off the end bent over through a right angle makes an excellent hook. The body of the file can be bound with layers of cloth and insulating tape to make a comfortable handle. If a broad, flat file is used, a couple of fingers can be slipped over the end beside the tang to get a really strong pull on any really obstinate bits of stopping. When the seams are being cleaned out, care must be taken not to damage the edge of a plank which is not to be replaced.

The next item is to remove the fastenings. There is no possibility of sawing through these as there is with clinker planking. Rivets must be drilled off, and any screws or bolts will have to be unscrewed. The first problem will be finding all the screws, the heads of which will almost certainly be counterbored and stopped over. If the presence of a screw beneath some stopping is suspected, the stopping can be removed with the bent-over file tang, or with the aid of a small metalworking chisel and hammer. Once the stopping is out and the head of the screw exposed, the slot in the head must be cleared of stopping, for which job a broken-off portion of a hacksaw blade is ideal. With the slot cleared, the screw can (hopefully) be removed. As there must be no risk of the screwdriver

blade slipping and damaging the screw head, it is best to use a stout screwdriver bit in a carpenter's brace. Really hard pressure can be applied to hold the bit (which must be perfectly sharpened) in the slot, and enough leverage can usually be applied to start most screws turning. If steady turning pressure on the handle of the brace does not move the screw, then the effect of a smart blow with the side of a closed fist on the handle can be tried, or a helper can give the handle a smart rap with a mallet. The sudden jerk may start the screw turning. Both leverage and sudden tap may however shear the head off the screw, or shear the shank off the screw at the start of the thread. Old brass screws will almost certainly shear off, as probably much of the zinc will have leached out of them over the years and they will be brittle. Iron screws may be badly rusted in, but provided the head is still recognisable and a fairly clean slot can be cut with a portion of hacksaw blade, they can often be shifted. Bronze and gunmetal screws should come out easily once started, especially if they were greased when they were put in.

Bolts are easy to find, as the nuts will usually be exposed inside the hull. Whether they will prove so easy to undo is another matter.

Another type of fastening which may be found on larger, older boats is the wooden trenail or trunnel (literally 'tree nail'). This is a wooden dowel, usually of oak or juniper, which is held in by wedges driven into splits in the dowel ends. Trenails are usually driven right through the plank and frame, split each end, wedged, and then cleaned off, but they may be driven only part way through the frame into a blind hole. They will have to be drilled out. This is not difficult in theory, but usually it is almost impossible to follow the centre of the dowel perfectly. Slight eccentricity in drilling out trenails is not a serious matter, but if the drill drifts out until its centre comes outside the dowel, there will be some nasty problems in removing the remains of the dowel – not to mention the problems which will arise on fitting new planks.

Ordinary blind or barbed nails are removed by a 'brute force and ignorance'

Kate: *35ft x 33ft x 10ft x 4ft: Essex oyster smack
built at Pagglesham in 1883. Shown finishing in
the 1965 ECOG Race when she was owned by
R. B. Pitt of Maldon*

Dreva: *34ft x 30ft x 10ft x 6ft: sturdy cruising cutter
designed by N. Warington-Smyth and built by
Frazier of Mevagissey in 1936 for G. Romney Fox
who sailed her for some thirty years*

process with the aid of a stout claw-hammer or, if available, a large case-opener.

The worst type of fastening likely to be encountered on old carvel-built hulls is a metal dump. This is just a plain, stout metal dowel which is usually driven through the plank into a blind hole in a frame. Sometimes a hole can be drilled into the end of a large dump, and the hole can then be tapped with a thread about 6 mm ($\frac{1}{4}$ in) diameter. A bolt can be screwed into this hole, and the dump can then be levered out with a stout crowbar. Bronze dumps are often movable, but old iron dumps may be well rusted in. Sometimes it is possible to drill out iron ones, but as they are much harder than the wood around them, great care must be taken to keep the drill well centred in the dump, as it will run out into the wood if it can.

Part of the fun of trying to remove carvel planks from larger old boats is in locating all the fastenings, but once the first plank has been successfully unfastened (or in extreme cases knocked and broken away to expose the hidden dumps or screws), the rest are usually somewhat easier as the fastenings in the planks can be expected to follow some more or less regular pattern.

Planks, of which a portion is to be replaced, are cut through as already described for clinker planking, but the operation is easier because there is no risk of damage to the lands of planks above or below. Edges of adjacent planks can be protected from an inadvertent saw cut by a piece of celluloid or stiff plastic slid between the planks.

If all the old fastenings are successfully removed, the portion of the plank to be replaced will fall out – but the more usual case is that there will still be some hidden fastenings. If there are any totally unremovable dumps, or screws with broken heads, the plank will have to be forced off. If claw hammers or similar metal levers are used to prise off the old plank, then pieces of hardwood should be used to protect the edges of adjacent planks or the faces of frames.

Replacement lengths of carvel planks can be scarph jointed, but since carvel planking is usually substantially thicker than clinker, it is not usually easy (or perhaps even possible) to spring out the ends of the old planks to facilitate cutting the scarphs. Butt joints are much less disadvantageous in carvel planking than they are in clinker. The butt plates can be cut to overlap the planks above and below the one being joined, so there is much less chance of a leak. Carvel planking is thicker and stiffer than clinker so the discontinuity in strength and the increase in rigidity at the butt plate is of less significance. When butt joints are used, there is no need to disturb fastenings beyond the actual areas of planking to be replaced.

On carvel-planked hulls, the garboards can be replaced without removing the next plank out, but the replacement of a garboard strake in the forward third of the hull can be a very tricky operation, as there is often a considerable twist to the plank.

When all the old planks have been unfastened or knocked out, the exposed faces of all ribs and frames must be cleaned up. Holes left by fastenings which have been removed must be plugged, and any immovable metal fastenings such as old dumps must be cut off flush with the face of the frame. Sometimes it is possible to get at an old fastening with a hacksaw with the blade set sideways, and make a useful cut before the frame of the saw hits the next frame of the boat, but all too often the only tool possible is a hacksaw blade held in a pad-saw handle and used with great care. Often it will be necessary to work with a slight curve in the blade so that the blade will cut the metal as near as possible to the wood without the operator's fingers getting excessively damaged by the planking. This is a slow, tedious job – often painful if a stout glove is not worn. But it can be done, and in time the old fastening will be cut through. The author sustains himself during such tedious cutting jobs by thinking of the wartime prisoners in Colditz Castle, who cut through metal bars by similar means, but with added hazards not normally found where old boats are repaired!

When the old planks have been removed, all frames cleaned and old holes plugged, the butt plates can be fitted, and replacement planks cut. The wood for these replacement planks needs to be thicker than the finished size of the original planking to allow for curvature. The planks should be cut slightly wide, so that they will enter the space in which they are to be fitted, but will not seat fully home. Thus as the planks are finally fitted, this extra width will tend to force closed any small gaps in adjacent planks. Since carvel planks can be edge bent, it may be possible to cut the replacement planks with one edge straight. A check with a spare piece of timber slightly narrower than the plank to be replaced will soon show whether this is possible. Edge bending is not usually possible when only a short length of planking is to be replaced; it is easiest when the replacement plank runs out to the transom, as then the end of the plank is accessible and considerable leverage can be applied. Edgewise bending should not be attempted within 0.6–1 m (2–3 ft) of the end of the portion of plank to be replaced on small craft – more on larger hulls on which the planking is thicker. If one edge of the plank can be cut straight, the width required can be marked on the plank by spiling.

The replacement plank is cut to shape and planed to be a tight fit between the existing planks. The edges are left square for two-thirds of the thickness, and a caulking chamfer is planed on the front third of each edge. Depending on where in the hull the plank is to be fitted, the inside face of the plank may be left flat, but it is more likely that it will have to be planed to a hollow curve to fit outside steam-bent ribs (Fig 79). The proper tool for this job is a curved-sole plane, but that is something the average amateur is unlikely to have so improvisation must be the order of the day. Anybody lucky enough to own one of the multi-bladed rebate and moulding planes with a variety of fences and other attachments will have no difficulty in planing a very close approximation to the required curve, but they are not much more common than curved-sole planes. However, the blade of a narrow 13 mm ($\frac{1}{2}$ in) rebate or block plane can be mis-sharpened to a curve, or if the boat owner does not possess any suit-

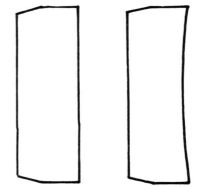

Fig 79 *Replacement plank with edges shaped for caulking (left) and with inner face hollowed (right)*

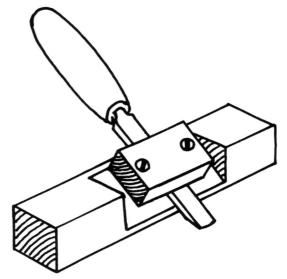

Fig 80 *Chisel mounted on block of wood to serve as a rebate plane*

able small planes, a chisel can be clamped between two blocks of wood to make a crude cross between a coarse-set spokeshave and a router plane (old woman's tooth). One of the advantages of such a crude home-made tool (Fig 80) is that blocks of wood can be nailed on to the sole to form fences to limit the position of the cut without any worries about spoiling an expensive tool.

Small rebate planes or an improvised tool can be used to rough out the curvature on the inner face of a plank, and it can then be finished off with medium-grade garnet

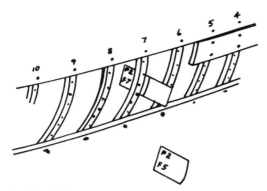

Fig 81 *Marking templates to gauge curvature on the inner faces of carvel planks*

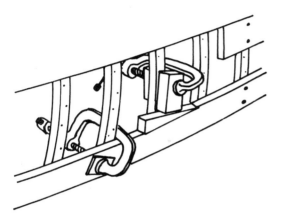

Fig 82 *A replacement carvel plank clamped in place: note that the wedge which forces the plank edge into contact with the next plank is driven home before the clamp holding the plank to the frame is finally tightened*

paper held over a block of wood whose face has been planed to an appropriate curvature. The depth and fairness of the curve can be checked with cardboard templates, which have been cut to marks made with the card held against the side of a rib. Each template cut must be very carefully marked with numbers to identify both the plank and the rib to which it refers. Numbers for the ribs can be painted on the outside of the hull above the area being repaired (Fig 81). If more than about a quarter of the length of any plank is being replaced, it will usually be found that the depth of curve required will vary along its length.

When the curve on the inner face and the caulking chamfers have been cut, the

replacement length of plank can be fitted. If only a single plank is being replaced, it is simply forced into place and riveted, bolted, screwed or otherwise fastened home against the ribs and frames. However, if more than one adjacent plank is to be replaced, then all but the last must be held very tightly against the next plank down before they are fastened. This is best done by driving a long – at least 203 mm (8 in) – hardwood wedge between the edge of the plank being fitted and a hardwood block clamped securely to a rib or frame (Fig 82). If only two or three planks are being replaced, the hardwood pressure-block can also be wedged to the underside of the existing planking above the repair but, even so, it is still important to see that the block is securely clamped to a rib. The wedging can impose considerable stresses in the plank being fitted and in the pressure-block and, as the fastenings pull the new plank firmly home, the slight movement can be sufficient to disturb the wedge and send both the wedge and an unclamped pressure-block flying across the yard with considerable force. The plank can also be clamped to the ribs to hold it in to the curvature of the hull, in which case the plank and ribs must be protected from damage from the metal jaws of the clamps by scrap pieces of timber.

The simultaneous clamping of a somewhat springy plank with a couple of scrap pieces of wood can prove somewhat frustrating to the single-handed operator, as first one piece slips out, then another. Naturally, if the worker is inside the hull, it is the outside-pressure piece which slips whilst, if he is outside, the inner one goes. Life is much easier when two people are working, as four hands usually suffice for the job. A good communication system is essential to avoid the operator on the business end of the cramp tightening whilst his mate's finger is still somewhere in the sandwich of timber. The single-handed worker will find a roll of masking tape or double-sided sticky tape of immense help when trying to clamp bits of wood into place with pressure-pads under the jaws of the cramps. Taping the pads loosely to the cramp-jaws saves a lot of fuss and bother. Also, it is a good policy to have ready a good supply of suitable pieces of wood for use as pressure-pads, kept handy in a cardboard box. Even better is to have one box of pads kept inside the hull and another box outside. The single-handed worker will spend a substantial amount of time moving in and out of the hull, and anything which can be done to minimise such movements is a great help – even to the extent of buying or borrowing extra tools so that one can have 'inside' and 'outside' hammers, wheelbraces, screwdrivers etc. Naturally, when this is done it is only a matter of time before the worker finds himself inside the hull with both hammers outside, which is twice as frustrating as it would be if he had only the one hammer!

A replacement carvel plank will probably need to be clamped to about every third rib, and wedged down at adjacent ribs. Four good stout G cramps is the minimum requirement for such work, pairs of cramps being moved along as the work progresses. Good quality G cramps are expensive, and the author, when he found the four he could borrow were not enough, made an adequate substitute for light work by sawing off 51 mm (2 in) lengths of channel-section RSJ and tapping a 9 mm ($\frac{3}{8}$ in) hole in one web. The limited throat depth and the need to use a spanner made these improvised clamps somewhat awkward to use, but the dozen clamps so made cost only an afternoon's work (Fig 83).

One difference between the fitting of carvel and clinker planks is that the rivets on the former are usually fitted with their heads in counterbored holes which are later filled with stopping. This complicates the drilling, making it well worthwhile acquiring another wheelbrace so that drills are not being perpetually changed over. It makes riveting easier for the helper, as there is no risk of a 'pipped' dolly slipping sideways off the rivet head.

Once the replacement planks are fitted and fastened home, all that remains to be done is to plane off the outsides of the planks to a smooth curve to match the rest of the hull and to caulk and stop the seams. Planing off is another of those jobs which seems simple enough, but which in practice

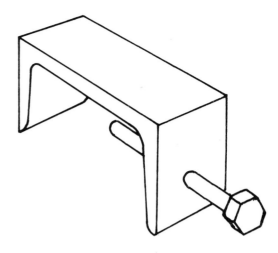

Fig 83 *Cheap home-made clamp*

turns out to be awkward and uncomfortable. The use of too small a plane results in a very uneven finish, whereas a large plane is far too tiring on the arms. A really sharp smoothing-plane must be used, and it is very important that it is kept absolutely sharp, since the weight of the plane is of no help in keeping it cutting.

Re-edging carvel planks

If the edges of otherwise sound carvel planks have been damaged to the point at which they will no longer hold the caulking properly, new edge-strips can be glued on to the planks without disturbing all the fastenings. The only really difficult part of this operation lies in cutting a clean edge on the old planks.

The job can be tackled in several ways. One of the most effective is to use a rebate or grooving plane of appropriate thickness – usually 13-19 mm ($\frac{1}{2}$–$\frac{3}{4}$ in). A guide batten about 38 mm ($1\frac{1}{2}$ in) square is nailed on to the outside of the hull with fine wire-nails, its upper edge being half the width of the groove to be cut below the centre of the afflicted seam. The plane is then run along the upper face of the batten so that it can cut down into the sides of the seam (Fig 84). Care must be taken to keep the side of the plane held firmly in contact with the face of the batten, so that successive cuts will leave a clean-sided groove. The first

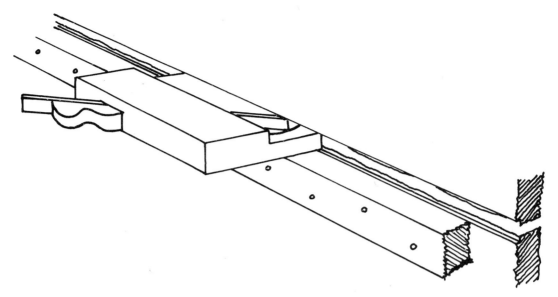

Fig 84   *Planing off rough plank edges ready to fit new lips or splines*

few cuts are usually fairly tricky to control, as the plane will tend to catch on the various irregularities on the plank edges, but once the groove has been started the work is easier. The groove can run straight out at the end over a transom stern; but there will be problems at the forward end on all types of hulls, and at the aft end of double-enders or where planks run into a deadwood. These portions of the groove will have to be hand cut with a sharp chisel, taking great care to keep the sides of the groove smooth. Cutting the groove gets tricky towards the end. Once the plane cuts right through the plank edges, it will catch against all the ribs and it will be very difficult to clean out the odd remaining bits which still need cutting. Once about three-quarters of the depth has been cut, it is advisable to check the depth of cut carefully, and to concentrate on any shallow spots so that the final breakthrough will occur fairly uniformly over the length of the hull. Once the plane does cut right through, the rest of the groove is best finished off with a chisel.

New edge-strips are planed up out of suitable timber, not forgetting to add caulking chamfers. The strips should be cut about 3 mm ($\frac{1}{8}$ in) wider than the thickness

Fig 85   *New plank edges glued in place*

of the planking, to leave a small overhang which can be cleaned off later (Fig 85). The strips are glued on to the edges of the old planks with resorcinol resin, and the best way of holding them firmly in place whilst the resin sets is to caulk the seam immediately. If the repairer is dubious of his ability to caulk the whole seam before the resin starts to set, very broad, short wedges of wood softer than the new plank edges can be lightly knocked into the seam. When the resin has set firmly, the edging-strips can be cleaned off flush with the surface of the planks.

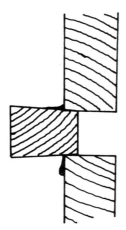

Fig 86   *Spline being glued into a seam*

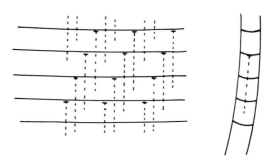

Fig 87   *Normal pattern of edge fastenings in a strip-planked hull*

Splining a hull is a very similar process to re-edging the planks, the difference being that instead of two separate edging-strips with caulking chamfers being glued into the groove, a single spline is glued to the edges of both planks (Fig 86). The spline is cut with a slight taper so that it can be forced home to make a thoroughly tight hull – until the natural movement of the planking with changes in moisture-content splits a plank, since there are no longer any caulked seams at which such small movements can be absorbed.

When new edging-strips or splines are being glued into seams, it is advisable to have a helper available to wipe away any runs of surplus glue as they appear. If these runs are allowed to harden they become brittle and difficult to remove. Hardened resin glues blunt a plane iron very quickly, and if the sole of a metal-bodied plane hits a hardened blob of resin it can shatter the resin, which usually flies straight into the nearest eye! Also it is not unknown for a blob of hardened resin to pull a sliver out of the surface of the plank to which it is stuck.

Strip-planked hulls

Edge-fastened strip planking, where all strips are the same width, with radiused upper and lower edges, and where the fastenings pass down through two and a half strips (Fig 87) was at one time regarded by many as the ideal way for an amateur to build a really good hull. The system does have much in its favour, as it results in a very strong, light hull which does not need heavy internal framing. However, it has two major disadvantages. The first is that it is liable to split along the strips adjacent to the glue-lines; the second is that it is just about as near to an unrepairable wooden hull as it is possible to get. The usual building system adopted was to plank up with the constant-width strips until just below the water line at the ends, then to use progressively shorter strips over the bulge of the bilges amidships until the upper edge of all this lower-hull planking could be cleaned off parallel to the sheerline. A radius was then cut to leave the extra midships-strips with ends which tapered away to nothing, and the topsides were then planked up with further constant-width strips.

Damaged topsides can be repaired by removing strips successively down from the upper edge of the hull. Since the strips should have been bonded with resin glue, this is not an easy process, but as each strip is removed – usually in splinters – the fastenings holding the next strip below can be withdrawn, again with difficulty as they are usually ring-barbed nails (or they should be on a well-built hull). Replacement strips can be scarph jointed to the ends of old strips, but the scarph joints will run from top to bottom of the strip instead of from inside to outside as on normal planking. Since a reasonable separation must be allowed between joints in adjacent strips, and the replacement portion of an

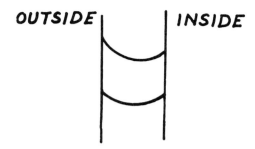

OUTSIDE | **INSIDE**

Fig 88   *Different radii used on the last strip of a repair to a strip-planked hull*

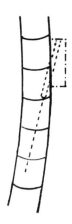

Fig 89   *Drilling the re-planked area for edge fastenings*

upper strip must always be longer than that in the strip below it, the damaged area does not have to be far down the planking before one finds it necessary to replace the whole length of the uppermost strips in the hull.

Below the turn of the bilge, any repair which restores the hull to its original construction must involve a total rebuild of the topsides. A fair repair can however be made by replacing only the strips in the affected area. The first difficulty lies in removing the damaged wood. Since the fastenings cannot be removed, all the cutting out will have to be done with a hacksaw blade in a pad-saw handle. Exposed ends of fastenings on the lower side of the cut-out area can be punched down into the wood with a nail punch so that woodworking tools can be used, but the upper edge will have to be cleaned with metal-working tools – usually a broad flat file. Each end of the area to be replaced will have to be treated as a large single scarph joint. Replacement strips are planed up and fitted, putting in the normal edge fastenings, usually up to two strips below the top of the area to be replaced. Shorter nails, put in at an angle so they can be hammered home with the aid of a punch held against the planking above the hole, must be used to hold the penultimate strip.

The final strip cannot be fitted in the normal way. The upper curve for this strip must be cut to a smaller radius than the lower curve, and the centre of the upper radius must be offset towards the inner face of the hull. This allows the last strip, which is best cut from over-thickness timber, to be twisted down into position until the radii lock (Fig 88). Edgewise fastenings can

be put through the last strip of a repair only by drilling down through the next strip above at a very fine angle. This can be done by wedging or tying a block of wood against the side of the hull so that the hole can start in the scrap block and pass through into the plank (Fig 89). The scrap block must be the same timber as the hull planking, the grain must run the same way, it must be shaped to fit closely against the planking, and it must be held securely in place. If this is not done properly, the result will be a ragged-edged hole in the planking which will be almost impossible to plug decently with a dowel. The hole should be large enough to accept the head of the nail to be fitted, but no larger. If a scrap block of reasonable length is used, holes for several fastenings can be drilled at each setting. Considerable care in drilling is necessary to ensure that the nails can be hammered in without their breaking out of the planking. Some of the nails to be fitted will be securing the last plank of the repair to the one below it; others will be holding the plank above to the repaired section. When all the nails have been fitted, the access holes drilled for them must be plugged with dowels glued in place.

Small areas of damage can be repaired (but not to restore the hull to its original state) by setting in patches, which will be large graving pieces. First (Fig 90, A) the inner side of the planking in the damaged area is cut away until the chisel starts to

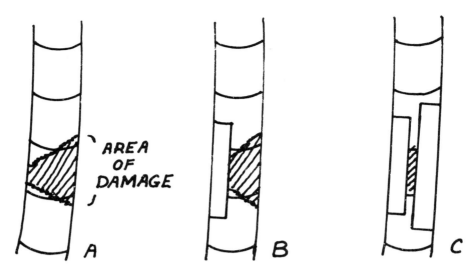

Fig 90   *Repairing damaged strip planking with graving pieces*

hit the fastenings (which, hopefully, should be fairly well in the middle of the planking). A suitable patch is then cut and glued in place (B). When the glue has set, a similar, larger patch is fitted on the outside (C), again working to the maximum depth the fastenings will allow. Having worked on a small strip-planked hull, and built a carvel hull from scratch, the author's method of coping with any substantial area of damage on a strip-planked hull would be to strip the planking off to the keel and rebuild the hull with conventional carvel planking!

If this is considered too drastic, a substantial area of damage can be repaired by the techniques described for moulded-plywood hulls (page 73-5), except that the repair would be done working from the middle layer outwards. If the area to be repaired is so large as to require a temporary internal mould, this mould would have its face packed out to support the middle-layer veneers. The middle and outer layers are completed with the mould in place, then the inside can be dealt with. Substantial area rebates must be chiselled into the old strip planking around the damaged area to accommodate the ends of the strips of veneer. As a strip-planked hull is usually thicker than a conventionally moulded hull, it will probably be found better to use a five-ply

build for a moulded repair, in which case the inner-layer veneers can be run to match the run of the original strip planking.

Local decay and graving pieces

One common cause of trouble in old boats is that bolts, especially those which hold on chainplates or go through the planking to metal floors, may have worked in the wood, bruising and destroying the wood fibres so that the hull leaks round the bolts. Also it is not unknown for metals of quite different electrochemical potentials to be used on older boats. Nor is it unknown to find that some well-intentioned previous owner has replaced iron or steel bolts holding iron chainplates with nice new corrosion-resistant bronze bolts. This is simply asking for trouble, which manifests itself in accelerated corrosion of the metal – which is easily replaced – and also in breakdown of the wood fibres around the fastening – which is not quite so easy to cure. There can be other reasons for wanting to replace a small portion of a plank (or deck plank, cabin side etc). Perhaps a cleat may have been re-positioned, leaving a couple of ugly bolt-holes in a nicely-varnished cockpit coaming. Any such 'cosmetic' repairs, and the making good of

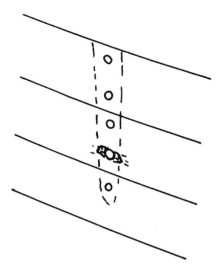

Fig 91   *Local decay behind a chainplate*

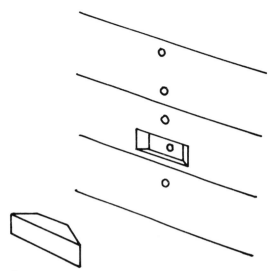

Fig 92   *Rectangular graving piece ready to be glued in*

local damage around fastenings, can be carried out by fitting graving pieces, which are simply small pieces of new wood let into the original.

To consider a typical example, a chainplate may show somewhat excessive corrosion, and it may be possible to detect softening of the plank to which it is bolted. Removal of the chainplate can reveal an almost total breakdown of the wood in the way of a bolt-hole – a soggy mess, some of which can be removed with a finger (Fig 91). If prodding with a stronger implement reveals that the damage is purely local and there is no evidence of fungal decay (call in a fully qualified surveyor of wooden boats if in any doubt), it will probably not be necessary to replace the entire plank.

All the damaged wood must first be removed, and cut back until clean, sound timber is reached. It is better not to dig right through the plank if this can be avoided. This type of trouble round bolt-holes usually occurs over ribs, frames or floors, and it is best not to glue the graving piece right through the plank and on to the face of the rib etc. The well-known Law of Natural Cussedness guarantees that if this is done the next major job, in a couple of years' time, will be the replacement of that rib, frame or floor, so it is as well to leave a thin piece of the original planking be-

tween the graving piece and the inner member. Of course, if the inner timber is to be replaced as part of the same job, it can be removed before the graving piece is fitted into the planking, and replaced after the repair to the planking has been finished. Thus the graving piece is set right through the plank.

The cavity in the face of the plank must be tidied up to a recognisable and reproducible shape, usually with parallel edges, well-tapered ends and a clean, flat bottom (Fig 92). A graving piece is then cut to be a nice snug fit in the cavity, and is glued in place with a good quality resin glue. When a graving piece is to be fitted into wood which will be varnished, care should be taken to make it from timber which will match the grain of the original planking. It is advisable to cut a graving piece from over-thickness wood and to clean off the surplus after the glue has set.

There is no need for a graving piece to be rectangular. They can be cut to any shape, but they must be a really good fit in the hole they are to fill, and the ends should be tapered. The amount of slope on the taper is not critical, but it should be enough to ensure a good glued joint between the two pieces of wood, which cannot be achieved if the ends of the graving piece are simply cut square across the grain.

The task of removing damaged wood can be made easier by the use of special but home-made tools. One 6 metre of the author's acquaintance required a large number of graving pieces in her otherwise sound bottom planking, and the replacement of all the oak frames. Since this allowed access to the inner face of the planking, all the graving pieces could be fitted right through. Her owner made up two special tapered circular cutters. One was a large, toothed, truncated cone which could be used in a carpenter's brace to open out the soggy holes in the mahogany planking back to sound wood all round, leaving a clean, tapering hole about 38 mm (1½ in) in diameter (Fig 93). The other matching tool bore a slight resemblance to a plumber's or engineer's tank cutter, without its centre pin (or for non-plumbers and non-engineers, it could be likened to a rotating pastry cutter). Its inner face was bored to a taper to match the hole-cutter, and was deeply toothed; and it had a hollow stem about 13 mm (½ in) in diameter (Fig 94). Mounted in a heavy duty bench drill, and brought down on to the face of a mahogany plank about twice the thickness of the boat's planking, it cut down through the wood, generating a considerable amount of dust and smoke, until it broke through. The cutter was then removed from the drilling machine and a piece of rod poked down the hollow stem to knock out a perfectly fitting tapered plug, which could be glued straight into the hole in the planking.

The number of pieces to be fitted justified making the two special cutters, but the plug-cutter was a somewhat fearsome tool to watch in operation. It could probably have been improved by drilling some large holes through the side walls to allow the dust generated to escape, and by turning a taper on the outside so that it did not rub in the hole it was cutting (Fig 95). As well as allowing the swarf to escape, holes in the side of the tool would allow the finished plugs to be knocked out without having to remove the tool from the chuck.

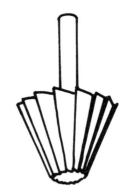

Fig 93   *Special cutter for making tapered holes in planks*

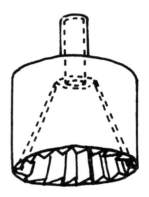

Fig 94   *Cutter for making tapered plugs*

Fig 95   *Improved version of plug cutter*

Chapter 10

Repairs to framing

Bent ribs

On older hulls in which all the ribs are steam-bent timbers, it is not uncommon to find some of the ribs are broken at the turn of the bilge amidships. On clinker hulls such breaks in ribs are often associated with badly split lands on the planks. If a shoal-draft carvel hull is found to leak badly at the turn of the bilge, cracked ribs can be suspected. Clearly, if ribs on a carvel hull are cracked or broken, there will be nothing to hold the hull in shape at that point. The caulking cannot hold it tight – it will merely force the hull further out of shape if attempts are made to harden it up. Such damage to ribs may occur behind a bilge stringer, where it is not immediately obvious.

The traditional remedy for such cracked or broken ribs was to insert a doubling rib beside the broken one (Fig 96). Whilst this made a temporary cure, unfortunately it could never be a good long-term repair. This was often not appreciated, and one used to hear about hulls 'getting tired' or having 'fallen out of shape' or even having

been built with ribs which were never strong enough to do their job, to explain the fact that the doubling ribs often broke, as did trebling ribs when these were fitted. Such excuses are hard to swallow, especially when one looks at some of the older class racing dinghies which have been sailed hard for well over sixty years without breaking any ribs.

The root cause of the premature breaking of doubling ribs is the presence of the old, broken rib immediately beside the new one. The pair share the loading right down to the break point in the old rib, where the entire load is abruptly transferred to new timber. The whole hull is made stiffer by the presence of the adjacent ribs, so any flexing will naturally be concentrated at the break point in the old rib; the doubler is therefore being asked to carry a greater load than the designer intended the ribs to carry, and has the full load transferred to it abruptly at the break point. Thus in the same way that a badly fitted tingle put on to cure minor leaking can be the cause of much more serious problems in the future, doubled ribs should be regarded as trouble-makers and not trouble-curers.

The correct cure for a rib which has cracked at the turn of the bilge is to replace the rib, not to double it. However, whilst this may be easy enough in an open dinghy, it can be almost impossible on a decked boat, so some alternative must be used. Either a new portion can be scarph jointed into the old rib, or some other means must be adopted to ensure that the replacement rib is not unfairly loaded by having an old rib with an abrupt break beside it.

Before considering the actual process of fitting new ribs, the alternatives to total replacement should be considered. On a decked boat on which the ends of the ribs

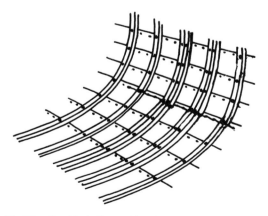

Fig 96 *Doubled ribs and lands of planks broken at the turn of the bilge*

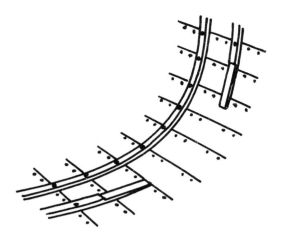

Fig 97 *Damaged portion of rib cut out and scarph joints cut*

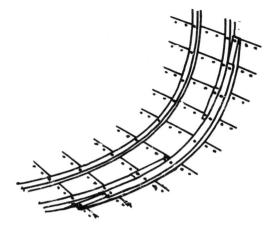

Fig 99 *Replacement portion of bent frame fitted beside the original: note tapered ends to both old and new frames*

are accessible only with considerable extra work, the best solution is to scarph in a new section of rib. The joints must be cut at places where there is minimal curvature of the rib, and the joints should extend over at least two of the normal fastenings through the rib (Fig 97). The steps at each end of the joint should be about a fifth to a quarter of the thickness of the rib. When the joints have been made, an extra rivet should be put in through the middle of the joint. On clinker hulls, a small wedge will have to be cut to pack the back of the rib to the face of the planking so this mid-joint rivet can be closed down hard (Fig 98). The wedge should be cut to leave a clear waterway behind the rib at the edge of the next plank in. If it is not thought possible to make good scarph joints, then a doubling rib may have to be fitted. To avoid risks of this doubler breaking, the ends of the old rib should be cut back at least one plank's width away from the break point, and then tapered off over at least the pitch of two fastenings. The doubling rib also has its ends tapered off, and should overlap at full thickness the full

size of the old rib by the width of one plank (Fig 99). When the doubler is fitted, soft bedding material such as Secomastic should be used between it and the old rib.

If several adjacent ribs are to be repaired, a neater job can be made if all the old ribs are cut back to the same length and new part-ribs are fitted round the turn of the bilge, midway between the old ribs (Fig 100). The ends must be tapered off, and all lengths should be as described above for doublers. If there is substantial reason to believe that the original ribs were too light for their job, then such part-ribs can be cut slightly larger than the original timbers. However, undersize ribs are not common, and the author can think of only two boats

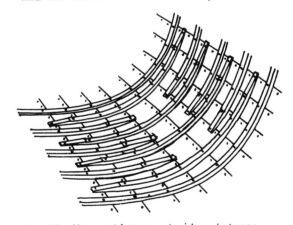

Fig 100 *New part-frames set midway between the originals along the turn of the bilge*

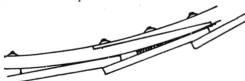

Fig 98 *Detail of scarph joint in a bent frame*

98

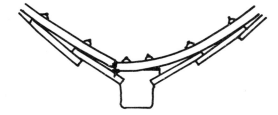

Fig 101   *A frame well up in the bows cracked near the keel is best left and reinforced with a floor timber*

on which there was good reason to believe the ribs were inadequate. All other instances of broken ribs have been caused either by bad workmanship, or by mechanical damage such as a dinghy being squeezed between two large boats or between its parent boat and a quay. In many cases the original damage was probably to only one or two ribs, but the incorrect fitting of doublers had caused the damage to spread over most of the midships third of the length of the hull.

Bent ribs are sometimes found to be cracked very near the bows of small clinker boats, where the rib has to make a very sharp U bend over the keel (Fig 101). Usually the first continuous rib has broken at the keel, putting an unfair strain on the fastenings between the garboard and the keel at that point. It is possible to replace the entire centre portion of such a rib with the new piece scarphed in well up the sides where there is little curvature in the hull, but such a replacement may not be easy, and it might be better to leave the old broken rib in place and to fit a transverse floor beside it (see page 149). If a replacement rib can be successfully bent to fit alongside the old rib, the lower part of the old rib can be cut out and the new piece cut to length and scarphed in.

But before any new bent ribs are actually cut, arrangements must be made for steaming them to shape. Clear access from the steam-chest or steam-pipe to the boat is essential, and the inside of the hull must be cleared so that the new ribs can be slid into place. Any stringers which lie over the ribs should have their fastenings to adjacent ribs removed, and should be sprung and wedged clear of the planking to leave a

space at least 3 mm ($\frac{1}{8}$ in) more than the thickness of the new ribs. All the old ribs should have been cut back and any scarph joints cut on their ends (except, as mentioned earlier, for a rib right across in the bows), and an ample supply of wedges and shores should be ready to hand to hold the steamed timbers in place.

The replacement ribs are cut to size from straight-grained, freshly cut timber, either English oak, Canadian rock elm, or ash. Obviously, the wood must be straight-grained if it is not to split on bending, and any lengths which have knots must be rejected. The author can recall watching an elm trunk well over 0.6 m (2 ft) in diameter being cut up to yield only eleven usable ribs, 25 mm × 19 mm (1 in × $\frac{3}{4}$ in). The remainder of the tree suffered from minute knots around which the grain meandered sufficiently to make whole planks unsuitable for use as ribs.

Not only must the timber be straight-grained, it must also be cut in the proper direction relative to the grain of the tree. The growth rings in the timber should lie parallel to the hull planking in the finished ribs (Fig 102). If a tree is being cut up primarily for timber for steamed ribs, it should be sliced into planks first, the thickness of the outer planks being such as will plane down to the thickness of the ribs, whilst that of the two or three planks which pass through the centre of the tree being such as to plane to the width of the ribs (Fig 103). The planks are then cut down to individual ribs, the first cut being made by eye on a large circular saw so as to follow as closely as possible the best line of the grain. The centre of the tree is usually unusable, and care must be taken not to use any of the lighter-coloured sapwood, which is non-durable.

It is essential for good steaming that the

Fig 102   *Correct run of the grain for bent ribs*

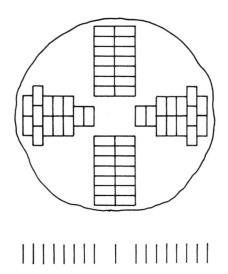

Fig 103 *Section of a small tree showing how it should be sliced into planks to cut the best timber for bent frames*

timber be as fresh as possible. Bends can be steamed into what today is sometimes passed off as 'seasoned timber', but any hardwood which has been cut into planks and stacked to air-dry will not bend well. With the careful cutting required and the need for the timber to be fresh, it is clear that suitable material for ribs cannot be bought from a DIY shop or any small local timber yard, but will have to come from a proper sawmill or from a large boatyard which has facilities for cutting timber from logs. A couple of planks through the centre of a reasonable-sized tree should provide more than enough ribs for the average boat repair, and a chat with the hardwoods manager of a sawmill will usually result in a supply of suitable cut planks the next time the mill cuts up an appropriate log. John Sadd & Sons Ltd of Maldon were found to be particularly helpful in providing timber for ribs.

When the timbers have been obtained and planed to size, a small chamfer should be planed on what will be the inner corners of the rib, ie on the side of the rib nearer to the outside of the tree, and the sharpness of the other two corners should be removed by a single cut from a fine-set plane.

Steam should be raised whilst the timbers are being planed. When the steam-chest is nicely hot inside and full of steam, the first two or three timbers can be popped in. Depending on the number of ribs to be replaced, the operator can then either plane up the next batch or take a coffee break (this assumes he has an assistant who is keeping the fire going and seeing that the steamer does not boil dry). Like any cooking operation, steaming time varies slightly depending on the age of the wood, the size of the ribs and the pressure (if any) of steam which can be built up in the chest. Normal time for most ribs is 20 minutes to about $\frac{3}{4}$ hour. If steam is plentiful, a small rib can be tried after about $\frac{1}{4}$ hour. Removing the timbers from the steam-chest or steam-pipe is made easier if a nail is hammered into an end of the timber and a length of string is tied round the nail.

A pair of stout gauntlets should be worn for handling freshly steamed ribs. The end-plug for the chest or pipe is removed, a rib pulled out by its string, and the plug replaced before too much steam is lost. If the rib is ready for fitting, it will have lost all stiffness and will 'flop' under its own weight rather like a piece of stout new manila hawser. A properly steamed rib will be very flexible, very hot, and will look and feel dry. The rib should be put into place as rapidly as possible, sliding it under any stringers etc as necessary. If the new rib is to be scarph jointed to the old one, it should be laid beside the old rib on the side which has the sharper curve and, if possible, blocks should be placed under the ends of the new portion so that it bends to a slightly tighter curve than will ultimately be needed. At this stage the new portion of a rib which is to be scarphed, or a total replacement rib, will not have been trimmed off to length. If partial doublers or intermediate ribs with a reasonable overlap are being fitted, and all the new ribs are the same length, then they can be cut to length and have the end-tapers cut before steaming. If different lengths of new ribs are required, either some very positive identification for each rib must be provided, such as a numbered (wooden) label tied to the end of the piece of string used to pull the rib out of the steam-box, or the ribs should be steamed one at a time. From when the steam-box is opened until the rib is bent into its final position there is no time to spare to sort out where or which way up a rib should go. The real flexibility lasts only a minute or two. The shipwrights who taught the author how to steam and fit ribs stated that any rib which was not finally in place inside three minutes should be abandoned. The chamfers on the inner edges identify instantly which is the 'inside' and 'outside' of the new rib.

On a carvel hull with reasonably stout planking, a freshly steamed rib can be held in place with a couple of fine nails hammered at opposing angles into the plank at the sharpest point of the bend (Fig 104); but on a clinker hull it will have to be held with shores to appropriate points (Fig 77). If the new ribs are being steamed one at a time, or if enough helpers are available, doubling, intermediate or replacement ribs can be riveted in as they are bent. On full-length ribs the riveting must be started at the keel and then worked up the side of the hull, fitting one rivet in each side alternately if the rib runs right across the hull – keeps the outside helper awake, dashing round the end of the hull when a midships rib is being fitted! When only a partial rib is being fitted, one or two rivets at the tightest point in the bend will hold it adequately until it can be completely riveted in. Doublers and intermediate ribs over the turn of the bilge should be riveted at their centre first, then the rest of the rivets fitted out to the ends. Ribs which are to be scarph jointed in cannot be riveted at this stage.

It should be noted that as well as bending round to the curve of the hull, all the ribs towards the ends of the boat will require some edgewise bending to keep the line of the rib square to the keel whilst the face of the rib lies against the tapering-in planking.

Portions of new ribs which are to be scarph jointed must be left to cool and set for a few hours, preferably overnight. Any packing blocks which were inserted to get a slight overbend must be removed, and the new portion held against the old so that the positions of the two scarph joints can be marked accurately. The new portion of

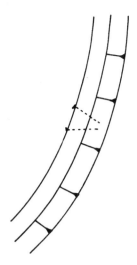

Fig 104   *Freshly bent frame tacked in place with wire nails*

the rib is then removed from the hull and the two joints are cut, remembering that on ribs near the ends of the hull the new portion was lying on the tighter-bend side of the old rib so the joints will have to be cut minutely larger than marked. Once removed from the hull, the rib will straighten out very slightly, and this must be allowed for when the fit of the joints is checked.

Before the new portion of the rib is glued and riveted in place, pieces of thin polythene sheet should be slid between the ends of the old rib and the planking to ensure that glue squeezed out of the joints cannot bond the rib to the planks. The lower joint should be closed first, then the new rib is riveted in place up to the upper joint, taking care to see that the upper end of the new portion does not pull sideways as successive rivets are closed down. To avoid too much of the resin glue used running off the upper joint face before the joint is finally made, it is better to spread the adhesive only on the lower joint initially. The glue can be applied to the upper joint with a thin knife-blade when the new portion has been riveted to within a couple of planks of the joint.

Sideways movement of the upper end of the new portion of the rib can be prevented by clamping a couple of pieces of scrap wood wrapped in thin polythene sheet on either side of the old rib, so that they cover the top third or quarter of the length of the joint.

When all the adhesive has set, the pieces of polythene slid beneath the ribs can be trimmed off flush with the sides of the rib.

Sawn and grown frames

It is rare to find sawn or grown frames that have cracked or broken in the way that steamed ribs break. The more usual faults to occasion repair or replacement are forms of nail sickness and rot.

Problems with isolated fastenings are best dealt with by small local repairs, which will usually involve removing the afflicted fastening and making good the hole it leaves ready to fit a new fastening. This can sometimes be managed by opening out the wood to a clean hole and fitting a larger bolt, screw or nail. More commonly, the hole will have to be plugged with a well-fitting oak dowel glued in after the hole has been opened out to expose clean timber all round. If a hole is to be bored through the plug to take a bolt, it is not a bad idea to set an oak graving piece into the face of the frame over the dowel so as to give the bolt head (or more usually washer and nut) a clean, flat, bearing surface. If this is done the graving piece should be slightly wider than the dowel fitted, its flat base should be at least twice the diameter of the dowel, and the slope on each end should be about two-thirds the length of the flat base. The depth of the graving piece should be about equal to its width.

One of the problems in a repair of this nature is in opening out the hole in the frame and gluing in the dowel without affecting the plank on the outside of the frame. If that plank is being replaced, then there is no problem, the dowel can be run right through whilst the plank is out of the way. If a graving piece is to be set into the plank, more care is necessary. The easiest way to handle such a repair whilst ensuring that the glue used to bond in the various new pieces cannot bond the plank to the

frame, is to cut the hole for the graving piece in the plank right through to the face of the frame, bore right through the frame for the dowel, and cut the hole for the graving piece on the inner face of the frame. The dowel is then glued in place in the frame, and any excess glue wiped off both faces before it can cure. When the glue is fully cured, the projecting ends of the dowel are chiselled off flush. The face of the frame exposed at the bottom of the hole for the graving piece in the plank is then masked with Sellotape, cut so that it extends for about 2 mm ($\frac{1}{16}$ in) up the bevelled ends of the hole, and put in so that it makes a small but positive overlap onto the sides of the hole. Since the hole will usually be wider than the roll of tape available, it is as well to put in two layers of tape so that the joints between the strips in the first layer are covered by the strips of the second layer. The graving pieces are then glued in, taking care not to spread any glue on the base of the piece to be set into the plank. If the plank outside the hole does not require any repair, the hole in the frame for the dowel must be drilled only to within 3 mm ($\frac{1}{8}$ in) of the outer face and, when the dowel is fitted, glue is applied only to the dowel so that none can be squeezed out ahead of the dowel to bond the frame to the plank.

Larger areas of damage or decay can be repaired by scarphing in a new length of frame. This job is just a grown-up version of scarphing in a new length of bent frame, the only difference being that the new piece will be sawn from wood with an appropriate curve to the grain and planed, chiselled or adzed to shape and to fit. At least, that is the only difference in theory. In practice, the differences usually start in the removal of the fastenings, which can vary between very difficult and totally impossible (see page 84). In extreme cases, the damaged frame may have to be split out with a hand axe, large chisel, and maul and steel wedges, leaving the fastenings to be cut off clean flush with the inner face of the planking or knocked out through the plank. If a frame is being split out with an axe or adze, extreme care must be taken to avoid the axe hitting any metal

Emma Goody: *15ft 6in x 15ft x 6ft x 1ft: dinghy of unknown origin and age restored and rigged with scaled down traditional Bawley rig (L. H. A. Weigall)*

Alma: 60ft x 22ft: San Francisco Bay Scow Schooner built in 1891 and preserved in sailing order in the California State Maritime Historic Park, San Francisco (W. E. Vaughan)

fastening. The first result is certain to be a chip out of the axe's sharp edge; the immediately subsequent result is usually a significantly larger chip out of the nearest arm or leg. The reader may ask how he (or she) avoids fastenings which are in unknown positions, to which the honest reply is: 'I don't know'. One could always get very technical about it and employ various clever ultrasonic devices, but the real way to do it is to take the job very slowly and cautiously, making sure that there are no fastenings in the immediate area which is being attacked with the axe. The use of wedges to split the frame into layers is one of the best ways of finding where the fastenings are, without hitting them with a sharp-edged tool. The split can be started with a good firmer chisel, going in only to a depth at which one can be certain there are no buried dumps, bolts or screws. One point to be watched in repairs to grown-oak frames in old boats is that whilst the exposed faces of the frame may be in very poor condition and possibly even somewhat soggy, the inner wood can be very, very hard indeed.

On bigger boats the replacement of part of a frame may be facilitated by the frame originally having been built up of pairs of separate futtocks or sections, with the joints staggered, so that replacement can be confined to possibly two or three sections (Fig 105). This simplifies worries about joints, but can give rise to more problems in removal of the damaged or decayed timber as not only are there fastenings through the planks and the frame, there are also the fore and aft fastenings between the futtocks. Removal or drilling out of these fastenings can be complicated by close spacing of the frames, and a splinter-by-splinter removal technique may have to be adopted.

Having removed various sections of built-up frames, cleared away all old fastenings in the vicinity, and cut new sections, the problem of how to fasten these securely to the originals has to be faced. Putting fastenings through the planking into the new sections is easy; the problem lies in providing adequate fore and aft fastenings between the overlapping frame sections.

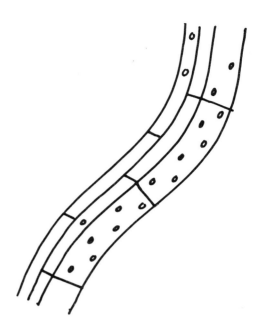

Fig 105   Sawn frame built up from separate sections

It may be possible to join two new sections together before they are fitted in place, but generally this is likely to make it much more difficult to fit them at all. Holes will have to be bored through new and old sections to take either bolts or trenails, and these holes will have to be bored with the next frame along possibly only 100–150 mm (4–6 in) away. Clearly it will be impossible to provide true fore and aft fastenings. Amidships, fastenings will have to be put in from either side of the frame, angling the holes as little as possible so that the drill used avoids the adjacent frames (Fig 106). Towards the bow and

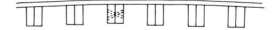

Fig 106   Angled fastenings between new and old frame sections in the middle of the hull

the stern, access for drilling is possible only from one side of the frame, but the curve-in of the side of the hull means that the holes can be drilled more nearly fore and aft (Fig 107).

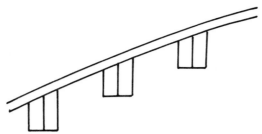

Fig 107 *Frames are more accessible for fore and aft fastenings near the bow and stern*

Boring holes in awkward places

The author's solution to this problem was to make up an extension fitting for a carpenter's brace. The end of a 0.6 m (2 ft) length of thick-walled (about 6 mm/¼ in) steel tube of about 10 mm (⅜ in) bore was heated to bright red, and the squared end of an old auger-bit hammered in until the enlarged squared end was a fair fit in the tube, with about 10 mm (⅜ in) of the tube projecting beyond the enlarged end of the bit. This portion of the tube was cross-drilled eccentrically to take a pin which just cleared the shank of the bit, thus enabling the bit to be pulled out of the hole it was cutting (Fig 108). The other end of the tube was heated and beaten into an approximate square to fit the chuck of a carpenter's brace. This end was also cross-drilled so that the extension could be pulled back by putting a tommy bar through the hole. The finished extension was distinctly 'floppy' in use, and until the bit got fairly well into the wood it tended to jump from side to side. This undesirable effect could be reduced by sliding a loose-fitting bearing plate cut from a piece of

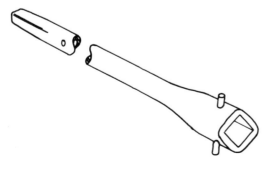

Fig 108 *A useful bit extension to fit a carpenter's brace*

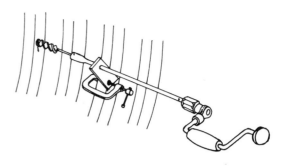

Fig 109 *Using the bit extension with a steadying bearing clamped to a frame*

13 mm (½ in) reinforced plastic sheet (Tufnol) over the extension and clamping the bearing plate onto any suitable adjacent piece of timber, such as a next frame along (Fig 109).

This somewhat fearsome contraption was originally devised to drill out holes for bolts through deadwoods, when the requirement was for holes over 300 mm (1 ft) long, and the longest bit the author owned was about 200 mm (8 in) long. On such deep holes it worked admirably provided the bit was withdrawn and cleared of chips at frequent intervals. The author can still recall the feeling of dismay when a bit jammed and for an hour or two it seemed possible that a friend's boat would have to sail around with a three-quarter inch bit buried in its bow knee and apron! Somehow or other it was freed, and after that bits were withdrawn and cleared at very frequent intervals. Since then the extension has been used on a wide variety of awkward jobs.

It might appear that even better results would be obtained by deliberately allowing a universal-joint action where the bit enters the extension. This idea does not work, as it becomes impossible to apply enough pressure to the end of the system to keep the bit cutting (old oak frames can be very tough). When working in confined spaces, a ratchet-action brace is a great help.

Metal bolts can be fitted in the angled holes drilled through pairs of futtocks, but trenails seem more appropriate and easier to fit because there is no need to provide an angled face for the bolt head and washers to bear on. If bolts are used, either a flat, square to the hole, must be chiselled

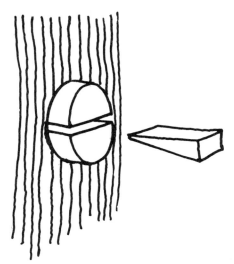

Fig 110 *Trenail and wedge: note that the wedge must be fitted across the grain of the timber being nailed*

into the sides of the frame, or suitably tapered blocks of oak must be made up.

Trenails

Trenails are easy to cut and fit. If only a few are required they can be planed and sanded round, but if several are needed it is worth making a dowel plate. This is merely a piece of stout steel plate drilled with a series of progressively larger holes. The trenail or dowel is cut roughly to size and to a more or less octagonal shape, then it is hammered through the successive holes in the plate until it has been reduced to the required diameter. It is then cut off to about 6 mm ($\frac{1}{4}$ in) overlength, and the two ends are cut into with a fine-bladed saw such as a Junior hacksaw. The saw cuts are made so that when the trenail is in place the cuts lie across the grain of the wood into which it is to be fitted (Fig 110). Oak wedges are cut, slightly narrower than the diameter of the trenail, and the latter is driven through the hole drilled for it. The two wedges are then placed in the sawcuts and driven home, opening out the ends of the trenail and locking it securely. The depth of saw cut necessary and the slope of the wedge will depend on the size and type of timber being fastened. A couple of experiments can be made on

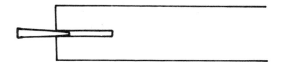

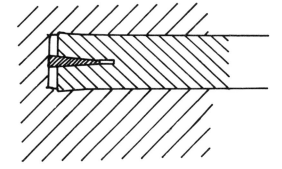

Fig 111 *Trenail wedged in blind hole*

scrap timber to establish the best proportions to use for any particular job.

Trenails can be driven and wedged into blind holes in large timbers. When this is to be done, the first essential is to check that the trenail is a good, but not binding, fit in the hole, and that it can be pushed in for the hole's full depth. The saw cut is then made in the end of the dowel, and the wedge cut. The wedge should be no longer than the depth of the saw cut, and it should be possible to enter the first quarter of the length of the wedge into the cut without it opening out the end of the dowel (Fig 111). The dowel with the wedge in the slot is then driven into the hole. As the wedge hits the bottom of the hole, it starts to open up the end of the trenail, which is driven in until it locks immovably against the hole sides. This same technique can be applied to mortise and tenon joints, when it is known as a fox-wedged joint. Whilst the principle of such blind wedging is simple, selecting the right length and slope of wedge must be a matter of experience and judgement. Clearly, the softer the wood into which a trenail is to be wedged blind, the wider the wedge can be before the system locks immovably.

Replacing part-frames

Work on the upper portions of grown or sawn frames can be further complicated if the original frame extended through the deck to support the bulwarks. Some boats were built so that these upper portions of the frames can be replaced fairly easily without removing half the deck and the entire beam shelf and clamp: other boats were not built with such repairs in mind, and repairs may entail a fairly substantial redesign of the structure so as to fit a removable top portion, suitably dowelled or bolted, to the main body of the frame. Unfortunately, the waterways beneath the bulwark planking on an old boat can easily get blocked, setting up a nice little trap in which rain-water can lodge, and then it may be only a question of time (and sometimes a surprisingly short time) before the frame head, beam shelf, covering board and a deck beam or two are all affected by rot. If this is found in one frame, it may well be present in others, and what might have started by looking like a minor replacement of part of a frame or two can end up as a major rebuild of the whole structure above the turn of the bilges.

If this is the case, a careful review must be made of time and funds available, and as to whether the boat was bought to provide enjoyable sailing or to provide spare-time work! There is absolutely no reason why, with time to learn the techniques and sufficient funds to buy the necessary timber, any amateur who is keen enough should not be able to complete quite a massive rebuilding job, but it is as well to be aware of what one is tackling at the outset.

The actual processes to be followed for replacing frames up to deck level cannot be described in detail. It is very largely a matter of discovering exactly how the boat was built, removing whatever has to be removed piece by piece and then rebuilding. Common sense usually provides the best guide for the order in which the work should be carried out.

If damage to a frame does not extend up to deck level but is confined to the bilges, it may be possible to effect repairs by removing all traces of damaged or decayed timber and then providing some alternative means of achieving the necessary strength rather than trying to make a direct replacement to restore the hull to its original condition. One such alternative is the fitting of a metal part-frame in place of the removed wood. This can take the form of a stout steel plate hammered (hot) to a suitable curve to fit over what is left of the old wooden frame, or an angle-section frame can be welded up from plate. Any such steel frames or floors should be hot-dip galvanised (never use electro-tinned steel on boat-work – it will not last). If the galvanised steel frames are bedded into hot tar, and fastened with dip-galvanised steel bolts which are also tar-dipped, the structure can be expected to last for many years. In one of the most fascinating books on amateur boat-building, John Wray described how he fastened his kauri pine cruiser *Ngataki* with lengths of galvanised fence-wire dipped into hot tar laboriously scraped up from the road verges. That was in 1933, and the last time the author heard of her in the mid-1970s she was still in good order, sailing around Auckland.

Another alternative is to laminate new wooden frames in situ, possibly laminating up to a scarph joint with the upper portions of the original frames. Really good grown oak of suitable curvature for grown frames is now hard to come by. Gone are the days when retired admirals planted acorns on their walks and trimmed and trained young trees to grow into fine curved stems and frames! However, really diligent searching can often unearth some suitable curved logs. But even if good curved wood can be found, cutting it to shape may prove too much for an amateur who does not have access to a large bandsaw. Frames can, of course, be cut out by hand from a rough log, but this is a task for the really dedicated enthusiast. Faced with the difficulty of finding suitable timber, and further difficulty in sawing it to shape, few can blame the owner who decides to laminate new frames from thinner, easily cut, readily available straight-grained timber.

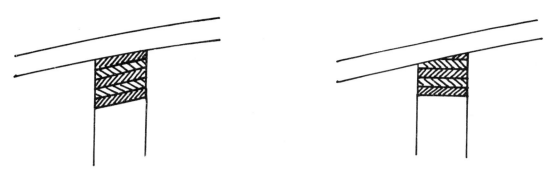

Fig 112 *Sections through frames laminated in the hull (left) and laminated externally (right)*

Laminated frames

In these days of readily available resin glues which can be relied upon to give a bond which, once cured, is much stronger than the wood it joins, the lamination of very large or shaped wooden structures is a practical proposition for anyone whose skills slightly exceed those of the cartoon 'home handyman'. When the lamination of replacement frames for a boat is being considered, two main areas of choice must be resolved.

The first is whether to use several thin layers, thin enough for the wood to be bent fairly easily without steaming; or whether to use fewer thicker layers and steam-bend them to shape. The second is whether to laminate in situ so that the separate laminates lie parallel to the hull planking and the thickness of the finished frame is determined by the number and thickness of the laminates, or whether to laminate out of the hull to build up a piece of curved-grain timber out of which the required frame shape can be cut (Fig 112). That is, the laminates of an externally moulded frame will all lie parallel to the centre-line of the hull, and any bevel on the outer face will possibly cut through into a second or even a third layer of the lamination.

These two choices must be made together. If the frame is to be moulded in situ, probably thin laminations will have to be used. The hull planking (which will already be minus one frame at least) can withstand only a certain amount of force without deforming, and the object of the exercise is to produce a frame which will fit the shape of the hull, not to distort the hull to a laminated shape which happened to bend most easily out of excessively thick and tough layers! If the moulding is done outside the hull, much more force can be applied to bend thick laminates. The author has seen a powerful hydraulic jack used to hold the curvature in a laminated deck beam whilst the resin cured.

A frame laminated in situ should be stronger, because most of the timber used in its construction remains in the finished frame. Also, provided the planking is not overstressed during the lamination, the fit of the frame to the hull is almost guaranteed. Against these advantages must be offset the disadvantages that the replacement frames with their inner faces parallel to the planking will not match any old frames which are left; in the bow and the stern there will be ugly acute corners to the frames; it is advisable to replace only one frame at a time to avoid distorting the hull and, worst of all, such replacement frames will use up very much more timber than would externally moulded frames. Apart from a midships frame where all the planking lies parallel to the centre line of the hull, the laminates for a frame moulded in situ must be cut with curved sides so that, when they are bent round to lie against the tapering in hull-planking, the sides of the finished frame will be square to the keel (Fig 113). Since it is far from easy to cut this shaping of the laminates perfectly, and also not very easy to bond them absolutely flush, the sides of frames moulded in the hull can be expected to

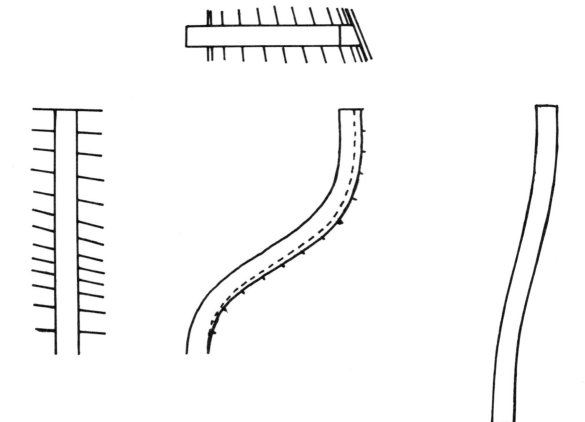

Fig 113 *The cut strips for a frame laminated in the hull may not be straight*

require more cleaning up than those of an externally moulded frame.

An externally moulded frame will have its outer face bevelled to fit the hull planking, but the sides should need little cleaning off. Once installed and painted, an externally moulded frame should be quite indistinguishable from an adjacent original grown frame.

If a good resin glue, such as pure resorcinol, is used, there is little virtue in using few layers and having to steam them into shape. However, if layers are to be steamed, they should be steamed and bent in a bending jig, then when they have cooled and dried out to a normal moisture-content of around 18 per cent, the layers can be bonded together. It is unwise to attempt to bond freshly steamed timbers as they are bent. The high temperature of the wood will accelerate the curing of the resin, possibly causing curing before the laminates are finally clamped home, and the excessive moisture-content of the freshly steamed wood will seriously degrade the bond strength. If layers are steamed and pre-bent, it is advisable to prepare the surfaces for bonding by going over them with coarse sandpaper after the wood has dried to a normal moisture-content.

Tables of suitable bend radii for laminated timber structures are available; but the best way for an amateur doing a repair job to establish the right thickness to use is for him to take a piece of wood of appropriate size and which looks as if it might be about the right thickness for the tightest bend to be made, and then try it. If it can be bent to the appropriate curve without any mechanical aids, and the thickness is such that there will not be an excessive number of layers, then that thickness will do. If (as is more usually the case) the wood creaks alarmingly before it reaches the final curvature, then it should be planed down and another trial made. If the frames are to be moulded in the hull, the pressure used to make the bend will be established by the strength of the hull, as well as by the ability to bend the individual layers. The availability of suitable points in the hull from which to rig struts to hold the layers in place during bonding will also have to be considered.

One other point which must be borne in mind when considering laminating frames in situ is that the frame will need to be taken out to have its edges cleaned off after the resin has cured, if a really good job is to be made of the replacement. But if subsequent removal of the frame poses real problems and the frame will normally be hidden from view, the edges can be left as bonded. In really awkward corners of a boat, a frame or two laminated in situ and left uncleaned may make the difference between a fairly quick repair and a major rebuild (for instance, of cockpit, quarter berth and engine bearers). If a frame is to be laminated in situ, the planking in the way of the frame should be protected from squeezed-out resin by a layer of thin polythene sheeting about three times the width of the frame, held to the planking by lengths of masking tape or by staples. The shape to which the individual laminates must be cut can be established by laying a strip of cardboard in place and marking the shape at a constant distance from an adjacent frame.

If the frames are to be laminated outside the hull and then bevelled and cleaned off to fit, some form of bending jig will be required. For smaller boats, a single sheet of stout blockboard can be used as a base for the jig, but on larger boats this may not offer an adequate area. A fairly light strong framework can be built up from one of the drilled angle-iron systems offered for instant shelving etc (eg Dexion). If a basic rectangle larger than the largest piece to be moulded is built up and braced with a pair of diagonals, intermediate bars can be

bolted on as necessary to provide suitable anchor and pressure points for each different shape to be moulded. Such a steel-framed jig can be faced with thin T and G boards or with a sheet of plywood. Some form of facing is advisable (though not essential) both to provide a flat surface against which the frame can be moulded, and to provide a clean surface on which the required shape can be marked out accurately.

If only one or two frames (or other items) are to be moulded, it is hardly worth the trouble of providing a specially made jig base. Some suitable flat surface can usually be found, such as a well-braced barn door, the back end of a wooden garage, or even the floor of a building, provided the owner of the building will not object to holes being drilled (and later plugged). The required shape for the inner curve of the moulding is marked out on the base of the jig, and the base is then covered with thin polythene sheeting. Stout blocks of wood are bolted to the baseboard to define the profile of the moulding. The faces of the blocks should be radiused to match the required curve, and two bolts should be used for each block so that they will not turn under load. If a blockboard base is being used, large wooden bobbins can be used as forming-blocks. Being circular, they need only one fixing bolt. For most boat-work, the blocks should be about 75 to 100 mm (3–4 in) apart.

A second row of blocks must be bolted down with their faces about 50 mm (2 in) beyond where the outer edge of the finished frame will lie, to provide clamping pressure-points. Unless the layers to be used are so thin that they can be hand-bent and slid in place against the inner set of blocks, some of the blocks in this second row will have to be removable to allow layers to be put into the jig and bent round to the required curve (Fig 114). If a partially open-framed jig is being used it may be possible to secure the removable blocks with G cramps. On solid-based jigs, the removable blocks can be counterbored on their underside and bolts and nuts fitted so that as each block is needed it can be slipped into place quickly. On wall- or door-jigs, a helper can

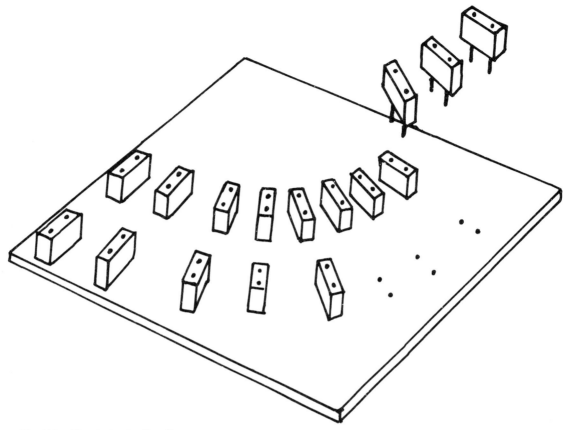

Fig 114 *Simple laminating jig*

put on nuts to hold the blocks as they are fitted. A supply of hardwood wedges, wooden pressure-pads of varying thickness, and a plentiful supply of pieces of thin polythene sheet complete the preparations.

The individual laminates can then be prepared. Each piece should be cut slightly overwidth and some centimetres (a few inches) overlength, so that the finished lamination can be cleaned-down to size. The surface condition of the individual laminates is important. There must be no 'glaze' present on the surface, such as will be present if the wood has been machine planed, or hand planed with an iron which has lost its initial sharpness. Machine-finished timber suffers from having been passed between the cutters and the back-up rollers: it is these back-up rollers which impart the glaze to the surface. The best surface finish for laminating is a very fine saw-cut finish. Since this is difficult for an amateur to achieve (or buy), it is as well to go over every surface to be bonded with medium-coarse garnet paper.

When all is ready, the temperature must be checked. The curing times of modern adhesives are temperature dependent, and it is most important that the recommendations of the resin manufacturers are observed. The adhesives make their bonds by penetrating into the the surface fibres of the wood during their liquid phase (or 'pot life'), and then the molecular structure of the resin changes and it bonds to the cells of the wood. If the joint is moved whilst these molecular changes are occurring, a low-strength bond will result. Low working temperatures inhibit the setting of the resins, and usually a lower-limit temperature is stated, below which a proper cure will not occur. Thus the best time to do laminating (or other work using modern resins) is mid-morning on a fine day, when the temperature is rising. The pot life will be reasonable, and the midday and afternoon heat will ensure a good cure. Unfortunately, circumstances often dictate that the work must be done in evenings or in the winter, when the air temperature will be too low for good curing. In such cases some form of heating must be provided. This need to keep up the temperature of bonded structures may well be the determining factor in deciding whether to laminate new frames in the hull or externally. Externally moulded frames can be taken into a suitably heated building.

If resin glues are being used on an open site during cold weather, there is not too much of a problem in providing some form of heating, but there will often be an attendant fire risk. On larger cruising yachts, there may well be a solid-fuel stove which can raise the temperature inside the hull to a suitable level and hold it there for as long as the resin takes to cure. For glued work on the outside of the hull, heat can be provided by placing one (or more) primus stoves under an inverted large oil drum stood up on bricks to allow the necessary supply of oxygen. A 'tent' of an old sail, or other piece of canvas over a wooden framework, can be rigged so that the air heated by the drum is contained against the side of the hull where the glue is setting. To do this, one edge of the canvas is held in place on the deck of the boat by a row of bricks or small ballast pigs; the outer edges of the canvas must hang about half a metre (1-2 ft) below the glued work. Provided the stoves are not placed too near the edge of the drum, the surface of the drum will not get dangerously hot, and provided the system can be shielded from direct wind or excessive draughts, it can hold up the temperature over a limited area of a hull. If mains electricity is available, fan heaters or oil-filled electric radiators can be used, again with a canvas tent if the work is being done outside the hull. But whatever form of heating is provided, it is essential that it is watched all the time. Gas appliances can leak gas until an explosive mixture is built up, and any heating system

can start a small fire – which can grow surprisingly quickly if it is not quenched in its earlier stages.

If any form of heating (other than electric) is being used in or near a boat which is hauled up ashore, it is a wise precaution to keep a couple of 180 l (40 gal) drums of water and a bucket on the site. At least one boat has been seriously damaged whilst old paint was being burnt off, when a fire started in the old paint, shavings and other rubbish under the hull. It is also obvious that the fire risk will be reduced if the whole working site is kept clear of shavings, old rags etc. Time spent sweeping the whole working site after each 'mess-generating session' may seem like time wasted, especially when it is obvious that the next session of work is going to generate even more shavings, but in the long run such cleanliness not only reduces the fire hazard, it also saves time searching for the inevitable dropped small tools.

The resin to be used – pure resorcinol resin is easy to use and gives the best results with a wide range of timbers, especially hardwoods – must be mixed carefully in a clean container, to the proportions stated by the manufacturers. If the work to be tackled is going to involve a number of gluing operations, it is well worthwhile working out pre-calibrated measuring systems for the two components of the mixture. Waxed-paper baking cases stood in empty round 28 g (1 oz) tobacco tins make almost ideal measuring and mixing containers for resin glues.

Laminated frames may have to be built up layer by layer, but it is usually possible to start with three. If the frame is being built up inside the hull, struts and wedges must be used to hold the layers together and in contact with the hull planking (or rather the polythene sheet which protects the planks). All wedges and pressure-pads which come into contact with the frame during moulding should be protected with polythene sheet. Pressure should be applied to the middle of the frame first, then subsequent struts or shores added out to the ends. If the frame is being laminated in a jig, it may be possible to laminate the entire frame in a single session, coating one face of each layer (except the outer one) with adhesive, placing all the layers in the jig, clamping securely at one end with a wedge and pressure-pad, then working along to the other end inserting pressure-pads and wedges against the outer row of blocks. The individual layers will have to be pulled round one by one to get each successive wedge started, and it is advisable to wear thin disposable polythene gloves for this work. Pressure-pads of various thicknesses should be ready to hand so that the distance the wedges will have to be driven can be minimised. As the laminates are bent round and wedged in place at successive blocks, it may be necessary to replace the pressure-pad and wedge at a previously tightened block with a thicker or thinner pad or wedge so the wedge can move further along to allow space for the next one to be tightened properly.

An amateur's first attempt at laminating may turn out to be a somewhat panic-stricken occasion, with frantic searches for wedges of the right thickness, worries about whether the layers will, after all, bend to the tightest radius necessary, and on top of all this concern that all the glue will run off the layers before they are finally locked in place with puddles of surplus glue running into the most awkward and unforeseen places. One worry which should not be present is over the strength of the bending jig. It must be remembered that, until the glue sets, the system contains a large and quite powerful laminated spring rather like some giant crossbow or medieval stone-throwing device, and the jig must be made with plenty of strength in hand to accommodate the stresses involved. Attempts to nail the pressure-blocks to the base of the jig are liable to result in some of the blocks being projected across the working site at high velocity, and damage to any fingers in the vicinity of the jig can be regarded as a near certainty.

A cautious, somewhat dubious amateur is well advised to build up his laminated frames one layer at a time, until he gains confidence and experience. Obviously, once a layer has been clamped in place, the resin bonding must be allowed to cure

fully before any of the clamps holding it are opened. This point may seem too obvious to mention, but it has been known for a worker, having finally clamped a jig, to attempt to loosen the first clamp ready to insert the next layer!

Plain blocks, pressure-pads and wedges provide the simplest and cheapest form of jig for the amateur who has only a few frames (or other curved parts) to laminate. A rather more sophisticated system, made up for laminating a full set of deck beams to a constant curve, consists of round bobbins cut from an old solid boom and held down to a solid baseboard of framed timber with coach-bolts. The bobbins on the inner side of the curve have the bolts in their centres, and are bolted down hard. The outer set of bobbins have their bolts about 20 mm ($\frac{3}{4}$ in) off-centre and are left just free to turn on the bolts (Fig 115). Clamping pressure is applied by means of wooden levers nailed across the tops of the bobbins, and as each one was locked home its lever was tacked down to the next bobbin along. Not only was this system quite simple to build and quick and easy to clamp and lock, it was also very much easier than a wedged system to undo once the resin had set.

When wooden structures are being laminated, it is most important that the final bond-lines contain the right amount of resin. As an old woodwork teacher once said, 'Glue is supposed to hold joints together, not apart.' There is little risk on a smoothly curved, well-clamped system of there being too much resin left in the final joints, so the natural tendency of the amateur who is not trying to make the last halfpenny of possible profit out of the job is to use an excess of glue and allow the surplus to squeeze out. There is nothing wrong with this policy, and it is far better to waste some resin than to end up with a glue-starved joint; but it is as well to keep all surplus glue wiped up as fast as it emerges from the joint. Even with polythene sheet over the face of the jig and all pressure points, surplus glue can find its way to all sorts of places, and even if it does not do any unwanted bonding (such as bonding what should be a removable

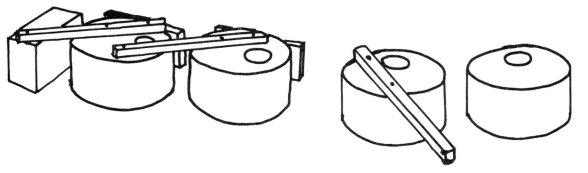

Fig 115 *Quick-action cams on a moulding jig, with two cams closed and two open*

block to the face of the jig, or bonding a wedge to its block), it can build up into lumps which make it difficult to re-use the jig.

If a frame is being built up slowly out of successive laminations, it will probably spring back as the jig is opened after bonding the first few layers; but as more layers are added it will hold better to its final shape. Slight spring-back will not do any harm, but the partly laminated frame must not be allowed to spring too far. Spring-back of the first few layers can be prevented by cutting the earlier layers sufficiently well over length to allow restraining blocks to be screwed to the base to hold the ends whilst the clamps are opened to allow a next, shorter, laminate to be bonded in place.

When all the layers have been bonded, the sides of the frame are planed flat and clean and, for jig-laminated frames, the face is bevelled as necessary to fit against the planking. Scarph joints to fit onto original portions of frames can be cut just as if they were being cut in a single new piece of grown timber. There is no point in treating a laminated frame any differently from this. If there is any risk of any of the bonding coming unstuck, it is very much better that it should happen before the new frame is fastened into the hull. It is most discouraging to discover that what may well be the result of a week or more of spare-time work is unusable; but it is very much better to accept the unpalatable fact and to try again, than it is to end up with a weak frame in a boat. At some time the

hull may be severely stressed in a gale off an exposed coast, and the last thing any owner wants then is niggling doubts about the quality of his repair work.

Failures of laminated structures are usually caused by attempts to glue at unsuitable temperatures, inadequate surface preparation of the wood, or incorrect mixing of the resin. Older hands at the boating game, well versed in the use of gasworks' tar and various oily compounds, may scoff at the worker who washes his hands before picking up timber to be laminated, and who lays a sheet of cardboard over the oily top of a workbench. They may suggest that only cissies and pansies need to provide heating when working on a boat in the winter, and tell of how when they were lads they had to break the ice which held their adze to the wall of the open boatshed before starting their day's healthful joyous work. Let them scoff. The full strength of modern glues cannot be achieved unless the working conditions are right, and whenever there is any doubt, the amateur should always err on the side of over-cautiousness. After all, he is not working to make a profit, nor is he working against any time deadline, so there is nothing to be gained by rushing the job or trying to take short cuts. On a seagoing boat, there may be a lot to lose if the work is not done properly.

Lest the foregoing paragraph suggests that 'gasworks' tar and various oily compounds' should be thoroughly condemned along with ideas of using children to haul tubs of coal in the mines, the reader might well pause to reflect that a far from insignificant number of boats treated with such 'unscientific' materials have survived for over seventy-five years, and there are more than a few centenarian wooden boats still in regular use. Those who feel that the techniques and materials of the later twentieth century should totally supersede the old ways will have to wait many years before their case can be regarded as proven. At the present rate, it appears likely that the case for using plastic materials derived from oil for building durable boats may be proven just as the last of the world's supply of oil is used up (equally it may never be proven); so our descendants will have to revert to the only self-renewing structural material – timber!

Chapter 11

Plank-ends

A not uncommon fault in old boats is failure of the planks at their ends, either through splitting at the fastenings or (on transom-sterned boats) by abrasion and mechanical damage. Any such failures can result in the fastenings losing their grip on the plank and in annoying leaks. They can also result in rot starting in planks, stem or stern timbers. If there is any rot, probably substantial lengths of planking will have to be replaced (as well as stem, transom, and whatever).

It may be felt that a section on repairs to the ends of planks should have been fitted in with the sections on replacing planks, and not mixed up with framing. However, it is more logical to consider such repairs together with framing repairs because often the cheapest and easiest cure lies in modifying the framing of the boat so that new fastenings can be fitted back from the somewhat mangled plank-ends. If all the planks are sound up to the last few centimetres (inch or two), it is a pity to have to re-plank what may amount to a fifth or a sixth of the hull simply to scarph new ends onto the planks.

On counter-sterned boats, the simplest cure for defective plank ends may well be to shorten the counter slightly, fitting a new arch timber at a point where all planks are sound and capable of taking new fastenings.

Transom-sterns with outboard rudders are not quite so easily cured. It may be possible to move the sternpost forward 51–76 mm (2–3 in), make a new, wider transom and shorten the whole boat slightly; but this, like major re-planking, means doing rather a lot of work which can be avoided. The simplest solution is to double the edges of the transom inside, with pieces of wood thick enough to take two fastenings through each plank, and wide enough

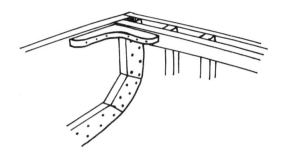

Fig 116   *Doubling frame fitted to a transom*

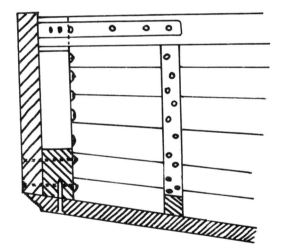

Fig 117   *Section through transom doubling frame*

to take at least a double row of rivets through the transom (Figs 116 and 117).

The doubling pieces must be cut to as perfect a fit against the planking as possible (see page 69 and Fig 55), and it will generally be found easier to cut the doublers in several pieces rather than to try and get one or two large pieces to fit each side of the hull. Without doing a lot of work on the deck structure, the presence of the aft end of the beam shelf and its

117

associated knee will make it impossible to run the doublers right up to the top of the transom. Often this is not necessary as the shear strake is protected from damage by a rubbing strip or a deck-edge beading. If the end of the shear strake does require extra fastenings, the space between the beam shelf or knee and the back of the plank will have to be packed with a well-fitting block, and long fastenings run right through into the shelf or clamp timber. All these doubling and packing pieces should be cut from knot-free oak, and should be well soaked with wood preservative before they are bedded and fastened in place.

The importance of ensuring that all doubling pieces really do fit the inside of the planks (and against the surface of the transom) cannot be over-emphasised. It is on this fit that the water-tightness of the modified stern will depend. Possibly not quite so obvious is the fact that the butting ends of the separate pieces must fit against one another – and that fit needs to be 'fag paper fit', not 'fits where it touches'. The bedding used must be thick enough to provide a proper seal, but no thicker. Any attempts to improve the seal by using too much mastic will result in the doubling piece not fitting right up into the corner between the transom and the planks. If it is not fitted right up into the corner, either the fastenings through the planks will be trying to hold it clear of the transom, or the rivets through the transom will hold it clear of the planking. Since the planking tapers in to the stern, the doublers should be riveted to the transom first and then the fastenings through the planks put in. Rivets have much more 'pulling power' than screws, and will ensure that the doublers are firmly in contact with the transom. The tapering in of the planks will help to ensure a tight seal against the planking. It is as well to force the doublers into good contact with the planking by shores and wedges before riveting to the transom.

It may be possible to use rivets through the planking and the doublers instead of screws, but before drilling for rivets it is as well to have a few 'dummy run' hammer swings to make sure that there is enough

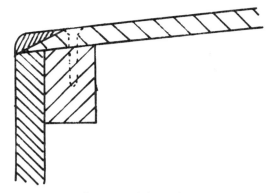

Fig 118   *Section through framed transom*

space to get a free swing to close down all the rivets properly. If the work is being done without removing the aft deck, access may not be all that easy – and if it is being done curled up in the space at the end of a quarter berth and partially behind a watertight cockpit, it can prove very difficult indeed.

Some boats have substantial, solid transoms; others have thinner planking over a framed edge which takes the plank-end fastenings (Fig 118). If the plank-ends need to be refitted further in on such a framed transom, the choice must be made whether to remove the original framing pieces and fit new ones of thicker wood which will enable the fastenings through the planks to be put through sound wood; whether to double the original framing; or whether to fit larger doublers which have been rebated to fit over the framing pieces.

Of the three alternatives, replacement of the original frame with a thicker frame will make the neatest job and, provided the old frame can be removed without too much difficulty, should not pose any insuperable problems. Doubling the original framing as in Fig 117 is the easiest of the three alternatives, but generally it is also the weakest. Unless the original frame pieces are unusually broad, the doubling pieces will not have a sufficient bearing area on the transom to support any loading imposed by the fastenings through the planks, and the fastenings through the transom, original frame and the doublers will be easily strained. Clearly if these fastenings are strained it will be only a

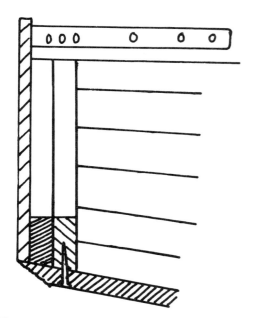

Fig 119 *Doubling frame fitted beside original transom frame*

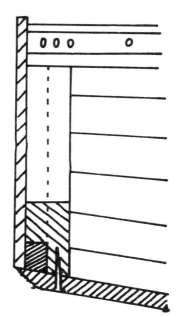

Fig 120 *Doubling frame fitted over original transom frame*

question of time before leaks are noticed. As a very crude guide, it is unwise to fit doubling frames to a transom unless the width of the old frame is at least one and a half times the distance from the outer face of the transom to the proposed new fastenings through the planks. (NB Fig 119 shows a frame which does not meet this minimum requirement – these illustrations must not be regarded as scale drawings.)

If the original frame is narrow and is considered too difficult to remove, the third alternative of rebated doublers must be used (Fig 120). These are difficult to cut and fit properly. They must fit closely against the face of the transom and the planking, with no risk of being held clear of either, because one of the faces of the rebate is bearing against the old frame; but equally important, they must not leave any gaps between the doubler and the frame. Any such pockets would act as first-class nurseries for rot. Probably the easiest way round the problem is to laminate the doublers, fitting pieces against the transom first to pack it out to the depth of the old frame, then using resin glue to bond in a second layer into which the plank ends can be fastened.

Once internal framing has been fitted and the planks have been properly fastened, attention can be turned to the actual plank-ends. These may be in very poor state, with splits around the fastenings and severe bruising; if left, as well as marring the appearance of the boat, they can become infected with rot if they are not tidied up and made watertight. One way of doing this is to chisel off the ends from a line immediately outboard of the new fastenings to the edge of the transom at the end of the planks, and glue on new ends after plugging any screw-holes or large splits (Fig 118). The glued-on pieces carry no actual load, so do not need any through fastenings. Oak or mahogany is the best timber to use for these facing pieces, even if the original planking is pine or another softwood.

If the plank-ends are not in good enough condition to glue on small facing pieces, their appearance and ability to keep out water can be improved by a combination of plastic impregnation and plastic wood moulding. First the plank-ends must be prepared, by cleaning back as far as possible to expose clean, sound wood fibres. For this job it does not matter how

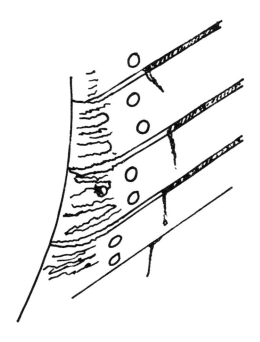

Fig 121 *Damaged plank-ends with caulking
cleared back*

splintered and fragmented the plank-end
appears, but it must be free of paint and
any rubbish which may have got mixed up
with the wood whilst the boat was in com-
mission. On carvel hulls, the seams should
be cleared back to just beyond the fastenings into the doubling pieces (Fig 121).
Thin wooden slips, or small pieces of metal
or plastic such as Formica are wrapped in
thin polythene sheet and wedged into the
seams, making sure that they go right into
the seam below the depth to which the
caulking will go.

Pieces of polythene sheet are now cut
ready to hold the resin in place. On clinker
hulls each piece needs to be about 25 mm
(1 in) wider than the plank it is to mask;
on carvel hulls the strips of polythene need
to be a nice fit between the slips packed
into the seams. The strips of polythene
should be about 203 mm (8 in) long. Pieces
of wood will be needed to act as pressure-
pads to hold the polythene sheet against
the planks, and some means of holding
these pressure-pads against the hull must
be provided. On a hull with no reverse turn
at the transom this can be a rope round
the hull – no great pressure is necessary.

The polythene sheet backed by the pressure-blocks, together with the slips in the
seams of a carvel hull, will form a mould
in which the resin can set to the required
shape.

When all preparations have been made
the resin can be mixed. This is no job for
normal wood glues such as resorcinol,
phenolic or urea formaldehyde, which
would be too brittle in large mouldings.
Polyester resins (as used for making GRP
hulls) may be readily available, but their
use is not recommended as it can be difficult
to control the setting reaction when they are
used in bulk, and the resins are not formu-
lated for use as casting resin or as adhesives. Epoxy resins are best for this job,
the easiest to use being Araldite 103, made
by Ciba Ltd, of Duxford, Cambridge. This
is a liquid resin, which must be mixed with
the correct proportion of an appropriate
hardener. The author has used 10 per cent
hardener HY951, but Ciba (who are most
helpful with advice on the use of their
products) recommend 40 per cent of hardener HY991 for marine work. They also
suggest that resin MY778 can be used with
hardener HY941.

The resin should be mixed thoroughly in
a clean container. About a fifth of it can
then be poured into a smaller container,
and the remainder 'loaded' with clean, dry
sawdust, stirred well in until it has the con-
sistency of thick porridge. All the exposed
wood fibres of the plank-end must now be
thoroughly soaked with the pure resin. This
would be a nice easy job if the boat could
be stood on its stem and the resin poured
into the mould formed by the polythene
sheet and pressure-pads. Since this cannot usually be done, the resin must be
introduced by pouring some against the
plank-end, damming as much as possible
with polythene sheet, and poking into the
plank-end with a resin-loaded spatula.
Wooden sticks from ice lollies are ideal on
larger planks, cocktail sticks on smaller
work. When it seems that all the exposed
ends of wood are as well coated as possible,
the sawdust-loaded resin can be trowelled
in with an ice-lolly stick until the end of the
plank is built up to the required volume.
The polythene sheet is then wrapped round

Amity: *37ft x 11ft x 3ft 4in: Norfolk beach boat*
built by Chambers of Great Yarmouth in 1912,
and now owned by Peter Crofts of Wisbech

Undine: 32ft x 27ft 6in x 7ft 9in x 5ft 6in: racing
cutter built by Edwards of Menai in 1889, and
originally fitted with heavy lead ballast keel and
rigged with over 1,000 sq ft of sail. Now owned
by P. G. Meakins of Woodbridge

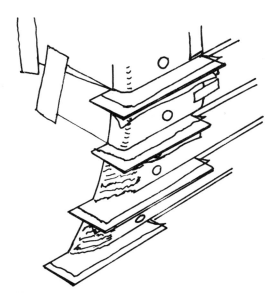

Fig 122   *Shims inserted in seams, and two plank-ends built up and covered with polythene sheet*

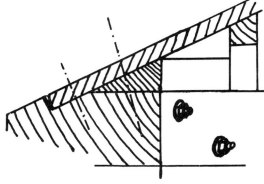

Fig 123   *Horizontal section through stem showing packing piece to take extra plank-end fastening*

over the end of the plank and secured to the transom, either with pieces of sticky tape or by staples from an office stapler. Fig 122 shows how the work might look after two plank-ends have have been treated, with the wooden pressure-pads omitted for clarity.

It is unlikely that it will be possible to hold the polythene sheet and the sawdust-loaded resin to a perfect shape, and gravity will ensure that some of the resin will 'slip' to the lower edges of the topside planks, so it is as well to 'overbuild' somewhat.

The liquid epoxy resins flow well, and there will inevitably be leakages of resin around the polythene sheets. These resins are unpleasant if they get on one's skin, and people who suffer from allergic reactions may find that splashes of hardeners can cause dermatitis. It is best to be on the safe side and wear polythene gloves when working with these resins. By the time a couple of plank-ends have been moulded in, there will probably be drips and smears of resin down the hull below the working area and even if a helper is standing by to wipe up all such drips as they start, the resin seems to have a disconcerting way of getting onto one's clothes, so it is advisable to wear old clothes or overalls. If any resin

does get on the worker's skin, it is easily washed off with warm soapy water. It is as well to see that a basin and a kettle of hot water are prepared before mixing the resin.

The resin usually takes about a day to cure, after which any surplus can be faired off to make a neat job. Since the resin is not as brittle as the usual wood glues, it is easily cleaned off with a plane or sharp chisel. One point to be watched is to make sure there are no traces of uncured resin around the area if a plane is used to clean off the ends. Once such traces of resin get onto and into a plane they take a long time to clean off. It may be found that the first lot of loaded resin applied has run too much and has not left enough to clean off properly to the desired shape, in which case a second layer can be applied.

When the plank-ends have been built up sufficiently with resin, the slips which were used to keep the seams of a carvel hull clear can be removed. If the slips were a tight fit in the seams there should be no need for any cleaning out, but if the slips did not fit too well, it may be necessary to clean off the sides of the seams with a sharp chisel.

Hood-ends of planks, that is those ends which fit into the rebate of a stem, pointed stern, or deadwood, can be dealt with in a similar manner. Triangular packing pieces can be inserted between the ends of the planks and the sides of bow and stern knees or deadwood timbers to take the new fastenings necessary (Fig 123). Some of the narrower plank-ends on a canoe-stern or

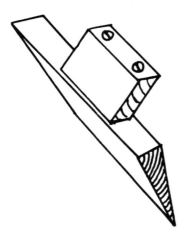

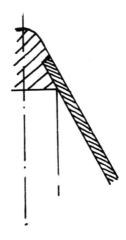

Fig 124 *Block of scrap wood screwed to back of packing piece to facilitate cutting and fitting*

Fig 125 *Section through stem with rebate run out to the inner face*

up the stem might be badly split and in need of filling with sawdust-loaded resin, but generally any such patching necessary is much simpler than it is on an exposed corner of a transom.

The fitting of the triangular filler pieces will usually be complicated by the presence of ribs or frames which make it necessary to cut and fit the filler pieces in short lengths. Since both ends and both faces of the filler must be cut to a good fit, this can prove somewhat tricky. The first problem to be overcome is that when a piece being cut is tried in position, it can prove difficult to get it out again. This is solved by screwing a piece of scrap wood on the back of the filler piece being fitted, so that it acts as a handle both for getting the piece out and also for holding it whilst it is shaped to fit (Fig 124).

The next problem is usually to establish the size and shape of the filler piece without wasting too much timber. This can be done scientifically by taking detailed measurements of lengths, widths, and angles; or it can be done much more easily by taking a roughly cut piece of softwood which more or less fits the space, coating it with a layer of plasticine, and pressing it firmly into place. If the plasticine sticks to the planking, frames or deadwood, these can be covered with thin polythene sheet. The oak filler piece can then be cut to match the plasticine impression.

On some boats, the rebate in which the planking is fitted may run right to the inner face of the stem or sternpost, leaving no space in which triangular fillers and extra fastenings can be fitted (Fig 125). In such cases, a piece of timber will have to be fitted as an apron right across the inner face of the stem (Fig 126). (To save repetition, all comments in this section about stem or bows can be applied to the sternpost of a double-ended hull). On the other hand the boat might have been built with an apron behind the stem, in which case it will probably be through-bolted. When this is the case, the bolts should be removed and replaced with new ones through the new inner piece as well. It is unlikely to be practicable to remove the original apron and simply to replace it with a thicker piece, as the breasthook, forward ends of the beam shelves and a portion of the decking would all have to be removed to get at the top of the apron. When a stem is being internally doubled in this way, it may well be found that the bearding line of the rebate (that is, the line at which the planking first contacts the side of the stem, knee or deadwood) may leave small flat sides to the stem at its lower end, so that when a new apron is fitted very small triangular gaps are left (Fig 127). These gaps will have to be filled with packing pieces before the apron is fitted.

It may be found that iron or steel bolts

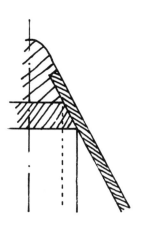

Fig 126   *Section through stem with apron fitted*

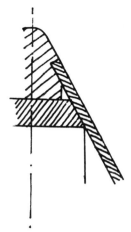

Fig 127   *An apron fitted to a stem might leave small triangular gaps. These must be filled before the apron is fitted*

through the stem are well and truly rusted in, and cannot be undone. If so, a decision must be taken on whether to rely on these bolts any longer, or whether to replace them with new bolts fitted midway between the old ones. If the bolts appear sound enough to leave in place, clearance holes should be bored in the new apron so that it can be fitted without touching the bolt-ends. To avoid moisture traps it is best to bore these clearance holes right through the apron. If any doubt is felt about the strength of the old bolts, every effort should be made to remove at least the exposed end of the bolt with its washer and nut so that the new apron can be fitted without having to bore into it.

The presence of any such badly corroded bolts in the stem should be taken as a warning to examine the whole stem assembly thoroughly. (Work in the area was started because of inadequate plank-ends!) It may well be found that the whole structure is in poor condition, and the correct cure could well be the fitting of a new stem instead of simply re-fastening the plank-ends to a doubling apron.

Corroded nuts and bolts can be treated with one of the proprietary rust removers available from most garages, and also with penetrating oil. Adjustable or open-ended flat spanners should never be used on very tight nuts, because they will almost certainly slip off and damage both the nut and the

operator's knuckles. Box or ring spanners should always be used. It may be necessary to hammer a ring spanner onto a badly rusted nut, but once the spanner is on the nut, one can be sure that all the force applied will be used in trying to undo the nut, and will not be wasted in converting what remains of the flats on the nut to a mangled curve, as usually happens with open-ended spanners. Sometimes a smart tap on the nut with a hammer whilst force is being applied to a good spanner will break the bond of rust which is locking the nut to the bolt.

All packing, filling or apron pieces fitted to the main backbone of a boat should be cut from well seasoned hardwood. Sapwood must be avoided, and all pieces should be thoroughly soaked with wood preservative before they are fitted. The use of odd off-cuts of wood found lying around may appear expedient, especially for small packing pieces, but odd bits of wood may contain fungal spores, and if the use of any old piece of wood for packing leads to rot in the keel or deadwood, one would have a classic instance of 'spoiling the ship for a ha'porth of tar'.

A ha'porth of tar can come in very handy when packing pieces are being fitted to take extra fastenings at plank-ends. As built, the internal structure of the framing should have been such as to leave clear waterways which would allow any bilge water to drain down to the lowest point of the hull, and the fitting of packing pieces may close off some of these waterways below frame ends, so a path will have to be made which will carry any water over the frame. Further wooden filler pieces can be put in to fill up any spaces which might otherwise act as water traps, but a simpler and very effective solution is to run hot tar or pitch down beside the stem or stern post (after temporarily blocking all unobstructed waterways with suitable plugs). When this is done great care must be taken not to set fire to the tar (and the whole boat). One owner used an electrically heated soldering iron for melting pitch into odd corners. Another essential precaution is to ensure there is full ventilation through the hull. The first smell of hot tar is usually considered pleasant, but after that it loses its pleasure, and in a confined space it is positively dangerous. Tar or pitch should never be heated unless there is a helper on the spot ready to cope with any emergencies, either fire or incipient asphyxiation.

Good quality tar and pitch may not be all that easy to obtain, so liquid epoxy resins (Araldite 103) can be used instead. As well as eliminating water-traps, the tar, pitch or epoxy will also help to fill any slight cavities left around the packing pieces (there should not be any, but it is not always possible to make everything absolutely perfectly).

Chapter 12

Repairs to the backbone of the hull

Keel

Replacing a keel

The keel may be one single piece of timber, into which the rebates for the garboard strakes are cut (Fig 128) or it may comprise the keel and a separate upper timber (the hog) which forms the rebate for the planks (Fig 129). The single keel timber is most likely to be found on deeper-keeled boats with a reverse turn to the bilges. Shoal-draft hulls with fairly flat floors will usually be built with a separate hog.

At the forward end of the keel, the bow knee and stem are usually through-bolted on top of the keel (Fig 130). The basic construction method is usually substantially the same whether the hull has a well cut-away forefoot and considerable slope to the lower part of the stem, or whether the stem is totally upright. At the aft end, the sternpost is tenoned into the end of the keel, and a knee or substantial deadwood timbers through-bolted to the keel and sternpost (Fig 131). If the boat has an external ballast keel, there will usually be separate blocks fitted below the main keel timber to form a fair profile to the external keel. Usually the junction between the external metal-ballast keel and the wooden fairing or false keel will be stepped. On some boats the step is made to allow the ballast keel to be dropped clear easily; on other boats the step (or steps) is shaped so that the wooden fairing helps to support the weight of the ballast (Fig 132). It has been suggested that iron keels should be fitted so that they can be dropped clear, whilst lead keels should be fitted with the extra support from the wooden fairings. This appears logical, but is certainly not followed universally.

Internally, the keel structure may be complicated by a centreboard-case, which

Fig 128   *One-piece keel*

Fig 129   *Keel with separate hog*

Fig 130   *Stem, keel and bow knee joints*

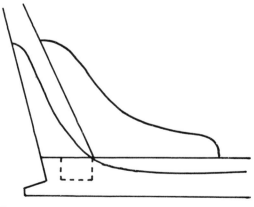

Fig 131   *Sternpost to keel joint*

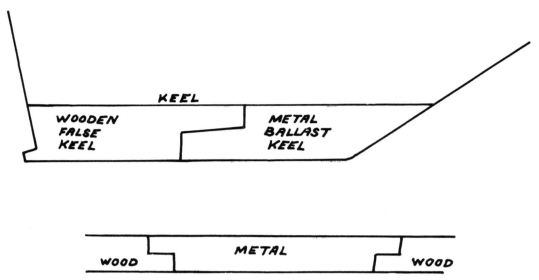

Fig 132 *Alternative joints between ballast keel and false keel*

will probably be supported either by knees to transverse floors, or by a thwart in smaller boats. Transverse floors can be expected to be through-bolted to the keel, possibly by the bolts holding the ballast keel. On smaller boats, floors may be screwed down or held with coach-bolts. Sawn or grown frames may be run over the keel and through-bolted, or they may be notched into the keel. It is not unknown for the frames to stop short clear of the keel, leaving heavy transverse floors to connect the two sides of the hull. Bent ribs may be run over the keel on shoal-draft boats. On deeper hulls with reverse curve to the bilges, steamed ribs may be notched into the keel, or they may merely butt on to the top of the keel, usually with a nail through.

Before the keel can be dropped out of the hull, the garboard strakes will have to be removed. Even if the keel has a separate hog which forms the rebate for the planking, the rebate will angle into the keel proper at the stem. It is possible on small, lightly built carvel hulls to unfasten the garboards for about a quarter of their length back from the stem and spring the forward ends out enough to allow the keel to be dropped away from the hog, leaving the rest of the length of the garboards still riveted to it.

On hulls which are too heavy to be turned on their side or upside down, removal of the garboards is easiest if the boat is supported on narrow keel-blocks, with shores or struts as far out on the bilges as possible, or even with side struts to beams over the deck (Figs 15 and 19). On clinker-built hulls the garboards and the second plank out each side will have to be removed, unless the keel is very shallow, so that the garboards can be twisted out (and in again) beneath the lands of the second planks. Once the garboards are out, the main support for the hull will have to be provided by rows of blocks under the bilges each side, placed as close in to the centre-line of the hull as possible. These blocks should be positioned under the heaviest transverse floors, and should not obstruct too much access to the keel-blocks from the side (Fig 133). The keel-blocks can then be released by knocking back the lower of the opposed wedges. If the boat has a ballast keel of any significant weight, this is best got out of the way first.

If height will permit, a long greased skid and slider can be placed on the ground under the keel, and wedged blocks built up on the slider so that the ballast keel is supported clear of all its keel-bolts. The nuts and washers on the inner ends of the

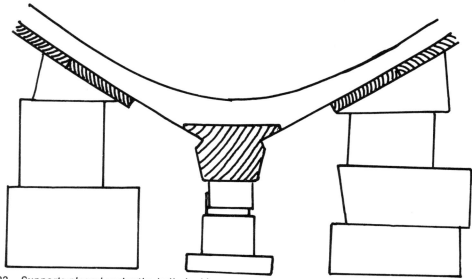

Fig 133 *Supports placed under the hull planking preparatory to dropping the keel*

keel-bolts are then undone, and the bolts knocked out down through the ballast keel but, for this to be possible, the height from the top of the slider to the underside of the ballast keel must be greater than the length of the longest keel-bolt. All too often this is not the case, and it is not unknown to see an owner operating beneath the boat with pick-axe and spade, digging holes into which the keel-bolts can be allowed to drop. Often this cannot be blamed on lack of foresight, as it may well be only after other work has been started that it is discovered that the keel needs to be removed.

If the height above a slider is not sufficient to allow the bolts to be removed, the ballast keel should be supported inboard of the outermost keel-bolts, with the wedges laid on substantial transverse baulks, which in turn rest on blocks far enough apart to allow a greased way and slider to be inserted from one end (Fig 134). Once the keel-bolts have been knocked out, the way and slider can be inserted and the weight of the keel taken by pairs of opposed wedges on the slider, at each end of the keel. When the first set of supports and their bridge timbers have been removed, the ballast keel can then be lowered to the slider by knocking back the opposed wedges. The lowering will usually have to

be done in several stages, inserting a second, lower pile of wedges and blocks as the wedges in the first set are drawn back to their full extent. It is as well to leave a pair of wedges under each end of the ballast keel so that when the time comes to raise it into place again there will be an easy start. Once the metal is low enough to clear the rest of the keel, it can be skidded out endways. If there is plenty of space clear at each end of the boat, the ballast keel can be slid out one end and left on the skidway, leaving the other end free to pull out the wooden keel. More commonly, there will be space available at only one end, and the ballast keel will have to be rolled or skidded over sideways to leave room for getting the wooden keel out and the new one in.

Usually the work does not go smoothly. The nuts on the keel-bolts can be difficult to shift, and then the bolts can be very resistant indeed to being driven out. One point to be watched here is that if a bolt has to be hammered out, the thread at the end must be protected by leaving a nut on the thread, with the upper face of the nut level with the end of the bolt. Once the bolt has started to move out, it can usually be driven the rest of the way without too much difficulty. Once the end of the bolt gets too low to leave a nut on to protect the end

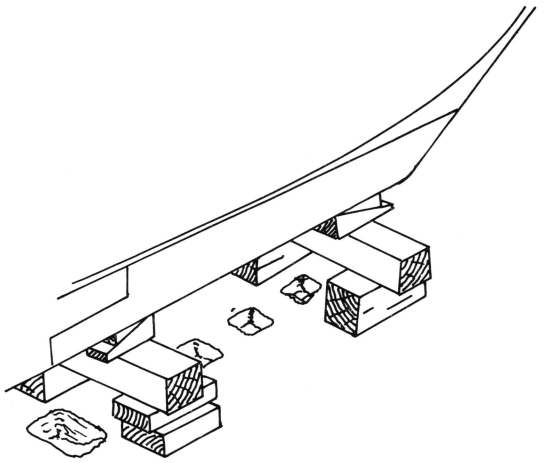

Fig 134 *Bridge supports which will enable a greased way and skid to be inserted under the keel: note holes dug to allow the keel-bolts to be dropped out. Supports under the bilge are not shown for clarity*

thread, it should be knocked down with a round-ended drift – a piece of steel rod a bit smaller in diameter than the bolt, with its end tapered-in to less than the core diameter of the bolt, and slightly domed. It is unwise to use another bolt of the same size as a drift, even if there is one handy. This can result in the original keel-bolt dropping clear and leaving the bolt which was used as a drift well and truly stuck in the hole – and hammering it out from underneath may not be at all easy!

The next snag may be a reluctance on the part of the ballast to part company with the wooden keel as the supporting blocks are eased back. Judicious application of

force may have to be used after making sure that all bolts have been removed. A bricklayer's broad steel chisel hammered in between the metal and the wood, with the blocks below the keel eased to allow a drop of about 6 mm ($\frac{1}{4}$ in), will usually prove effective. If a heavy ballast keel is being dropped onto wedged blocks which have been eased back, the piles of blocks should be secured with battens nailed up the sides of the piles, and the ends of the wedges should be dogged so that there can be no risk of the pile slipping when the weight comes on it.

With the ballast keel out of the way, the wooden keel can be taken out. All bolts

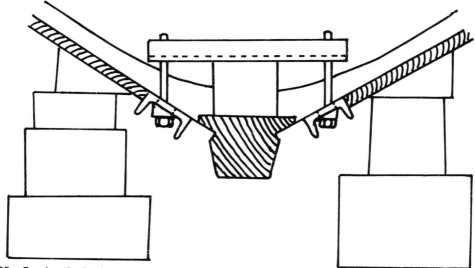

Fig 135 *Forcing the keel away from the frames with bolts through channel sections: note the heavily tapered washers necessary under the bolt heads*

and other fastenings must be removed. If the boat has a centreboard, care must be taken to ensure that any transverse fastenings through the keel into the sides or the ends of the case are located and removed or, if the case is being taken out with the keel, that any fastenings between the case and knees, thwarts or floors are removed. It is unlikely that the keel will drop clear when the last fastening is taken out, especially if ribs or frames are notched into it, and quite substantial force may have to be applied. The necessary force can be provided by screw or hydraulic jacks, and it is usually easy enough to find suitable places on the keel on which improvised jacks can be stood, but it may not be quite so simple to find suitable points for the jacks to push against. Coachroofs or deck beams are quite unsuitable, as they are not usually built to withstand pressure from inside the hull. On deeper-keeled hulls, it is usually possible to wedge a stout beam across the hull beneath the bilge stringers. A channel-section steel girder is the best, and its ends should be wedged under oak blocks which will spread the load as far as possible along the bilge stringers. On shallower hulls, a short length of girder can be held down by long, stout bolts through lengths of

channel- or angle-section girder placed under the hull where the garboards have been removed (Fig 135). Note that the holes in the pieces of girder outside the hull need to be drilled well oversize so that the bolts can pass through at an angle, and angled pads will have to be fitted under the bolt heads. When this is possible, the inner girder can be packed directly down to the keel with oak blocks, and the force to move the keel is supplied by tightening down the bolts through the girders. If broad, flat U section girders are used, they can be laid directly on the wooden frames or keel, but if narrow girders have to be used, pieces of stout, flat metal plate should be used to spread the load.

Once the keel has been persuaded to start parting company with the bow knee, stem, deadwoods etc, it can be helped on its way by driving in broad wedges. When the keel is clear, it is taken out endways from under the hull, and the replacement made as an accurate copy, usually from a baulk of elm. If all the work has to be done by hand, this can be a considerable undertaking. Access to a bandsaw or other power tools can ease the work.

One problem which may have to be faced when the new keel is lifted into place is the simultaneous fitting of the heels of all the ribs or frames into their sockets in the keel. This would be extremely difficult if all the sockets were cut square to the correct size, so it is better to accept that this cannot be done and to taper one side of each socket for two-thirds of its depth so that all the frames will enter easily and the gaps can be closed with wedges. All other features of the new keel should be copied as accurately as possible from the original and, on completion, thoroughly soaked with wood preservative.

The keel is then slid under the hull and all surfaces which will contact the bow knee, deadwoods etc, are well coated with bedding material, either a modern synthetic compound, or the traditional hot tar. The new keel can then be lifted into place, taking great care to ensure that the tenon on the sternpost and all frames enter their sockets properly. This can best be done by raising the keel on blocks with opposed wedges, so that its position is easily adjusted as necessary. Once in place, all bolt-holes can be bored and the bolts fitted. Wrought-iron bolts are the most durable (if the boat has an iron ballast keel) but these are very hard to find, so it is likely that mild-steel bolts, hot-dip galvanised, will have to be used. If all the bolts are heated and dipped in hot tar before they are fitted they should last for many years without corrosion problems. One point to watch when galvanised bolts are used is that all holes must be drilled large enough to be a nice sliding fit for the bolts. If the holes are undersize, so that the bolts have to be hammered home, the galvanising may be stripped. Do not forget to put a grommet of twisted caulking cotton round each bolt, beneath the head. Putting in tarred bolts is a very messy business, and all-over protective clothing is advisable. If the boat has lead ballast, bronze or gunmetal bolts may be used, but care must be taken to avoid mixing ferrous and cuprous metals.

The last operation in replacing the keel is to fit stopwaters. These are softwood plugs which are fitted into holes bored transversely through the keel and the heel of the stem where the planking rebate crosses the joint-line between the two

pieces. A stopwater should also be fitted between the keel and the aft deadwood if the rebate for the planking runs up over the latter. When only the keel has been replaced, the half-holes from the old stop-waters should still be present on the under-side of the heel of the stem and the dead-wood. These half-holes should be plugged with pieces of wood carved to shape, so that when the new holes are drilled the drill will be cutting into more or less uniform wood all round and not trying to cut just the lower half of a hole. The softwood stopwaters should be a tight fit in the holes, and should be well soaked with wood preservative before they are hammered in. Stopwaters must be cut overlength and the excess at the ends is cleaned off down to the face of the rebates when they have been driven through.

With the stopwaters safely in place, the garboards can be refitted, and any interior work which had to be undone to get the old keel out is replaced.

Fitting a false keel

Most of the foregoing description has been written as a description of replacing the keel on a sizeable cruising boat. Clearly the operations can be scaled-down to suit smaller craft. On small open dinghies or pulling boats where the reason for replacing the keel is to repair mechanical damage or abrasion, it may be found better to clean the old one off until it is flush with the planking and then to laminate on a new false keel, fitting rivets through to the old keel and hog. Obviously this must not be attempted if the old keel is suffering from fungal attack, but if the old keel can be cut back to expose clean, sound, dry timber, the new false keel can be laminated on with resorcinol resin which will result in a very strong structure without any great increase in keel size. However, if there is any doubt about the suitability of the old wood for bonding with resin glue, it is better to make up a false keel which will have sufficient strength in itself, and to bed it in place with a soft bedding compound, fastening it on with bolts to the bow and stern knees and rivets to the flat portions of the old keel.

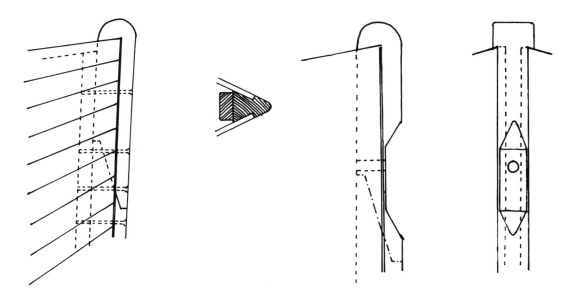

Fig 136 *New upper end scarphed on a stem and reinforced with a narrow apron*

Fig 137 *Stem cut back and hole bored*

Stem

Local damage to the stem of a boat may be repairable by fitting graving pieces, or by laminating on a new false point; but a stem in which rot has been discovered, or which has broken, will have to be properly repaired or replaced. Replacement of the stem is probably one of the worst tasks on a wooden hull. Most, if not all, the planks are fastened to it; its upper end is attached to the breasthook and beam shelves, and if the stem is raked or curved the forward ribs or frames will be attached to it.

An upright stem on a dinghy or small boat can usually be unfastened and withdrawn upwards, and it may be possible to withdraw a raked, straight stem in a similar way if ribs or frames are not socketed into it.

If the damage is confined to the upper portion of the stem, a partial replacement can be made, with the new upper portion scarphed on to the original lower end of the stem (Fig 136). Any such scarph in a stem must be cut with its outer end downwards, and when the new upper portion of the stem has been glued in place it is advisable to reinforce the stem with an apron timber. If the hood-ends of the planks are in good condition, the apron can be cut narrower than the back face of the stem for ease of fitting (Fig 136). The scarph joint and the apron timber, if fitted, should be through-bolted. The only real problem in such a repair lies in how to cut through the old stem without damaging the plank-ends. The easiest safe way is to saw and chisel back the face of the portion of the stem to be removed to just clear of the plank-ends, then to bore a hole through the middle of the stem, using the largest bit which will comfortably clear the inner faces of the planks (Fig 137). The wood either side of this hole can then be chiselled away down to the rebate, exposing the ends of the planks (Fig 138).

Strips of thin metal (which can be cut from an empty tin) are slid in between the planks and the stem, and a hacksaw blade can be used to cut through the stem to the back of the planks without any risk of damage. On large boats it may be possible to drill several holes about 25 mm (1 in) in diameter. Whenever this is possible, the outer holes can be angled to reduce the thickness to be sawn through.

Once the upper portion of the stem has been removed it is not too difficult to cut the scarph joint. To avoid leaving a fine

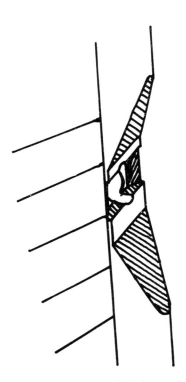

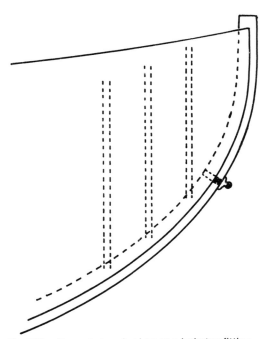

Fig 138 *Hole in the stem ready to be opened out to the inner faces of the planks*

Fig 139 *Curved stem broken at a bobstay fitting*

feathered edge on the new portion of the stem a stopped scarph should be used, the depth of the stop at the end depending on the sharpness of the radius which forms the point of the stem.

Cutting a new stem or portion of a stem requires careful measurement and accurate workmanship because the angle of the rebates for the plank-ends changes along the length of the stem. When a boat is being built this angle can be adjusted if necessary as the planks are fitted, but when a new stem is being fitted into existing planking the rebates must be cut correctly. English oak is the best wood for the job, and selected knot-free timber clear of any trace of sapwood should be used.

Replacing the stem in a hull with a well-rounded forefoot and raked, curved or clipper stem into which frames or ribs are socketed, is a much more difficult proposition. If the whole of the stem is rotten, the only practical solution may be to open up all the bow planking, and spring it all clear

of the stem and bow knee, removing all the frames which fit into the stem. Then the stem can be replaced and the whole of the bows rebuilt onto it. Such a repair is unlikely to be done, as probably if the whole stem was rotten the planking would also be affected, as would the forward frames, in which case a total rebuild would be the best course of action.

What is more likely is rot around the waterline, possibly originating at a loose bobstay fitting; or mechanical damage, again probably near or above the waterline. If the frames and most of the planking are sound, an adequate repair can be made by laminating a new stem in place. As an example, the case of a curved stem damaged at a bobstay fitting can be considered (Fig 139).

Laminating a new stem in place

The first operation is to remove all bolts etc from the inner face of the stem. If an

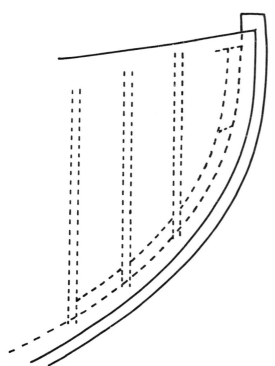

Fig 140 *Apron pieces fitted inside the stem between the frames: note that the upper apron piece must be fitted in two lengths with an angled joint*

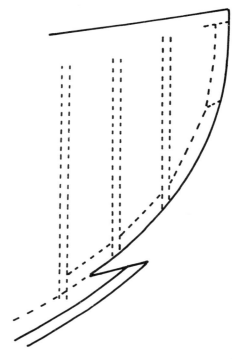

Fig 141 *Planks secured to the new apron, and the stem and plank-ends cut back to the face of the apron*

apron is fitted, this should also be removed. New apron pieces are then cut from oak, to fit onto the inner faces of the planking and round the lower ends of the frames which are fitted into the stem. The first length of this new apron, from below the breasthook down to the foreside of the first pair of frames, will have to be made in two butt-jointed pieces, as otherwise it will be impossible to get it in and out (Fig 140). The easiest way to cut and fit the pieces of the apron timbers round the ends of the frames is to butt the lower end of each piece against the foreside of the frame, and to cut the upper end of each piece to fit between the frames which lie forward of it. All the apron pieces must be as perfect a fit as possible to the planks and the frames, but whilst they should all touch the inner face of the stem over their full length, only the lowest one needs to be fitted accurately to the stem. Plasticine templates, as described on page 124, can be used, and the final fit against the planks should be checked

by chalking the inner faces of the planks, blowing away any loose dust, and seeing where the chalk is transferred to the face of the apron piece as it is pressed in place.

Bedding material is applied to the sides and ends of the apron pieces, taking care to leave the front face clean, and the pieces are fitted into the hull and shored and wedged firmly home, using pairs of shores running up to the corners between suitable frames and the beam shelves. The plank-ends are then screwed to the apron pieces.

Caulking and stopping can then be cleared from the ends of the planks, and the plank-ends are sawn off at the level of the inner face of the old stem, down to the level to which the stem is to be replaced. At this point the stem is sawn through, following a continuation of the line of a plank edge (Fig 141). Sawing off the plank-ends is easily said; on a sizeable hull it is less easily done. Cutting-lines must be carefully marked, and since the newly fitted apron pieces must not be damaged,

135

great care must be taken to ensure that any errors are on the pessimistic side. This means that the saw will be cutting into the back of the old stem. A hand-held electric circular saw can be used to cut through most of the planks, but this is quite a tricky operation better avoided by an amateur worker. The safest, surest way is to use a large two-handled crosscut saw. Anyone who has never used a two-handled saw may think it a very simple tool to use, and indeed it is, but there is quite a knack in getting the right swing into the work. Much of the success in using such a saw lies in pulling in the appropriate rhythm but never pushing – always wait for the other fellow to pull the saw. The fact that the saw must never be pushed usually results in some initial frustration as either or both operators are pulling hard or neither is pulling. However, an adequate if not truly efficient swing is soon established. The cutting will have to be taken in stages as the saw will follow only a straight line, and as the cut departs too far from the required curve the stem will have to be cut off and a fresh cut started at a new tangent to the curve. Starting the cut is made much easier if the stem head is first sawn off flush with the deck.

Such cutting usually leaves portions of the back of the old stem in place, but these are easily removed, exposing the faces of the new apron pieces. The plank-ends should be dressed back until they lie just behind the face of the apron, and a slight caulking chamfer is cut on the ends.

The new stem pieces are laminated in position. They should be cut from clean, straight-grained hardwood, and their lower ends must be cut to a really good fit in the vee notch left on the old stem. Each layer should be cut about 25 mm (1 in) wider than the desired finished width to provide an allowance for some 'run out' as the layer is bent. The edges can be angled to an approximate match to the final shape, as this bevelling will ease the bending of the layers. Before each layer is finally bonded in place, it is as well to have a 'dry run' to make quite sure that the laminate can be bent and that it will lie fairly in place. The lowest bolt should be put in to hold it in place during this dry run. If the laminate

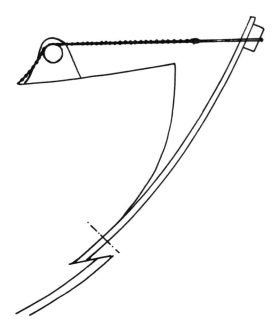

Fig 142 *Use of an anchor winch to bend a laminate into place*

will not take the necessary curve, it can be thinned down by 1.6 mm ($\frac{1}{16}$ in) and another attempt made. Resorcinol resin is applied to the faces of the apron pieces, and to the cut end of the old stem. The new laminate is seated properly in the notch and then bent round to the correct curve. On larger boats adequate power for the bending can be obtained by shackling the anchor chain to a wire strop which can be taken round a pressure-pad on the foreside of the new laminate (Fig 142). To avoid any possible mishaps, it is as well to through-bolt each laminate as it is fitted, fitting the bolts as soon as the wood is pulled into suitable contact.

Bolts should be lightly greased or oiled before they are fitted, and large washers should be used. Also, a wooden pad should be used on the outer face below the washer. To prevent any oil or grease from the bolt getting on to the face of the laminate, the bolt-hole should be drilled, the wooden pad held against the face, and the bolt pushed through the pad and the stem. The glued joint between the inner apron pieces and the first curved laminate must be well made, as this joint must withstand all the forces imposed by caulking the plank-ends. The number of bolts to be fitted will depend on the curvature of the stem and the thickness of the laminates used. It is advisable to fit as many as would be needed to hold the stem together in the absence of any glue, with at least three into each separate piece of the apron.

The holes for the bolts through the first laminate can be drilled from outside the hull, but on all subsequent laminates the holes will have to be drilled through from the inside, possibly using an extension on the bit as in Fig 109.

Laminating a stem in this way really needs three or four workers: one to work the winch or whatever means is used to bend the wood; one standing by to drill holes as soon as the wood is bent into place; one with a bolt, wooden pad and washer ready to push through; and one with washer, nut and spanner ready inside the hull. For all layers after the first, the helper inside the hull can alternate between drilling the holes and putting nuts on the bolts. Even with a full team, it takes quite a time to bend and bolt each layer into position, so it is as well to spread the glue 300 mm (1 ft) or so at a time so that it does not all run down before the laminate is pulled into contact. The length of time needed to bend and bolt each layer in place usually dictates that for successful gluing the work must be done in a morning when the weather will be cool enough to allow a good pot life for the resin, but when there is a reasonable certainty of enough warmth later in the day to cure the resin fully.

As the first layer is fitted, any resin which squeezes out over the plank-ends should be wiped clear. The seam between the plank-ends and the new face of the stem can be kept clear with paper tissues wrapped round an old credit card or similar piece of thin stiff plastic. As soon as the first layer is fitted and bolted into place, its edges can be trimmed off down to almost the final shape, leaving just a shaving or two to be taken off when all the layers are laminated in place. It is as well to leave the tension on whatever means was used to haul the top end of the laminate into place.

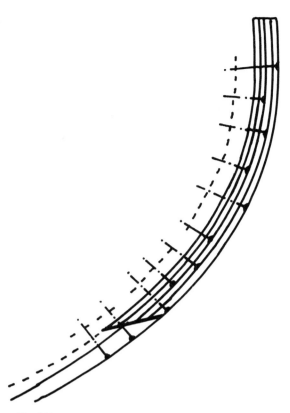

Fig 143 *The completed lamination showing bolt lengths needed*

When the resin has fully cured, the tension on the hauling mechanism can be slackened off, the bolts removed and the next layer bent, bonded and bolted into place. The number of layers to be added will depend on the size of the boat and the amount of curvature in the stem, but three of four layers will usually be needed to build up a facing which will radius off to a reasonably sharp stem. Not all the bolts need be continued through all layers, as the last layer can usually be regarded as ornamental and contributing little to the stem's strength. The uppermost and lowermost bolts through the laminated portion should be run through all layers, but after the second layer has been fitted, alternate bolts can be stopped short at each layer (Fig 143). The bolts which are to stop at any intermediate layer should be taken out when the layer has been bonded, and a counterbore to accept the bolt head and washer cut in the face of the layer. The bolt cannot then be simply fitted in the normal manner and the next layer bonded on, as this would leave an open space in the middle of the stem. This space must be filled before the next layer is fitted, the best filler being an epoxide resin very heavily loaded with sawdust, as described on page 120. Also, if a bolt is to be sealed into the stem in this way, the bolts must be truly corrosion resistant. Bronze, monel metal, or hot-dip galvanised bolts are usually safe, but 'stainless steel' should not be relied on. There are many grades of stainless steel, some of which do have excellent resistance to corrosion, but some grades are unsuitable for use in sea water or in contact with oak or other acidic hardwoods. An engineer with access to all the relevant specifications can have bolts made of a suitable grade of stainless steel, but the average amateur who buys over the counter could find the bolts he hoped would be almost everlasting are corroding badly after only a season or two.

Depending on the shape of the stem and the extent of the damage, it may be possible to use an alternative laminating system in which the lower ends of the laminated layers run out over the face of the old stem as shown in Fig 144 instead of being caught in a vee cut. This method is somewhat simpler, but it requires that considerably more of the original stem is sound and quite free of rot. As the plank-ends and the old stem are cut away, the lower end of the cut is allowed to run out to the front of the stem on a tangent to the curve of the inner face. The flat portion of this run-out should be of such a length that the outermost laminate will lie truly flat for at least 300 mm (1 ft) before it will need any bending. Successive laminations are bolted in the same way as when the layers are notched into the old stem.

If the stem comes to a fairly sharp point, there may be problems in hiding the heads of the bolts which hold the final lamination. The bolt heads will have to be sunk into the surface of the wood, which usually leaves an unsightly hole, and the width of a normal hexagon bolt head may require that the head be sunk almost right through the laminate in order to find enough width in the stem.

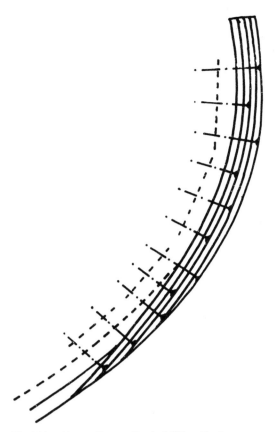

Fig 144 *Alternative method of fitting the lower ends of the laminated stem*

There is a threefold solution to such problems: (a) accept a greater radius on the front of the stem (which may well mean one less layer to laminate); (b) hacksaw and file off opposite faces of the heads of bronze, gunmetal, monel or stainless bolts to reduce the width to be hidden (warning – sawing and filing really good quality stainless steel is a job for only the most dedicated enthusiast); (c) fill the inevitable hole exposed in the outer faces of the finished stem with epoxy resin and sawdust.

When all layers have been bonded in place and finally bolted, the stem can be finished down to its final profile, leaving only the seams to be re-caulked and any ironmongery to be bolted back onto the stem-head. In the case of a really dedicated enthusiast, an extra lamination can be glued on the top foot or two and a proper figurehead carved on. One word of warning –

Cutlass: *47ft x 37ft x 10ft 8in x 6ft 6in: ketch,
built in Norway in 1886, allegedly as a day racer
for the King of Denmark. Shown racing in an
ECOG race in the 1960s. Now owned in France*

Peggy-H: *32ft x 30ft 6in x 9ft 8in x 5ft 9in: fishing boat of unknown origin and antiquity. Owned and restored by Ron Crick of Cowes (Harold Hayles)*

carving on the face of the stem involves working from all sorts of angles, and a really large working staging all round the stem at a height which will allow the artistic owner to sit in comfort is highly desirable. Some tricky bits are best reached by lying on the deck. When this is done, remember that the deck at the bows is of distinctly limited width before rolling over to change position!

Sternpost

On double-ended hulls, the sternpost can be repaired or replaced in the same way as a stem, the only point to be watched being the provision of strongpoints for the rudder attachments, which should always be through-bolted to an inner strength member. On deep-draught boats with a reverse turn to the bilges there will be some substantial deadwood timbers in the angle between the keel and the sternpost, and the fastenings through the sternpost and these deadwood timbers will be very much longer than those between the stem and bow knee, so work on the sternpost may well be considerably more difficult than on the stem.

Also the sternpost may be bored through for a propeller shaft. Since the shaft hole will usually pass through the deadwood timber, and will have to align with the engine bearers, it is preferable to bore the hole through the new sternpost from inside the hull. To do this, the engine will have to have been removed. Several keen sailing men, such as world circumnavigator Peter Tangvald, or small-boat sailor Charles Stock, would probably advise permanent removal of the engine and plugging of the hole in the deadwoods, leaving the sternpost unbored. Whilst there is no question that a boat which was designed for sailing only will sail faster without the drag of a propeller – even large and not too handy ex-fishing vessels can be (and still are) manoeuvred around crowded anchorages with the aid of warps, anchors and seamanship – most owners prefer to feel they do have the iron topsail available, and so will have to face the problems of boring the new sternpost for the propeller shaft.

Working from inside the hull clearly requires a very long bit indeed. Since the average amateur is most unlikely to have such a tool available, the best solution is to use an extension as shown in Fig 109. The other problem in boring from inside the hull lies in preventing the wood on the outside of the sternpost from splintering as the bit emerges. The best way is to have a helper outside the hull to warn the worker as soon as the tip of the bit breaks through to the outside. The hole can then be completed from outside. If no helper is available, a piece of scrap wood should be securely clamped, shored or screwed on the outer face of the sternpost. If for any reason (such as inability to remove a heavy engine) the hole cannot be bored from inside the hull, the position of the hole will have to be marked on the new sternpost very accurately indeed and the hole bored from outside. If the metal shaft-tube has been removed from the deadwood, a small pilot hole can be drilled through the sternpost, and its accuracy verified before it is opened out to full size.

If the metal shaft-tube is still in place and cannot be moved, the sternpost will have to be bored before it is fitted. Since it is almost impossible to guarantee adequate accuracy, the easiest technique is to bore the hole up to 25 mm (1 in) oversize, then when the new sternpost is in place to make up a hollow wooden plug which will fill the gap left around the tube and to glue it in place with resorcinol resin.

The hole for the propeller shaft should be bored (or bored and plugged) before the sides of the sternpost are bevelled to shape.

On transom-sterned hulls the sternpost will be very much more difficult to replace. Generally the transom will have to be taken out, and since the sternpost is usually tenoned into the keel, the deadwoods will have to be unbolted and a portion of the aft deck removed to allow the sternpost to be lifted. If the damage to be repaired is mechanical, either a break or severe gouging, the best repair is a major graving job: simply cut away as much as possible of the visible portion of the sternpost and glue on a new facing.

Counter-sterns pose the problems of a rudder trunking. On many yachts this may be a bronze tube, but on older working craft it is usually a built-up wooden box, which forms a favourite home for gribble or teredo worm and for most varieties of rot which can affect wooden hulls.

Replacement of a wooden rudder trunking and sternpost is not in itself a terribly difficult operation, but it is likely to involve the removal of several planks from the underside of the counter and also most of the aft deck. The trunking itself may be built up of four pieces of timber with their inner faces cut to form an approximate circle, with softwood strips set into grooves in the joint faces to act as stopwaters. If a new wooden trunking is to be built up, the construction of the original should be studied and copied. After all, it has probably kept the hull afloat for three-quarters of a century or more, so an exact copy should prove reasonably durable if sound timber is used.

One method of replacing a wooden rudder trunking which is too worm eaten or rotten to be repaired is to cut the trunking off flush with the top of the counter-horn timber and at the underside of the deck and to insert a flanged tube in its place. The tube can be welded up from sheet steel and galvanised, or a moulded fibreglass tube can be used. Some traditionalists who have heard about osmosis and the decay of gel coats on GRP hulls, and the accelerated rotting of wooden hulls when fibreglass sheathing is applied, may not like the idea of using a fibreglass rudder trunking, but in fact it can be an almost ideal job for fibreglass.

Since the tube is not normally visible, no pigment will be needed in the gel coat, and a pure, unfilled resin should be used. Since the tube will never be exposed to direct sunlight, ultra-violet light cannot affect the resin. The tube can be moulded in situ, using a cardboard tube of suitable diameter as the body of the mould, and moulding the top and bottom flanges directly against the planking (covering the planking with thin polythene sheet so that the flanges will not bond themselves in place). A sandwich construction should be used, with at least two layers of glass-cloth applied against the mould surface, then layers of chopped-strand mat to build the moulding up to the required thickness, and finally two more layers of glass-cloth. The moulding should be thickened up with extra layers of chopped-strand mat for about 25 mm (1 in) at the top and bottom of the tube, and a fillet of about 13 mm ($\frac{1}{2}$ in) radius should be built up between the tube and the flanges. Triangular pieces of thin hardboard can be embedded in the moulding to form gussets which will stiffen the angle between the tube and the flanges.

The inside diameter of a moulded tube should be at least 25 mm (1 in) larger than the original wooden trunking, and a separate top-bearing of oak, lignum vitae, greenheart, or Tufnol reinforced plastic should be fitted into the deck. If the rudder does not have a strong bearing at its lower end, it may be necessary to provide bearing surfaces at both the upper and lower ends of the moulded trunking to ensure that the rudder stock cannot touch the fibreglass tube. The upper bearing is best set into the deck where it can be supported by the deck beams which originally held the end of the wooden trunking; but if a lower bearing is needed, it may be necessary to place this clear above the horn timber or counter planking so that it will be incorporated into the moulded trunking (Fig 145).

If the moulding is done in situ in the hull, adequate ventilation is essential. If the boat has ventilators on the aft deck, the hose of an old vacuum cleaner can be connected on the outlet end of the cleaner and poked down a ventilator. If no electricity is available to run a vacuum cleaner to provide forced-air ventilation of the counter, it may be possible to rig up sails to provide a perceptible current of air through it. If ventilation cannot be provided, the moulding should not be done inside the hull. Templates can be made out of pieces of hardboard or thin plywood and softwood strips nailed together in place in the hull to ensure that all angles and lengths are correct, and a mould can then be made up out of plywood sheet and a suitable cardboard tube. If the lower flange of the moulded trunking has to be shaped,

Fig 145 *Moulded fibreglass rudder trunking*

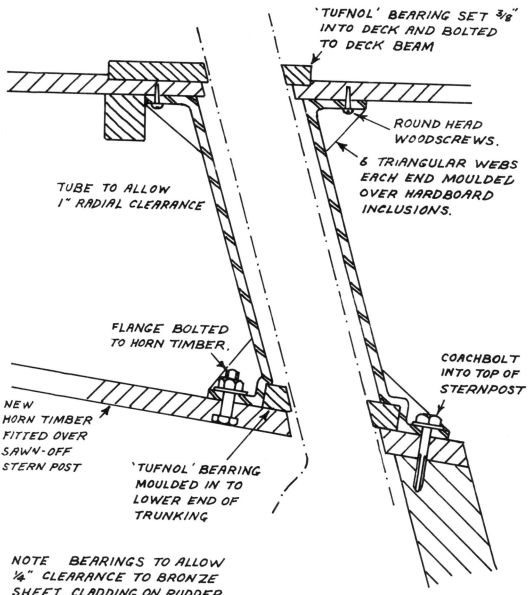

'TUFNOL' BEARING SET ³/₈"
INTO DECK AND BOLTED
TO DECK BEAM

ROUND HEAD
WOODSCREWS.

6 TRIANGULAR WEBS
EACH END MOULDED
OVER HARDBOARD
INCLUSIONS.

TUBE TO ALLOW
1" RADIAL CLEARANCE

FLANGE BOLTED
TO HORN TIMBER.

COACHBOLT
INTO TOP OF
STERNPOST

NEW
HORN TIMBER
FITTED OVER
SAWN-OFF
STERN POST

'TUFNOL' BEARING
MOULDED IN TO
LOWER END OF
TRUNKING

NOTE   BEARINGS TO ALLOW
¼" CLEARANCE TO BRONZE
SHEET CLADDING ON RUDDER.

TOP BEARING IS ¾" SMALLER
THAN LOWER BEARING.

DECK BEAM ON FORESIDE
OF OLD WOODEN TRUNKING
CUT AWAY BELOW THREE
CENTRE PLANKS.

MOULDING   TO BE UNPIGMENTED.
SANDWICH CONSTRUCTION :-
2 LAYERS FINE WEAVE CLOTH,
³/₁₆" MIN. CHOPPED STRAND MAT,
3 LAYERS MEDIUM WEAVE CLOTH.

AT LEAST 2 EXTRA LAYERS CLOTH AT WEBS & FLANGES.

as it might to fit over a thick horn timber and onto planks either side, a plaster cast can be taken of the area to be covered by the flange, and a reverse cast used as the lower face of the mould.

When the moulding has cured it is removed from the hull (or the mould), the ragged edges of the flanges are cleaned off, and the flanges are drilled for fixing holes. The upper flange can be held to the underside of the deck by round-headed woodscrews, but the lower flange should be bolted to the horn timber. The flanges should be well coated with soft bedding compound before the new trunking is finally fitted.

Bow knee and deadwoods

On many hulls the sternpost can be very difficult to replace, but the bow knee and deadwoods can be replaced only if the entire hull is virtually rebuilt. Possibly a third of the planking would have to be removed, and also a third of the frames to gain access to the deadwood timbers. Fortunately, these timbers are virtually immune to mechanical damage, so the only reason for wanting to replace them would be rot. Deadwood timbers are most likely to decay around the bolts which hold them together, or at any point which can form a trap for fresh water. The latter should be eliminated by filling with tar, sawdust-loaded resin, or wooden filler blocks.

If a periodic survey reveals any softening of the deadwoods around any of the fastenings, all the bolts should be removed and checked for soundness. The wood around the holes should be allowed to dry out and also checked. If there is any doubt about its condition, oak graving pieces should be glued into the face of the deadwood to provide a new, strong seating for the bolts (or more correctly for the washers and nuts). The holes in these graving pieces will have to be drilled through from outside the hull, which may well involve digging quite a deep hole in the ground beneath the latter so that a long enough bit can be poked up through the deadwood.

When all the graving pieces have been glued in place and bored, the lower ends of

all holes should be plugged with an ordinary cork wrapped in thin polythene sheeting. All the bolt-holes are then filled with the owner's favourite wood preservative and left for as long as possible – all winter is not too long – for the preservative to soak well into the wood. If the holes can be left for several months whilst other work is done on the hull, corks should be put in the tops of the holes to keep out dust. Every time the boat is visited, the level of preservative in the holes should be checked, and topped up as necessary until the wood is thoroughly impregnated. Rapid loss of preservative from the holes will indicate a crack or split somewhere, but so long as none of the fluid is seen to be dripping out on the outside of the hull this loss is nothing to worry about. Successive applications may 'gum up' the leak sufficiently to allow the upper levels of the holes to remain filled for long enough for some impregnation to occur. The 'lost' preservative from the holes will help to 'pickle' the keel, lower frame ends, or whatever other timbers it leaks out onto.

Counter horn-timber

The end of a long, fine counter is the most likely place to find rot in any older wooden hull. All too often the shapely counter sterns are unventilated, and even if ventilators are fitted, a long counter tends to become the last resting-place of torn sails and other unwanted gear – which blocks off the air flow and encourages rot. Since the rot usually occurs at the tip of the counter, many owners cure the problem by cutting half a metre or so (a foot or two) off the end and shortening the boat. In these days of high berthing-charges per foot of overall length (or perhaps per metre) such shortening of a boat can prove financially beneficial.

The horn-timber may need to be replaced together with the rudder trunking if the latter has decayed or been attacked by worm. If the horn-timber is forked to pass either side of the sternpost and the top of the aft deadwood, several planks each side will have to be removed to gain access to the transverse fastenings, and this amount of work may not be felt to be justifiable.

If the ends of the horn-timber either side of the sternpost are sound, the timber can be cut off short at the sternpost and a new, thicker one fitted over the sawn-off top of the sternpost, the deadwood and the ends of the old horn-timber. This new, thicker timber will have to have its upper surface notched to fit under the frames in the counter, which would usually have been fitted across the top of the original horn-timber.

Generally the work is similar to that involved in fitting a replacement keel, except that the replacement horn-timber will have to be tilted to get the forward end in place over the top of the sternpost, and then the aft end can be lifted into place, with a helper inside the hull to ensure that the frames in the counter enter their slots in the new timber. Because of this 'rocking' into place, the slots cannot be a perfect fit over the frames, so ample bedding compound must be used. Any gaps left once the horn-timber is in place should be closed with wedges hammered in. The new horn-timber is fastened down to the head of the sternpost and deadwood with long coach-bolts.

It may be possible to make a good watertight replacement for a horn-timber in a hull in which it is impossible to get a sound mechanical fastening to the sternpost without removing far too many planks and possibly a frame or two. If this appears to be so, the counter can be strengthened by running a pair of internal stringers either side of the sternpost. These stringers should extend for at least two-thirds of the length of the counter, and at least the same distance into the hull forward of the sternpost. They should be placed as close in to the sternpost as the curvature of the hull will allow. Straight-grained Columbian pine is the best timber to use for these stringers. Their size will obviously depend on the size and type of hull concerned; about 76 mm × 32 mm (3 in × $1\frac{1}{4}$ in) would be suitable for an average ten-tonner. A 'trial run' should be made with a somewhat lighter timber to make sure that the stringers can be bent into place. They are run over all frames, and are fastened by riveting right through the planks, frames and stringers,

with two rivets to each frame. The riveting should be started at the frame nearest the sternpost, back into the counter, then forward into the hull, allowing the stringers to take the most natural curve possible as the cross-sections of the hull change their shape. Some hulls were built with hardly any discernable horn-timber, the counter relying on the planking for its strength. These counter-sterns are easy to repair, but their lack of any main-strength member does render them liable to straining in a seaway, and a pair of stringers added to such a counter can help to eliminate annoying leaks.

Centreboard-case

Boats with centreboards pose extra problems in repair work. Most older centreboard-cases leak to some extent, and the case can also be a favourite place for attack by worms. Some boats of moderate draft were fitted with centreboards in the belief that their windward performance would be improved, but this turned out not to be the case, the boats performing better to windward when sailed a half-point further off the wind with the plate up. A significant number of seven- to ten-tonners with drafts of 1–1.2 m (3–4 ft) have been sailing round for years with their centreboards removed and the slot in the keel stopped up. So the first thing an owner who is plagued with a leaking centreboard-case should do is to see whether the boat really needs the centreboard. In marginal cases a centreboard can be replaced with a false keel some 102–152 mm (4–6 in) deep.

However, there are the very shoal-draft, full-bodied hulls, and the high-performance, light-displacement types of cruisers which will not perform at all well without a centreboard, and there are also the many older classes of dinghies, all of which need their boards or plates.

How easy it will be to repair or replace a centreboard-case depends on how it was fitted when the boat was built. Usually the end pieces of the case (the headledges) pass through the keel and the hog, whilst the sides pass only through the hog, with fastenings up through the keel into the side planks of the case. Normally a sill timber is screwed on to the outer faces of the sides and screwed or riveted down to the keel or hog.

If there are no transverse fastenings through the keel and the lower ends of the headledges, it is not difficult to take the entire case out of the average dinghy and fit a complete new one. Any sills should be taken out with the case. On a really well-built boat it may be found that the sills are riveted to the sides of the case. If it is found on attempting to remove the case that the headledges are fastened into the keel, the sides of the case will have to be removed separately. The headledges can then usually be broken out of the keel, and the transverse fastenings cut through with a hacksaw blade.

If the entire case is to be replaced, the original construction should be followed as closely as possible. The headledges are usually of oak, and the sides can be cut from iroko or mahogany, either of which should be readily available in sufficient width to cut the side out of one piece. If mahogany is used, it is as well to buy from a reputable timber merchant with some knowledge of marine work, as the name 'mahogany' is used to cover a wide variety of timbers, some of which are not all that durable. The sides of the case can be bonded to the headledges with resin glue, then riveted right through. Sills, which should be as substantial as the width of the keel will allow, can be cut from straight-grained pine. The lower faces of the sills may have to be notched to pass over the lower ends of the ribs.

The case can be stood in place in the hull to locate the sills, which should be temporarily fastened to the sides of the case with two or three screws through each sill. The case and sills are then removed from the hull and the sills bedded onto the sides and secured in place with bronze or gun-metal screws. If the plate is of the pivoted type, the hole for the pivot-bolt is drilled through the sills and the sides of the case before the latter is finally fitted into the hull. The hole must be a really tight-drive fit for the bolt, because any attempts to stop leaking round the bolt by tightening the nuts will merely result in closing in the sides of the case and straining the fastenings to the keel.

If timber of sufficient width to make the sides of the case in one piece is not available, two or more pieces will have to be edge-joined, which is a nice exercise in precision woodwork. The edges must be flat, smooth, and square to the face of the timber. The joint should be tongued and grooved, using a separate tongue set into a groove in each mating face. The tongue should be a quarter of the thickness of the case side, and the grooves should be twice as deep as they are wide. The grooves are cut first, then the tongue is carefully planed to size. When checking such a tongue for fit, try each end of it in the groove, and then use a micrometer, vernier gauge or sensitive calipers to check that it is of uniform section over its whole length. If it is checked by trying its whole length in the groove, it will be very difficult to get it out again if it really fits well! The joint is finally assembled with resorcinol resin.

If the case itself is sound, but leaks at the joint to the keel, a partial cure can be made by tightening the screws through the keel into the sides of the case, and perhaps putting in extra screws midway between the original fastenings. If the wooden sills do not cover the whole of the face of the hog either side of the keel, they can be removed and replaced with larger-section sills. When new sills are being fitted, all the holes left in the case sides by old fastenings should be plugged and new sites found for the new fastenings.

If the boat concerned is a 'knock about' dinghy or small cruiser of uncertain origin, it may well be worth having a close look at the overall design of the case and its support. Despite the work of designers like Morgan Giles and Maurice Griffiths, who demonstrated that centreplate-cases need not leak, many builders failed to appreciate the principles of fitting in cases able to withstand the stresses imposed by the plate or board when the boat is sailing hard. The cases fitted in the better-class clinker-built racing dinghies designed by Giles had long extended ends, the sides running well out beyond the headledges with the space between the sides blocked in. The extended

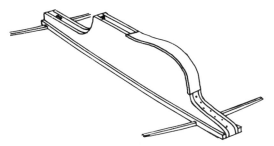

Fig 146 *Centreplate-case with elongated ends as fitted to good quality racing dinghies with light clinker hulls*

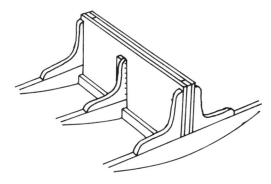

Fig 147 *Centreplate-case with side knees as fitted in heavy carvel hull*

ends could be riveted or bolted to the keel, making the joint between the case and keel very resistant to twisting stresses (Fig 146). These long cases were fitted in relatively lightly built, flexible clinker-planked hulls, so that most of the twisting forces are dissipated in the springiness of the frames and planking (which is one of the reasons why clinker sailing dinghies should have frames and planks repaired by replacement and not by doubling).

On the other hand, the case in a relatively stiff shoal-draft, carvel-planked cruising hull as designed by Griffiths needs to be well tied in to the entire bottom structure of the hull, usually by fairly stout knees between the case sides and main floor timbers. At each end of the case the floors should be continuous transverse timbers, and the head-ledges and case sides should be notched to sit over the floors. The pair of knees at each end are riveted right through the sides and headledges. If the plate is of the type which drops through ninety degrees, intermediate knees should be fitted at the aft edge of the plate when it is lowered. These knees are riveted to struts which are screwed on to the sides of the case (Fig 147).

Trouble can arise if attempts are made to mix the case and hull types. What can for convenience be called an 'end-supported case' will almost inevitably leak if it is fitted into a relatively rigid carvel hull, and a 'side-supported case' in a flexible clinker hull will be robbed of its essential support if the hull flexes at all. Of the two 'mixes', the end-supported case without knees in a carvel hull is by far the worse.

If it appears that inadequate side support is the cause of persistent leaking, knees can be fitted between the sides of the case and suitable floors. Really good grown-oak knees with the necessary right-angle bend and legs fine enough not to block off access past the case unduly can be very hard to come by. Suitable knees can be laminated from oak strips, with a solid block on the point of the corner (Fig 148), but they will still take up a lot of space, and also take quite a lot of work to make.

The author found that an elegant solution to the problem of finding good crooks or laminating suitable knees lay in having the knees cast in bronze. A pattern was simply made up out of 6 mm ($\frac{1}{4}$ in) plywood – an L shaped base with about 25 mm (1 in) radius in the point of the bend, and two plain strips glued and nailed on (Fig 149). All corners were rounded off. It took longer to paint and label the pattern than it did to make it, and Moyle Marine Ltd of Wokingham cast the knees in high-quality bronze at less than the cost of buying oak crooks! Bronze knees have several major advantages: fastenings can be put in through both webs; the projection into the boat is only 6 mm ($\frac{1}{4}$ in) other than right in the corner; they do not warp, twist, shrink or rot and, although they are slightly heavier than wooden knees, the extra weight is of no significance in the bilges of a boat. They should be fastened in with rivets whenever possible, or bronze or gunmetal screws where a through-fastening is impossible. The wood to which they are fitted should be shaped to fit as closely as possible into the angle section of the knee, and a soft bedding compound should be used.

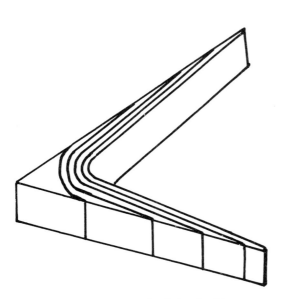

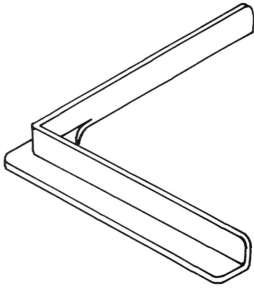

Fig 148   *Laminated knee for fitting beside centreplate-case*

Fig 149   *Cast-bronze knee for centreplate-case*

Whilst on the topic of centreplate-cases, there is a technique for dealing with minor annoying leaks which does not involve slipping the boat, but if not done very carefully, it can be messy. The boat is allowed to take the ground on a fairly hard surface, so that all the water will drain out of the plate-case as the tide recedes. When the tide returns, a careful watch is kept on the bottom of the keel, and as soon as the rising tide completely seals the bottom of the slot for the plate, a cupful of black varnish or thinned down gasworks' tar is poured into the top of the case. This spreads over the rising water in the case, and runs into all the minor crevices which cause the weeping. For a week or so after treatment the boat should be kept afloat or allowed to ground only in a soft mud berth which will keep some water in the case, so that the black varnish or tar cannot escape and foul other boats' topsides.

Floors and keelson

The transverse floors are a most important feature of any wooden hull other than light dinghies. They serve to tie the two sides of the hull together, and also to spread the loading of the ballast keel over the largest possible area of the bottom planking. On any boat which regularly takes the ground, the floors serve to spread the load imposed on the bilge as the boat settles on the ground.

Usually the floors will be of oak, and on boats with sawn frames the floors may form the lowest member of each pair of frames. The floors are bolted to the keel, and usually the planking is screwed to the floors, although dumps and blind nails or trenails may be used on larger boats. In hulls with all-bent frames, the floors will not be fastened directly to the frames; but when the hull has sawn or grown frames these are usually side-fastened to the wooden floors, often with dumps.

On some boats metal-strap floors are fitted. These are stout metal strips which are forged to lie over the top of the wooden keel – to which they are held by a keel-bolt – and up over the tops of the sawn frames (c in Fig 150). Strap floors are usually bolted through the frames and planks, but sometimes they are riveted through the planks. Often in these cases the floors are badly corroded, if copper rivets have been used to hold down iron floors. If the frames meet over the keel, a strap floor will run straight over the top of the frames.

Another type of metal floor is the plate floor, which is basically a stout metal plate

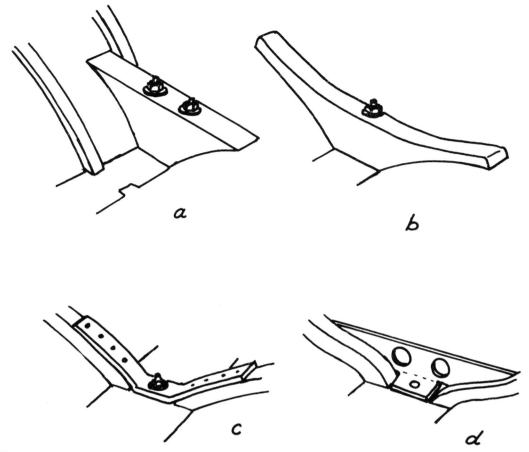

Fig 150   *Wooden and metal floors*

fitted across the hull beside a sawn or grown frame, to which it is bolted or riveted. Some plate floors have bent flanges which lie over the keel and through which a keel-bolt passes, and sometimes they have welded-on flanges which lie over the frames so that the planks can be through-bolted to the floors (D in Fig 150). Plate floors are more likely to be found on more expensively built yacht hulls than on ex-working craft, which used the cheaper strap floors or relied on an all-wooden construction.

Replacing wooden floors is quite a straightforward operation, the only pitfall for the unwary being the possible presence of side fastenings into an adjacent frame. New floors can generally be cut from a single piece of timber, as they do not usually have much curvature. Short block floors

like that of (A) in Fig 150 may be cut from elm or oak; longer armed floors as in (B) are usually cut from oak.

Metal-strap floors are fairly easy to replace, but unless one has access to a heavy engineering works, they must be forged to shape. A strap floor thin enough to be bent to shape without heating and beating or without the aid of an hydraulic press will not be strong enough to do its job properly. Plate floors present a little more of a problem. They can be cut from steel plate, and side flanges can be welded on to fit over the frames, but there is quite a lot of work involved. Welded-up plate frames should be hot-dip galvanised and bedded in, preferably in hot tar. However, they are very liable to corrode at the welds. A much better solution is to use cast floors. For a yacht with copper and bronze fastenings and keel-bolts, the floors can be cast in bronze from a plywood pattern. For iron-fastened boats, iron floors must be used. Ordinary cast iron is too brittle, and cast steel would corrode too quickly (and would be too expensive). There is however one ferrous metal which meets all the requirements for a plate floor, and that is a variety of iron called spheroidal graphite iron (SG iron). This material flows into the mould like ordinary iron but, after an annealing process, it develops the strength of mild steel, and has outstanding corrosion resistance, especially if unmachined and left with the 'skin' still on. It has the unusual property that after annealing the castings are the same size as the pattern (most other metals shrink slightly as they cool so that patterns need to be made oversize). SG iron castings are easily drilled for fixing holes. A simple pattern can be built up from 6 mm ($\frac{1}{4}$ in) plywood, working in the place the finished floor is to fit. One great advantage of cast-plate floors is that drainage holes can be cast in. The finished pattern must be sanded smooth and painted or varnished, and do not forget to paint a clear label on the pattern so that the foundry can identify it.

The only disadvantage of SG iron is that not all foundries can use the process. A local foundry may suggest that it is expensive, unsuitable, difficult to cast, or that no firm capable of casting SG iron will be interested in a 'one-off'. Ignore all such advice. The author heard all these tales when he wanted a large centreplate cast, but it did not take too long to find a foundry (in Cardiff) who could handle a casting 2.1 m × 0.6 m (7 ft × 2 ft), and the end product was in all respects most satisfactory – immensely strong, and virtually rustproof. After thirteen years that plate showed much less corrosion than any stainless steel fittings! SG iron is not normally encountered on wooden boats because it is a relatively new process, and did not come into significant use until the mid 1950s. Had the material been available earlier, there can be little doubt it could have found many marine uses. As it is, the author believes that his SG iron plate was the first time the metal was used on a yacht in the UK. Any amateurs wishing to contact foundries which handle this material could try enquiring at the Mond Nickel Company on Millbank in London; they supplied the author with a list of foundries using the process.

On larger boats, and more particularly ex-working boats, work on the floors may be hampered by the presence of a keelson – an inner keel timber which runs from the bow knee to the aft deadwood over all the floors or lower frames. Keel-bolts are fitted right through the keel, hog, floors and keelson. If one floor has to be replaced, all keel-bolts must be undone and the keelson removed first. Replacement of a rotted keelson is quite simple, as it is usually a plain rectangular baulk of timber. If the hull is flush-decked, there may be a problem in getting the old one out and getting the new one into the hull, and it may be necessary to remove a portion of the decking. On a boat which has a cockpit, the cockpit may have to be taken out to slide in a new keelson, but most hulls which have got to the state of needing a new one will usually be needing some other quite extensive repairs as well, so somewhere in the job it is likely that a hole can be opened to get the new timber in. Getting the old keelson out is no problem – it can be cut into short lengths.

If a boat is fitted with a keelson, the mast step may be cut into its upper face. This can be a starting point for decay, so should be examined carefully. Some boats simply had a rectangular slot cut into the keelson and a tenon cut on the end of the mast. The slot forms a first-class catching vessel for any rain water which leaks down the mast and into the hull, so both the keelson (or mast-step timber) and the heel of the mast can rot away together. The cure is very simple – provide a drainage path to the step. This is one of the few instances where an old hull can be improved by not following exactly the original construction.

If a keelson has limited local decay around the mast step, the best cure is a large graving piece set in, followed by a thorough dosing with wood preservative.

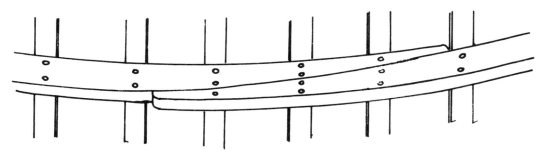

Fig 151   *Joint in a bilge stringer*

Bilge stringers

Of all the main structural timbers in a boat's hull (excluding the decking and its associated framing), a broken bilge stringer is the most difficult to replace. A bilge stringer is usually quite a substantial timber, and it normally runs the whole length of the hull. Because of the curvature of the stringer, it can be longer than the overall length of the hull, so fitting a new stringer without first removing a substantial amount of decking can be impossible. Even on totally undecked dinghies it may be necessary to remove a thwart to fit a full-length stringer.

Damage to bilge stringers most usually occurs in the middle third of their length, so replacement of just the damaged portion is normally the best policy. The bilge stringers are usually run over the frames, held down with two fastenings through each frame (and the planking).

Cutting and gluing two scarph joints on a substantial curved timber is almost impossible, so it is just as well to accept that this cannot reasonably be done and to adopt an alternative approach. The simplest solution which will give a reasonable transfer of strength from the old portion of the stringer to the new, is to run the new portion slightly further out from the keel than the original and to taper off the width of each portion over a length of three frame spacings. This allows each portion of the stringer to have two fastenings to the frame below the centre of the joint (Fig 151). Note that off-setting the new portion means that the fastenings will be in new locations, and the old holes in the frames and planks will have

to be plugged. It also allows the end of each portion to be left at about a third of its original width with no step cut at the broad end of the taper as would be needed with a stopped scarph joint. The advantage of such an offset joint is that the length of the replacement portion is not as critical as it would be if a stopped scarph were cut on each end.

Cutting through a bilge stringer is another of those very frustrating jobs one meets in boat repairs. Often there is just no way to get a really good saw cut unless one is either very small or has totally double-jointed arms. One technique which is not too frustrating is to clamp or nail a piece of scrap timber along the line of the taper to act as a guide, and then to run either a large tenon saw or the rounded end of an electrician's floorboard saw along beside this guide timber (Fig 152). On a large boat, cutting like this is not a quick job, but given company to chat to, the tedium can be relieved. Be careful not to get into too much of a rhythm and cut through the frames as well! The long feather-end of the section to be left is easily cut off once the defective portion has been removed.

When the replacement section has been cut, the joint faces should be covered with soft bedding compound, as should the faces of the frames where the stringer will fit. The new section can then be shored and wedged into place. It may be necessary to force a compound curvature into the stringer, with bending in both width and thickness and also a twist. Shores and wedges can fly out as the stringer is twisted into position, so all shores should be carefully placed and checked as the stringer is

151

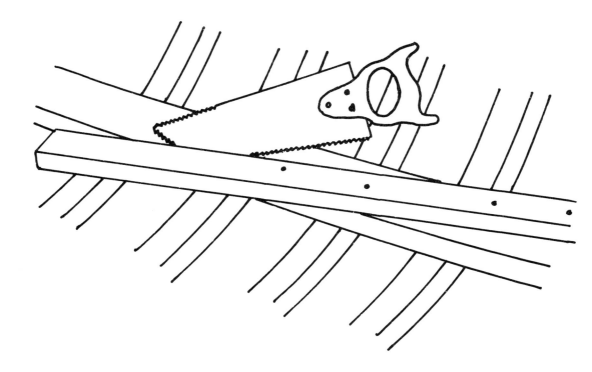

Fig 152 *Cutting a bilge stringer with a floorboard saw*

forced home. A good workable sequence is first to wedge the two ends with shores down from the beam shelf; next force the middle of the stringer into full contact with the face of the frames, then add further shores and wedges as necessary to force the stringer into its final place. Only when the whole of the stringer is properly in place and the joint faces at each end are closed as tightly as possible should any fastenings be put in.

If the stringer is not bearing firmly on all frames, it can twist as it is riveted home, and a small twist in the middle can result in one end moving some centimetres (inches) or, if the end cannot move, in the new section of stringer splitting. Riveting should be started from the middle of the new section, fastening alternate frames towards each end; G cramps can be used to hold the joint faces closed as riveting progresses.

When the new section is riveted to all frames, screws can be run through the tapered ends of the joints, screwing the new

section to the old (and vice versa). Drilling for and fitting these screws is always difficult since the stringers are usually fitted at the sharpest point in the turn of the bilge. They should be put in at the smallest angle possible to the face of the stringer, but it will probably have to be accepted that this smallest possible angle may be fairly large and the screws can be at best supplementary fastenings, with the real transfer of strength from the old section to the new being by the rivets and frames.

Transom

Replacing a transom is quite a straightforward job, the only real complication being that if the boat has any aft decking this may have to be removed to get at it. Unless the transom is small it will probably have to be built up from more than one plank and, since it will have to withstand being thoroughly soaked whilst sailing and then being baked by the sun (in the years

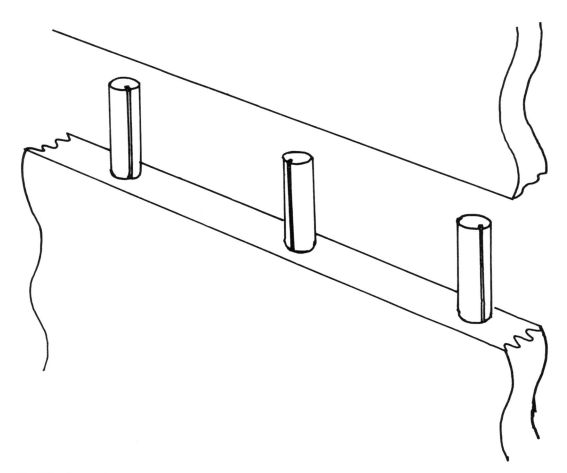

Fig 153 *Dumps between planks in a transom:
note the 'air escape' grooves in the dumps*

when we see some of it) whilst the boat lies on her mooring, it is inadvisable to try and glue up separate planks to make a 'one-piece' board. Such a large board may split as its moisture-content changes, so it is better to use the traditional method of fitting two boards together, either with a wooden tongue or key fitted into grooves in each part, or with long metal dumps and soft bedding compound on the joint faces and a thinner backing board bedded behind the joint.

If dumps are to be used, the two boards to be joined should be clamped together face to face and the positions for the pins marked on the edges of both boards simultaneously. The holes must be bored square to the joint face and, if the worker has any doubts about his or her ability to hold a drill truly square, it is well worthwhile making up a little checking jig. It is helpful to have somebody standing by the ends of the boards to warn if the drilling is going off square. The holes (and the dumps) should have a diameter of about three-eighths of the thickness of the board, and the holes should be just deep enough to take the full length of the pins. When long dumps are fitted into blind holes there can be a problem with air being trapped in the bottom of the holes, so a saw cut should be run along each dump to form a groove along which the air can escape (Fig 153). The holes should be well dosed with wood preservative before fitting the dumps.

Cutting the transom to shape must be done with care as the edge will be at an angle to the face, and the angle changes round the curve of the bilge. If the worker has any doubts of his ability to cut the correct angle first go, the transom must be cut oversize, and the excess removed with a spokeshave. The required angles are easily measured off the inside of the planking.

The transom may need doubling pieces up each side so that screws through the top-side planking can be run into the side of the wood instead of into the end-grain timber of the main transom. If doubling pieces are not fitted, and the fastenings have to be run into the end grain, long ring-barbed nails will hold better than screws. Internal framing for a transom or the arch board of a counter is described in the section on plank-ends, page 117.

Some boats have shapely curved transoms instead of flat boards. These may be made of separate planks or a sheet of plywood on a frame. Repairs to, or replacements of, such transoms should follow the original method of construction as closely as possible.

A transom might need a local repair around a through-bolted rudder pintle which has worked loose and bruised the timber. Provided the transom is free of rot, a substantial graving piece can be fitted. Such a graving piece can be fitted right up to the underside of the deck planking without the deck being lifted. Sellotape stuck on the underside of the deck planks will prevent the resin glue from bonding the graving piece to the deck.

Chapter 13

Decking and above

Beam shelves

A damaged beam shelf is one part of a decked boat which cannot be replaced to its original form without totally rebuilding the entire deck. The beam shelves are the longest continuous frame members in the entire hull, and usually all the deck beams are fitted into the shelves in some way – from above! Replacement of even part of a beam shelf is a job which makes replacing a bilge stringer seem very simple. If the deck planking is not lifted, one is working inside a fairly sharp angle, often less than a right angle in the bows, and some of the work will have to be done lying on one's back or side. Even cutting through the old shelf to remove a damaged portion becomes a major task.

Before starting any repairs to beam shelves which show signs of rot, it is advisable to check all the deck beams very carefully for rot. It may even be worth lifting one deck plank to expose the upper faces of all beams, whereupon it may be found that what appeared to be sound oak beams are in fact hollow shells of solid wood with a core of rot where water has crept in round the mast, down a cabin side, or just through a seam in the deck planking, and then run along the top of the beam to the side of the hull, leading to rot in the beams and beam shelf. If this has happened to any extent the best action is to strip off the entire deck – which at least simplifies the task of replacing the beam shelves.

If the deck beams are sound, and the damage to a beam shelf is local, the afflicted portion can be cut out and a new length fitted. How difficult this will be depends on how the deck beams are fitted into the shelves. The heaviest, most solid construction likely to be met is that which comprises two timbers – a vertical timber which

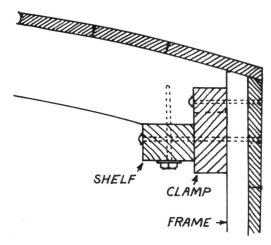

Fig 154 *Beam shelf, clamp, and deck beam*

lies against the inner faces of the frames and into which the deck beams are located by simple halving joints, and a horizontal timber below the deck beams, to which the beams are usually secured by coach-bolts driven up through the shelf (Fig 154). Both timbers are through-bolted or riveted to the planks and frames. Strictly, only the horizontal timber is the beam shelf, and the vertical timber should be called a clamp, but the term 'beam shelf' is frequently used to cover both (or either) timbers. Some boats have a shelf and clamp construction on which the horizontal shelf runs only for a third or a quarter of the length of the hull in the way of the mast.

If both shelf and clamp timbers run full length, the shelf timber should be replaced for at least two or more frame spaces each end than the clamp. If only a partial-length shelf is fitted, it is easiest to replace it entirely.

On hulls which have only a single shelf timber, the deck beams may be set in with a halving joint, but they are more likely to

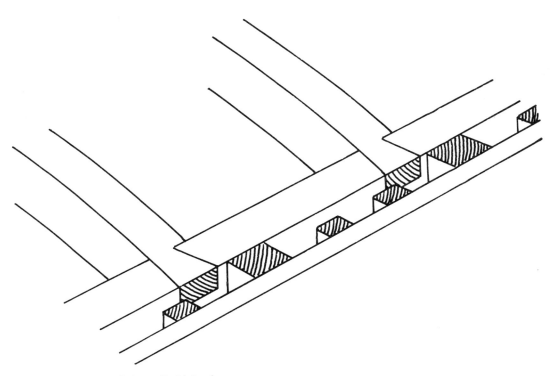

Fig 155 *Beams half-dovetailed into clamp timber*

be fitted with a half dovetail joint (Fig 155). The half tail is cut into the side of the beam nearest to the end of the hull. If only a single vertical timber is used for the shelf it may be set low so that the dovetail joint is only on the lower half of the deck beams, and the beams are usually run out to touch the inner face of the planking (Fig 156). Sometimes the shelves are set higher, so that they touch the underside of the deck, and the beam ends usually stop short at the face of the shelf (Fig 157). This type of construction makes it easier to cut and fit the joints in the beams, but it leaves a dead air space behind the shelves, so is more liable to rot in the latter than if the shelf is set lower to leave an all-round air space.

When a boat has a coachroof and side decks or hatches, replacement of a beam shelf will probably be complicated by the presence of tie rods. These are simply long metal rods, threaded at each end, which are fitted through the beam shelf and the carlin at the cabin or hatch side, with washers and

nuts on each end. These tie rods prevent the caulking in the seams of the side deck from simply pushing in the cabin sides. A glance up under the side decks of many an older yacht will reveal that the side-deck beams are pulled partially out of their joints into either the beam shelves or the carlins, because not enough tie rods were fitted when she was built (Fig 158). Any tie rods will have to be removed before the shelf can be replaced, and it is far from uncommon to find that the nut up behind the beam shelf is well and truly corroded in place, and the rod will have to be cut through with a hacksaw. Since the rods will be typically about 25 mm (1 in) away from the side of a deck beam, and probably no more than 51 mm (2 in) below the deck, this is a job for a junior hacksaw and a vast reserve of patience. On a yacht, the nut on the inner end of the tie rod will usually be hidden behind a mahogany facing timber fitted over the bottom of the cabin side and the face of the carlin.

Cutting out the damaged portion of a

156

Wender: *30ft x 26ft x 8ft 2in x 4ft: prawner designed by G. F. Holmes and built by Bond of Birkenhead in 1898. Now owned by A. J. (Sam) Poole of Dartmouth*

Restored Gaffers in a wide variety of shapes and
sizes racing down the Blackwater Estuary shortly
after the start of the 1974 East Coast Old Gaffers
Race

The author at work on his 4-tonner
Essex Melody with mast up, nearly completed

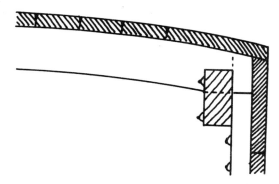

Fig 156   *Beam shelf set low with free air circulation around it*

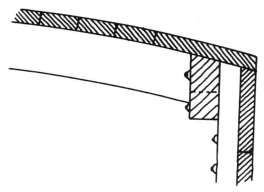

Fig 157   *Beam shelf fitted right up to the deck planking. This is bad practice as it leaves a dead air space*

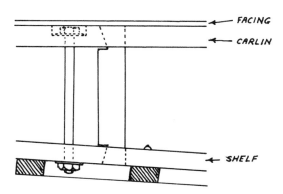

Fig 158   *Tie bolt alongside half beam under side deck, viewed from underside*

beam shelf is a difficult operation because of the lack of space, and efforts to cut a clean end may have to be abandoned in favour of boring a number of 25 mm (1 in) diameter holes and breaking the wood be-

tween the holes. The joint between old and new portions should be cut to give the longest taper possible, but the need to leave adequate strength around all beam ends may dictate that this taper is quite short. The new portion of the shelf is cut from close, straight-grained pine. Most beam shelves have compound curvature, that is they are bent to follow the curve of the deck plan of the boat and are also bent edgewise to follow the sheerline. Cutting and fitting simultaneously half a dozen or more halving or dovetail joints in a piece of wood which is to be bent with compound curvature is one of those jobs best left to experts; the average amateur is well advised to seek some easier alternative.

The first simplification which can be made is to cut the new shelf from overwidth timber, shaping it to the sheerline. This greatly simplifies the fitting as it leaves only a simple curvature to be forced into the timber. It also allows the new portion of the shelf to be thickened up at each end so that it will sit below the end of the original portion allowing extra fastenings through the frames (Fig 159). A cutting template can be made from a strip of thin plywood or hardboard.

With the aid of a template, adequately accurate joints for the beam ends can be cut in the new portion of the shelf, but this is not all that easy, and fitting will still be tricky. All the difficulties in fitting plain halving joints to the beams can be eliminated by cutting the sockets in the new shelf about 25 mm (1 in) overwidth and angling the ends of the sockets so that wedges can be glued in place to close the gaps after the shelf has been fastened in place (Fig 160). If the beams are half dovetailed into the shelf, the angled faces of all joints must be cut to fit on all beams, and wedges are fitted only on the plain sides of the beams (Fig 161). When such wedges are cut and fitted, they should be glued only to the new shelf and not to the side of the deck beam.

The newly cut shelf timber should be held in place just below the deck beams and forced into contact with all the frame faces by long wedged shores right across the hull. After a final check that all joint faces will match up correctly, it is eased up into its

159

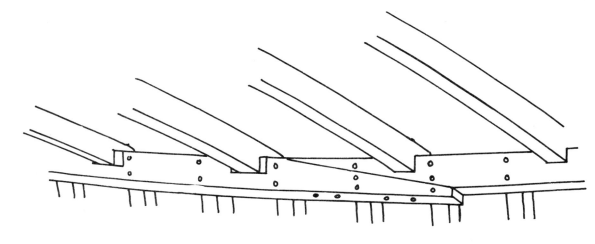

Fig 159 *New section of beam shelf joined in to lie partially below the original shelf*

final position either by tapping with a mallet or by further shores and wedges against a bilge stringer. If oversize joints to be closed later with wedges have been cut, bedding compound should be used only on the tapered ends which will butt against the ends of the original portions of the shelf.

Once properly in place, the new portion of the shelf is fastened, starting with the fastenings to the frame in the middle of the new section and working out towards each end. Wedged shores should be fitted under each end of the new portion to keep it up against the original sections as it is fastened. When all fastenings through the frames have been fitted, screws should be put in upwards through the end of the new portion into the old (Fig 159). If there is any doubt about the transfer of strength from old to new portions of the shelf, a metal strap or flitch plate cut to pass clear under the deck beams and drilled out so as not to sit on the ends of fastenings can be screwed over the joint (Fig 162). Such a flitch plate should never be needed with full shelf and clamp structures, as the joints in the shelf and clamp should be well staggered.

Fitting a new portion of a true horizontal beam shelf is quite straightforward. If only a partial shelf is fitted it should be cut to the curvature of the plan. Many boats with partial shelves had cut shelves whose width

Fig 160 *Gap round plain-ended deck beam closed with wedges*

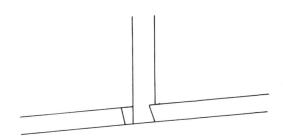

Fig 161 *A single-wedged gap should be left on the plain side of beams which are fitted with half dovetails*

Fig 162 *Metal strap for reinforcing repaired beam shelf*

varied, tapering from the narrow ends to a maximum under the mast beam.

Some boats, as already mentioned, are built with the ends of the deck beams simply resting on a low shelf timber. This type of construction has little resistance to any stresses which might open out the top of the hull, but it is the easiest type on which to replace part of the beam shelves.

Deck beams

Replacement of a deck beam is almost impossible without first removing the deck planking. The two main problems are what to do about the fastenings through the deck planking into the beam, and how to arrange a strong joint to the beam shelf without access from above.

If the reason for wishing to replace a deck beam is the presence of rot, then usually it will be advisable to lift the deck planking and do the job properly. If rot has been discovered in one beam, it is more than just possible that other beams are beginning to go, and often the rot is readily detectable only from the upper face of the beam. If the reason is of a mechanical nature – either a beam which is badly split or a beam which has been cut into by a previous owner in fitting a bulkhead or locker which is being (or has been) removed – the best solution may be to fit a doubling beam on the midships side of the old one. If the deck planking is held down to the beams with screws or nails which are accessible from the surface they can be removed and the deck beam can be replaced, with some modification to its fitting, into the beam shelf.

Once all fastenings through the deck into the beam and any fastenings through the beam shelf are removed, the easiest way to get the old beam out is to spring one of the deck planks near the middle of the beam up slightly by inserting a wedge between it and the beam, then slide in a piece of thin sheet material such as Formica. The beam is then sawn through from underneath, the plastic sheet protecting the deck plank from damage.

If there is any tendency for the saw to bind in the cut, spare ballast pigs can be loaded on the deck, or a heavy friend can be persuaded to stand over the beam being cut so that the load in the centre of the beam holds the saw cut open. Once the beam is cut through, the cut ends can be

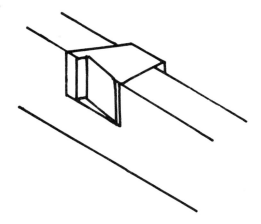

Fig 163 *Deck-beam joint in beam shelf plugged, with plug cut to take end of new beam*

wriggled gently to investigate the strength of the joints to the beam shelf. If these are plain halving joints, they will pull out without any fuss. Old dovetails in a hull which has worked a lot may pull out, but more usually a dovetail will jam, and attempts to force out the beam will split the shelf. If the joint is a usual half dovetail, a sharp chisel can be used to cut back the joint face in the shelf until the end of the beam can be released. The gaps left in the top of the shelf must be closed up by gluing in blocks of wood. On an old boat it will probably be necessary to chisel back the faces of the joint to expose clean wood. If this chiselling back is done to leave tapering faces, the plug will be much easier to fit, and there is no need to worry about the plug being cut off flush with the back face of the beam shelf (Fig 163).

The replacement beam is cut from well-seasoned oak, with its length an exact fit between the beam shelves on the midships side of its final position, and with the ends of the beam cut square. Recesses are chiselled into the plugs in the shelf, with the faces of the recesses parallel to the centre-line of the hull so that the new beam can be pushed into position (Fig 164). The underside of the beam should be cut with a flat at each end so that it can sit squarely on a horizontal shelf timber. If the boat already has shelf and clamp timbers, the new beam will be the same shape as the old. If the boat originally had only a vertical

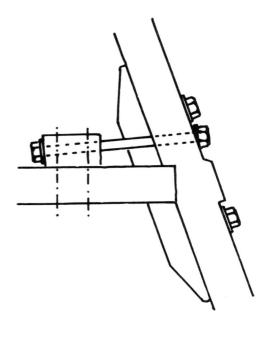

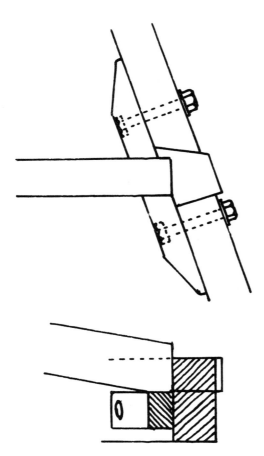

Fig 164 *New deck beam fitted with partial shelf*

Fig 165 *Short tie bar fitted to hold side of hull into new deck beams fitted without dovetails*

timber, short horizontal shelf timbers can be through-bolted to the existing timbers below the ends of the new beam (Fig 164).

A single replacement deck beam fitted in this way should be more than adequately strong, but if two or three adjacent beams are replaced there will be a lack of strength holding the sides of the boat together, and it may be advisable to fit a metal tie rod across the hull. If there is much camber to the deck, a long tie rod right across the hull could be very much in the way, so it is better to fit short rods from the beam shelf to oak blocks riveted or bolted to the face of the beam nearer the end of the hull (Fig 165).

Side deck beams, or half beams by hatches, pose special problems as they are usually dovetailed into the carlin, and often the carlin is the same depth as the beam so that a partial shelf cannot be fitted to support the vertical loading of the beam. If more than one beam needs to be replaced, there is little doubt that the best policy is to lift the deck planking and replace the beams properly. When only a single beam is involved, an adequate if somewhat crude repair can be made by plugging the old joint in the carlin, fitting the new beam with a square end, and driving a metal pin through the carlin into the end of the beam. The size of the pin relative to the beam must be carefully chosen – too thin and the pin will not do any good; too thick and it may split the beam. A pin diameter of about a third the thickness of the beam should be suitable.

Further strength can be obtained by screwing a T shaped metal flitch plate under the carlin and the end of the beam, and by riveting or bolting angled metal plates into the corners between the carlin and the beam. If a pin, flitch plate and angles are all used, great care must be taken in positioning all the fastenings so that they do not foul one another.

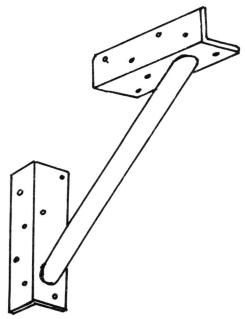

Fig 166 *Welded metal handgrip which can serve as a hanging knee*

Hanging and lodging knees and mast partners

The edge of the deck is the weakest part of a boat's hull (in an engineering sense) as the more or less right-angled joint could be easily distorted by a heavy sea, with virtually all the loading being taken by the joints of the beams into the shelves. Also any planked deck has little resistance to trapezoidal distortion. These potential weaknesses are usually overcome by the provision of grown-oak knees both horizontally between the beams and the shelves, and vertically between the beams and the frames.

One common problem with these knees on old boats is that over the years they change their shape slightly, and pull their fastenings until their effectiveness is greatly reduced. The simplest cure (if the wood is sound) is to remove all fastenings, plug the old holes, reface the knees and refit them. If the fastenings cannot easily be removed, they can usually be cut through with a hacksaw blade poked up behind the knee.

If the original knees have rotted, it may be possible to find good oak crooks to make

new ones, but it is more likely that replacements will have to be laminated.

Knees have always been the traditional way of strengthening the edges of a deck, but an owner with a good knowledge of engineering practice can devise some excellent alternatives to solid oak knees. For example, a length of tubing welded or brazed to two metal angle-sections can be used to replace a hanging knee, and will double as an excellent handgrip (Fig 166).

Lodging knees can be replaced with tubular metal struts across between the beam shelf and the deck beams; any such struts fitted will be found very convenient for hanging up damp clothing etc!

Mast partners are relatively massive chunks of wood set between the deck beams to take the loading of the mast. They are usually socketed into the deck beams, and can be replaced only after the deck planking has been lifted. Attempts to take short cuts here are liable to result in more extensive repairs being necessary later on – and possibly not all that much later. Unless a qualified boat designer or an experienced designer in another mechanical field who sails extensively has agreed that a proposed modification to the original structure will be satisfactory, the best practice if any repairs are needed is to copy exactly the original construction.

Deck planking and canvasing

The deck covering may be sheets of plywood, softwood planks covered with canvas, uncovered pine planking, or a 'yachts' laid deck. Owners, designers and builders of cruising yachts have sought almost endlessly for an ideal deck covering, and as well as the four 'basic' methods have tried almost all combinations of them in an attempt to get a leak-free, durable one. Proprietary variants of canvas have been introduced: either plastic materials which can be spread as a thick liquid and which set to an impervious solid film, or plastic impregnated woven materials which can be glued down over the wooden deck. Teak planks (for durability) laid on plywood (to stop the leaks) have been tried, and fibreglass sheathing over planks and plywood has had its advocates. Modern plastics' technology has attempted to produce new stoppings for laid or planked decks which will not leak. The results of all these efforts have had little success. Some decks, especially those laid in teak – or more recently iroko or afrormosia – and those of planked pitch pine are very durable but tend to leak, which may lead to rot in the deck beams. Others such as a newly canvased or plastic-coated planked deck or a plywood deck do not leak, but have to be classed as non-durable in terms of the eighty or so years' life one can expect from a wooden hull. Canvased or plastic-covered planked decks soon develop annoying leaks, whilst plywood continues to exhibit a regrettable tendency to delaminate if it is frozen.

If an owner has got so fed up with a leaking deck that he has decided to give up repairing the old one and try something different, he must think of the weight of the deck structure. Plywood and canvas over planks are basically lightweight decks, whilst planked or laid decks are usually considerably thicker and heavier. A plywood deck needs no lodging knees on the deck beams, so replacing a plywood deck with any other form can add considerably to the weight at the top of the hull.

Having tried all types except the 'working boat' pitch-pine planking, the author would settle for laid-teak decking, stopped with the flexible rubber compound produced by the International Paint Company Ltd, as giving the best combination of durability and imperviousness. This is also the most expensive way of covering a deck but since, unlike a motor car, a wooden boat can be regarded as a long-term asset, value for money rather than absolute cost should be considered. 'Second best' is probably a canvased deck, which should remain leak-proof until it is chafed in some way or until the working of a deck fitting such as a fairlead starts a small leak, and which is not too difficult or expensive to repair.

As well as weight, leak resistance and durability, the repairability of a deck should be considered. A planked or laid deck can be repaired locally as necessary; a canvased deck will have to be recanvased after replacing any plank, and a plywood deck may

have to be replaced completely. Combinations of plywood and planking or a plastic-sheathed deck will usually involve replacing a large area to cure even a very minor defect. Light planked decks covered with a plastic-coated woven base-material may appear to be repairable by peeling back the sheet of covering material until the damaged plank is exposed, then after replacing the plank the covering can be glued back in place. Unfortunately it is impossible to get the new glue right up to the point at which the original glued joint has been pulled apart by peeling back the covering. Thus when the sheet of material is laid back over the wood there will be a line which is not stuck down properly.

It may be thought that a very small unglued area under the sheet will be of no significance, but this is far from being the case. Any such discontinuity in the glue-line will lead to very high stress concentrations at its edge, as the wood and plastic coating move. These stress concentrations will be more than sufficient to break the glue-line at the edge of the discontinuity, so the unglued area will grow until it reaches an outer surface somewhere. Then water can get in, and the deck will leak, and the water trapped between the covering and the planking may set up rot. Much the same applies to attempts to make local repairs to a canvas-covered deck.

Plywood decks are repaired in exactly the same way as the sides or bottom of a ply hull (page 62). Covered decks are usually planked with fairly broad tongued and grooved planking, nailed to the deck beams. All beadings and deck fittings are removed, the covering is stripped off, and the planks can then be replaced with no difficulty. A minor annoyance is that if the damaged plank is near the centre-line of the boat, all planking out to the edge must be removed so that the tongues can be engaged properly in their grooves. Re-covering the repaired deck with a plastic sheeting is simple enough given sufficient helpers to spread the impact adhesive and to hold the rolled up sheet clear of the tacky adhesive until it can be put down in its correct position.

Recanvasing a deck is not difficult, but

it is as well to try to enlist the help of some-one who has done the job before. A couple of experienced men can cover the deck of a seven-tonner whilst half a dozen enthusi-astic and intelligent but inexperienced amateurs make a fine mess of the foredeck of a 5 m (14 ft) dinghy.

The canvas must first be cut and sewn up to the correct shape to cover the whole area, with an allowance to turn down over the edge of the deck and up round coam-ings etc. The completed canvas is laid in place on the deck and weighted down with ballast pigs laid on clean pieces of wood. An area of the canvas, perhaps the fore-deck, is left unweighted. This area is rolled back, and the deck planking is covered with old paint – most boatyards which worked on wooden boats kept a large tin into which all the odd remnants of paint could be stirred, to give a sticky greyish mess. There should not be too high a percentage of top-coat in the mess, undercoat and deck paint being the best constituents and in these days of epoxy and polyurethane paints, care must be taken to confine the contents of the 'canvasing' tin to the traditional oil-based variety. When the planking is covered with the old paint and the paint is nicely tacky and gooey, the canvas is dampened with plain water, either from a brush or a bottle fitted with a sprinkler, and rolled down carefully into the paint. The edges are pulled tight over the edge of the deck, taking care to avoid creases (which is where experience scores), and tacked to the edges of the deck planking with large-headed copper tacks at about 152 mm (6 in) centres. As soon as the edges nearest the unstuck area are tacked, the remainder of the canvas can be rolled back over the area already done, and the next length (usually the side decks) painted and covered, work-ing on area by area until the whole deck is finished.

It is important that all the canvas be laid before any of the paint can dry, but the haste necessary is not such as to preclude pausing for a cup of coffee. As soon as the canvas is down it must be given a coat of paint. Some people swear that ordinary undercoat must be used, some say that only varnish will do, whilst others use an 'un-loaded' deck paint. Most agree that the first coat should be thinned so that it will pene-trate the canvas properly, and also that the canvas should be dampened to swell the fibres before the paint is applied. This should be done with an almost worn-out stubby old paint-brush so that the paint is pressed down between the fibres of the canvas rather than brushed along over the cloth. Even if the canvas is well soaked it takes a surprising amount of paint to cover it properly.

The entire process is very similar to working with fibreglass: the first layer of old paint is analagous to the gel coat, into which the woven material is laid and then impregnated with further paint (resin). Several books on boatbuilding have des-cribed the process of canvasing a deck in greater or less detail, but nowhere has the author seen mentioned what he has found to be the biggest problem in the whole job, which is getting at the work without making a mess both of the job and of one's clothes or overalls. One can judge the success of the operation by the appearance of the canvas as it is laid and pressed down into the messy paint on the wood. The creamy colour of the new canvas turns greyish as the tacky paint comes up through the weave. If this colour change is uniform, and pushing the canvas down with an old brush or tacking it at the edges does not result in any significant change to the fine mottled colour, then all is well. But if one kneels or stands on the canvas the local pressure-points will bleed too much of the paint through the canvas and on to the operator's trousers, shoes or bare knees.

If one has a large team of helpers, the work can be done with one person in the forehatch, a couple on the cabin top or in the cockpit and others outside the hull so that at least one person can reach every part of the deck, but an owner and one helper working on a beamy 9 m (30 ft) hull without a forehatch have a major problem, unless they have unusually long arms. The area can be covered strip by strip so that the workers – kneeling on the uncovered foredeck and in grave danger of falling off as they work forward – can always reach the area to be painted, but working this way it is very difficult to avoid wrinkles; it is much better to get the canvas spread and tacked down over a reasonable area before any paint is applied over the canvas. On boats whose beam is such that the entire deck area cannot be reached without getting on the deck, the simplest solution is to build a 'working bridge' over the hull with a couple of high trestles and some stout planks.

If sufficient helpers are available, the various beadings round the deck edge and at any coamings etc can be bedded in place with a very soft bedding as soon as the area involved has been painted. If only two people are doing the job, the beadings are fitted after the canvas has been painted. Just as in working with fibreglass, the secret of success lies in getting the whole job finished before any of the first layer of old paint can dry. It is a great help to have all beadings pre-drilled for their fastenings, and positions for tacks to hold the canvas chalked on the planking, cabin sides etc. It is most frustrating to try and put a screw through a beading only to find the head of a tack in the way. Once the beadings are in place, any surplus canvas projecting beyond them is trimmed off with a sharp knife.

A deck can be covered with separate, unsewn pieces of canvas, but only with some risk of subsequent leaking. The overlap between unsewn cloths should always be made in such a direction that any water on the deck will run down over the joint and not into it, in the same way as the slates on the roof of a house are overlapped. Since, unlike houses, boats' decks tend to change their orientation, there will be occasions when water will lodge against the overlapped joints. Unsewn joints in the canvas are sometimes covered with a thin copper strip well-bedded in paint and tacked down through the canvas. If well made, such a joint should usually be good for a season's leak-free sailing, whereas a sewn joint usually lasts very much longer.

The difficulty likely to be experienced in making repairs to planked or laid decks depends on how the boat was built. Most boats with planked decks have covering boards – stout planks cut to shape to follow the sides of the hull. Sometimes these covering boards will be thicker than the rest of the deck planking and the upper surfaces of the deck beams will be stepped to take this extra thickness. The covering boards not only eliminate any exposed end-grain or feather-ends where straight planks would otherwise be cut off at the edge of the hull, they also add very significantly to the hull's overall strength since with the shear strakes and the beam shelf they form a stout curved girder around the otherwise weak edge of the hull. Boats with laid decks usually have a broad, thick kingplank down the centre-line of the hull. Sometimes this kingplank stands proud of the rest of the deck planking, forming a lovely hazard to be tripped over when changing headsails in a rough sea, but more usually its excess thickness is accommodated by notching the deck beams to leave the upper surface flush. The kingplank is usually rebated on its outer edges so that the next deck planks out lie over it (like garboards on an upside-down keel).

The planking between the kingplank and the covering board may be straight laid, with all planks parallel to the kingplank and of uniform width; or it may be laid curved, parallel to the covering board. On curved-laid planking the widths of the planks may vary to maintain a constant radius of curvature (or more or less constant) for each plank. The planks may be nailed or screwed to the deck beams. On ex-working boats, the screws or nails are usually obvious, but on yachts screws would have their heads dowelled over, and nails were usually put in as 'secret' nails run diagonally through the edge of each plank as it was fitted (Fig 167). The ends of straight-laid planks are usually cut off short and the inner edge of the covering board notched to avoid sharp feather-ends on the planks, whilst the ends of curved-laid planks are similarly notched into the kingplank. If the covering board or kingplank are thicker than the rest of the deck planking, with their upper surfaces flush, the notches for the plank-ends form rebates; if they are the same thickness, the notches should form a partial halving joint so that any loading on the plank-end is transferred to the kingplank or covering board.

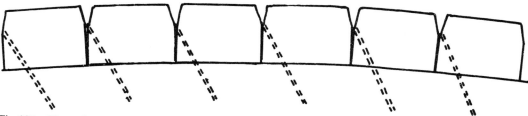

Fig 167 *'Secret' nailing of deck planking*

Working boats were sometimes built without these refinements to the deck, fairly broad straight-run planks simply being cut to fit against the covering board, usually with joggles in the edge of the covering board to avoid feather-ends, but not always. Of the planked decks, a curved-laid deck is easily the best because the curve of the planks adds significantly to the resistance of the top of the hull to any shearing distortion. Not only does it make the hull stronger, its extra strength helps to reduce the chance of leaks as the hull and deck work in a seaway. Since in this life everything has its price, a curved-laid deck is also the hardest and most expensive to fit.

Not unnaturally cheaper methods of construction, in which the plank-ends are not notched and rebated into the covering boards or kingplank, are much more likely to leak than properly laid decks.

Replacement of the plain deck planks on any type of deck is usually simple enough; remove all the stopping and caulking, find the fastenings and remove the old plank, cut and fit new plank. There are two problems. First is finding the fastenings if the deck is secret nailed; after which judicious use of oak wedges between the deck beams and the plank to be removed will usually force the plank out. Remember that a curved-plank deck is laid from the outside working in to the centre, so the nails will be on the inner edges of the planks; whereas a straight-laid deck is put down from the centre outwards, so the nails will be on the outer edges of the planks. It is at this point that an owner might discover that his deck planking has dumps or pins set in edgewise between adjacent planks, which means either fitting a graving piece into the damaged plank or replacing a minimum of three planks. The first plank out will have

to be cut or broken up to allow it to be pulled away from fastenings into both edges and the deck beams. Without replacing the whole deck, it is impossible to put edge fastenings into the last plank back on a local repair job.

The second problem is found in curved-laid decks, where it can be very difficult indeed to get the replacement plank into the curved gap without damage to the edges. The solution here is to place blocks of wood on the deck, cut carefully to length to run from the bulwarks or toe-rail to the outer edge of the slot. The plank to be inserted is then laid against these blocks and its middle is pressed outwards and wedged back to the cabin side, forehatch, or any other suitable strongpoints. Once the plank has been forced to the correct curvature over the slot, it is quite simple to push it down into place without any damage either to the new plank or to the edges of the old ones. When a plank is being forced into a curve in this way, it is important to make sure that all the blocks and wedges used are bearing squarely against whatever is used to support their outer ends, and that a line from outer support-point to outer support-point passes through the new plank and not below it. If the supports are allowed to follow the curve of a cambered deck, so that the end-to-end line can pass below the plank, the whole system will be unstable and, as the plank is bent, both planks and support blocks will fly out with considerable violence (Fig 168). Another point to watch is that as the plank is bent it will tend to draw the ends of the outer support-blocks inwards and the set-up may become unstable. This can usually be countered by angling the outer supports slightly outwards initially.

If the boat has no bulwarks or toe-rail

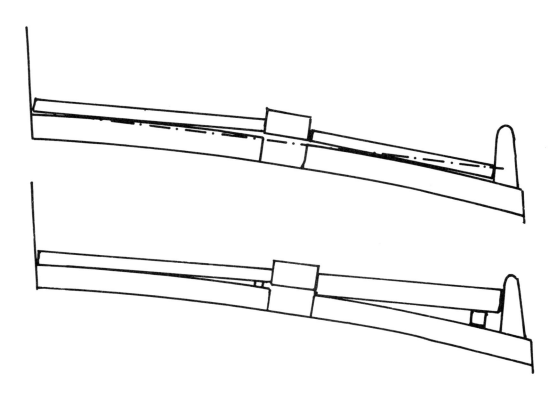

Fig 168 *Wedging a curved-laid deck plank into place: note that the upper arrangement is unstable and the plank will probably spring upwards rather violently. The lower arrangement is stable*

against which blocks can be wedged, posts can be stood up either side of the hull, with both upper and lower ends of the posts lashed together with wire or terylene ropes. If the hull is a reasonably fair shape, a support for each end of the plank will usually suffice.

If only part of a plank (or parts of several planks) is to be replaced, a butt joint over a butt plate can be used at each end; or a shallow-angle, short stopped scarph over a deck beam can be used. Such a joint is really half-way between a lap or halving joint and a scarph, and should be used only where the deck planks are reasonably thick. Two fastenings should be run through the joint into the deck beam.

If the kingplank on a straight-laid deck requires replacement, it may be necessary to replace the plank either side as well if the kingplank has rebated edges; but if the kingplank on a curved-laid deck has to be

replaced, the whole deck will have to be relaid. 'Bodge' type repairs could be made, but 'patching up' a curved-laid deck should be classed as a form of vandalism!

Covering boards do not pose so many problems, as a new covering board can be slipped in beneath the ends of a straight laid deck without having to disturb all the planks. With a curved-laid deck there is no problem with covering boards – other than those involved in producing some 9 m (30 ft) or so of plank with 1.2 m (4 ft) of 'bow' to the middle.

The biggest problem with covering boards is usually that owners (and many shipwrights) fail to appreciate the contribution a properly fitted covering board makes to to the strength of the hull, and they replace damaged sections piece by piece, often with no attempt whatsoever to ensure any real continuity of strength along the boards. All too often one sees covering boards which

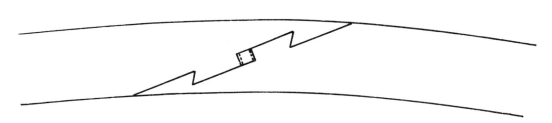

Fig 169 *Hooked and wedged scarph joint in a covering board*

have been 'repaired' by setting in a new, short length of timber, sometimes with a butt plate underneath, but sometimes butting onto the original over a deck beam, with the butt joints caulked and payed. If both covering boards have been cut about in this way, much of the strength of the whole deck structure may have been lost and it may work badly and leak in a seaway. There is no need to replace an entire covering board if only a short length has been damaged, but the new section must be fitted properly with a joint which will give the best possible continuity of strength along the board. The best way to joint in a new section is with a hooked and wedged scarph (Fig 169). These joints need to be cut carefully and accurately, especially if a new piece is being joined in the middle of a covering board and two joints must be fitted simultaneously. Before starting to set in a new length, the original should be examined to see where it was joined since most boats had their covering boards made from three or four lengths joined together.

Replacement of a portion of a covering board may be complicated by bulwark stanchions passing through it. Often the need for replacement will have been caused by these stanchions, as the point at which they pass through the board is one of the most likely places to find rot in a wooden hull. All the stanchions must be removed before the covering board can be replaced, and square holes to take new stanchions will have to be cut in the board before it can be fitted.

Replacement covering boards should be cut either from teak or iroko. Iroko is not found to any great extent on older boats simply because it was a relatively unknown timber in the earlier years of this century.

But there can be little doubt that, had it been readily available in earlier years, it would have been used extensively on boats where teak was regarded as too expensive.

The covering boards should be well secured to the shear strakes, either with barbed nails, screws or, on larger boats, dumps or trenails.

If the whole deck is in poor condition, an owner might decide to replace all the deck planking, possibly retaining the original kingplank and (less likely) the covering boards. In this case, it is worth having a critical look at the width of planking to be used. A curved-laid deck does not usually leave much room for choice; the planks will be fairly narrow so that they can be bent into position without too much force. It should however be noted that if a curved-laid deck is to be laid with all planks of uniform width, the bend radius of the innermost plank must determine the plank width usable. If a width is chosen which will bend easily to the curvature of the inner face of the covering board, all planks will have to be tapered in slightly towards their ends to maintain the same amount of bending on all planks.

Curved planks must be laid in pairs, one each side of the boat, working inwards from the covering boards. The way in which the planks are fitted will depend on the deck plan of the boat. If the first two or three planks in from the covering board can sweep right round from the foredeck, clear of all hatches, cabin sides, cockpit coamings etc, to run off over a transom (or counter) stern, they will be fitted starting from the forward end. Planks which run out beside the cabin or cockpit are more easily fitted starting at their aft end, with the forward end cut off to fit into the kingplank when the new plank has been bent to the required curvature and screwed or nailed down for most of its length, leaving the forward end sprung up just enough to cut the joint. Since the planks should be fitted in pairs, one on each side, the pair on which the joints are being cut can be held in to their correct curvature by a lashing across the foredeck about 300 mm (1 ft) short of where the ends are to be cut. The plank edges are protected with thin wooden packing pieces from being nipped by the lashing. When cutting joints on the end of planks which are sprung up out of position, it is as well to slide a sheet of plywood under the plank-end being cut so as to protect the kingplank from accidental damage.

As the planks are fitted they can be held out to contact the next plank out by clamps, blocks and wedges as in Fig 82, until they can be fastened down to the beams. The free ends of the pair of planks being fitted can be pulled in towards one another by a rope lashing.

It may seem that a straight-laid deck will be very much easier to fit than curved-laid, firstly because there is no bending, secondly because the planks can be wider and there will be fewer of them. This is true, but it is not the whole truth. Whilst the straight-laid deck is easier to fit, it does not have the great resistance to wringing and shearing stresses of a curved-laid deck. Wider and fewer planks can be used, but it must be remembered that the changes in width of the planks as they are alternately soaked and dried by the sun and wind will be greater on wider planks, and the seams will be more likely to leak. The mathematically minded can try plotting graphs of the total length of seams in the deck and the probability of any given seam leaking, against the plank-width used. The inconvenience and risk of rot involved with deck leaks can then be evaluated against the extra work in fitting narrower planks. For a cruising yacht, the usual result of such considerations is that the deck planks will be much the same width whether the decks are laid curved or straight.

It has been argued that many working boats were built with fairly wide deck planks, which is perfectly true. But it has to be borne in mind that leaks through the deck into a fish-hold are of slightly less consequence than leaks into what is meant for a comfortable cruising home!

Once the width of planking to be used has been determined, the method of fastening can be chosen. Secret nailing looks the neatest, and if pins are used to side-fasten adjacent planks as they are fitted it gives a very strong deck. However repairs and replacements are difficult, and since accidents can and do happen, the author would always opt for screws with their heads dowelled over. Only one screw through each plank into each deck beam is necessary, the screws being set one-third of the width of the plank in from the edge, alternating the sides for alternate deck beams. If a whole deck is to be laid, with screws dowelled over, it is well worth making a combined countersink and counterboring tool. This is simply a length of carbon steel of appropriate diameter with its end turned to the profile of a short pin to fit the drilled screw-hole, followed by an angle to form the countersink with a further parallel portion to allow the head of the screw to fit below the face of the dowel (Fig 170). After turning the end, four grooves are filed to leave four cutting edges, and the tool can then be hardened and tempered.

A dowel cutter can be made from a piece of steel tubing which is an easy fit over the counterboring tool, with half a dozen cutting edges filed on one end. The cutter should be made from carbon steel and hardened and tempered, but the author cut about 1,000 iroko dowels with a plain mild-steel cutter, unhardened. The dowels are cut by running the toothed end of the tube into the face of an offcut of the timber used for the planking. Dowels can be cut into both sides of the offcut, and cutting the dowels and their subsequent removal from the block are both made easier if successive cuts are allowed to overlap by about half the width of the cut.

The dowels can be broken off the block with the aid of a sharp chisel, their flat end is dipped into a tin of glue, and they are then tapped into the counterbores. Resorcinol glue can be used, but a better-

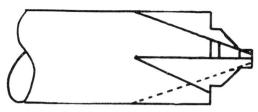 

Fig 170 *Combined countersink and counter-boring tool*

looking job results if a colourless urea formaldehyde is used.

As soon as the glue has set, any surplus length of dowel should be trimmed off. The cross-grain dowels are very liable to break off if they are knocked sideways, and if they are not properly trimmed they may get broken, in which case one can be sure that the break will occur just below the surface of the plank!

Bulwarks

One often hears a crew member, sailing for the first time on an older wooden-hulled boat with bulwarks instead of wire guard-lines, say, 'There's something about a real boat with bulwarks'. Often he is right: there is – rot! The sad thing is that so many owners appear to accept rotted bulwark stanchions and covering boards as inevitable, which they most certainly are not. If the waterways below the bulwarks are kept clear, and the wedges around the stanchions are replaced annually, there is no more reason for rot there than there is round the mast or a hatch.

Bulwark stanchions are usually made of oak, and they should be through-bolted to a frame head inside the hull. Sometimes they form the uppermost member of a double frame as in Fig 105, but when they do the planking should not be fastened to them. The holes in the covering board through which the stanchions pass should be cut oversize and the gaps closed with wooden wedges driven hard in. The side-planking of the bulwarks should leave an adequate waterway all round the stanchions so that there is nowhere for water to get trapped. One sometimes sees bulwark planking fitted right down to the covering board, with rounded-end cut-outs midway

between stanchions. Whilst this may look prettier than a plain plank set with its lower edge 38 mm (1½ in) or more clear of the deck, it is simply asking for trouble. Bulwarks should be fitted with a capping rail wider than the stanchions, so that no end-grain of the oak stanchions – which will almost inevitably have some small splits or cracks – is exposed to rain.

Properly fitted bulwarks and stanchions should present no problems in repair work. On any working boats, bulwarks are very likely to get damaged, and they were usually built so that they could be repaired or replaced quickly and cheaply.

Superstructure

Most of the work on the superstructure of a wooden boat, in which the cockpit can be included, is largely a matter of common sense. When any repairs are necessary, it is mainly a matter of dismantling the structure until the damaged part is reached, then replacing and rebuilding as before. Sometimes an owner may decide to alter the superstructure of his boat, either by adding a doghouse to an existing cabin, by adding a coachroof to an old working boat, or by removing a coachroof from an ex-working boat which had previously been converted (or perverted) to a yacht. Whenever such alterations are contemplated, care must be taken to preserve as far as possible the transverse strength of the top of the hull. Several owners have thought that the bridge deck between the cockpit and cabin hatch on their boat was a nuisance, and have removed it to give 'walk in' access from cockpit to cabin, only to discover later that the cabin and cockpit sides crack, the side-decks leak, and even the hull springs leaks at the turn of the bilge – simply because in removing the bridge deck they cut through the two deck beams which held the aft half of the hull in shape.

Most older boats have their coachroofs as 'built on additions' sitting on top of strong carlins which, had the boat been a working vessel, would have surrounded the hatch. The hull and deck structure of these boats does not depend on the coachroof for its strength, and the coachroof need be strong enough only to ensure that it cannot be torn off or knocked in by a rogue wave (which means quite strong). Alterations to the superstructure of such boats can be carried out as required. However some designers and builders recognised that the traditional construction is wasteful of material for what it does, and there are boats whose cabin sides and cockpit thwarts etc are designed to be integral parts of the deck structure, adding considerably to the overall strength of the hull. Before any alterations to the superstructure of any boat are started, a thorough check must therefore be made to ensure that the proposed changes will not in any way reduce the hull's strength. The story of the captain who objected to an obstructive pillar in his stateroom and ordered the shipwrights to cut it out, only to find his mizzen mast collapse, is an old and hoary one, but it contains a very sound moral for the would-be boat 'improver'. Fortunately, these days the trend is to restore older boats to their original condition rather than to convert them to something their designer never intended.

Repairs to a cockpit or cabin structure can be needed because the wood has split badly or rot is suspected. Many yachts have their coachroof sides cut from a single broad plank, which is often supported by vertical framing only at its two ends, and may be pierced for a number of deadlights. It is far from uncommon to find splits open up between the deadlights, and if two splits occur between the same pair of lights, the piece between the splits can be knocked in. The easiest cure for such splits is to chisel the afflicted area to clean edges, and fit large graving pieces in the same way as a strip-planked hull can be repaired. Care must be taken to use well-seasoned timber for any such pieces.

Any large deadlights set into cabin sides weaken the structure, and if large 'picture windows' are wanted, the cabin side should be properly framed. Tough transparent plastic can be used for large-area lights, and can contribute some of the structural strength provided they are fitted in adequately strengthened recesses and are securely bolted in place.

Rot may be found in cabin sides at the top where water has penetrated the cabin-top canvas and run down to the side. Sometimes the rot may have started at a badly fitted beading. The best repair is usually a large graving piece or patch set in; or an entire new top half can be glued onto the affected cabin side, following the principles of repairing a transom. Whenever a part of a cabin side is replaced in this way, it is as well to fit some vertical framing on the inside if the original was an unreinforced single piece of wood. An ingenious owner can usually manage to disguise any such internal framing by building on a little locker to hold cigarettes or some other 'light stores', or by using the frame as a base to mount a mirror, an electric-light fitting or some similar semi-luxury.

Whenever rot is found in the upper portion of a cabin side or front, the beams and cabin-top planking near the area must be examined thoroughly to check that they are free from rot, and also to find the cause of the rot if at all possible. This will usually be found to be fresh water penetrating and lodging somewhere.

Repairs to the upper half of cabin sides etc are fairly straightforward, but if rot is found in the bottom of a structure, at deck level, life can get much more complicated. The method adopted to effect repairs will depend on the original construction. Sometimes it is possible to remove an entire coachroof structure from the carlins, replace the affected area, and then refit the coachroof. If this is not possible, the repair will have to be done in the form of a large graving piece with reinforcing frames. Sometimes the complete cabin side or front may have to be replaced, following the original construction as closely as possible.

Beadings

Beadings fitted on a boat at such points as the deck edge, between decks and cabin sides, hatches etc, have an ornamental function in that they break what would otherwise be a sharp, harsh angle; but they have a very much more important technical function in acting as a seal over an edge which might otherwise leak. Deck-edge or cabin-top beadings may also be holding down the edges of a canvas or plastic covering, or they may be sealing the exposed edges of plywood sheets.

The fitting of such beadings should present no problems or offer any pitfalls for the unwary; but it is astonishing how often one finds, on starting work on a boat, that beadings have been badly, even stupidly fitted. The classic example is a neat half-round deck-edge beading round the edge of a canvased deck (or cabin top). All too often this is a flat-backed half-round bead, fitted 40 per cent over the canvas and its tacks and 60 per cent over the planking (or cabin side). Since the flat beading will not fit over two levels simultaneously, it often ends up touching the planking at the bottom and the edge of the canvas just above the middle, leaving a nice gap at the top, just waiting to collect rain water and start rotting the deck and shear strake.

If that pitfall is avoided, many such beadings have the screws holding them run into the joint between the top of the shear strake and the underside of the deck planking. Such screws offer little holding power, and if the deck is nailed on they tend to lift the deck away from the hull. Little better are screws which are put in so close to the upper edge of the shear strake that they simply split the edge off the plank.

The removal of a few such beadings can make an owner, embarked on what he thought would be a fairly minor recanvasing exercise, decide that some major structural rebuilding may be highly desirable.

Properly fastened beadings can still pose problems. They should be bedded down into a soft bedding material, which keeps the nicely fitting beading in watertight contact with the joint or edge it is sealing – which it does for a while. But water and sun over the years swell and shrink the beading until the thin film of bedding compound which was not squeezed out when the beading was fitted dries and gives up the unequal struggle, and the beading needs cleaning off and rebedding. Sometimes this becomes obvious only after water has penetrated behind the beading and rotting of the cabin side or deck starts.

The author's cure for the problems of beadings which dry out away from the edge or angle they are covering, is to cut the beading (or the edge) so that a hollow is left behind it which will remain filled with soft bedding material whilst the edges of the beading can bear hard against the wood they are sealing. Thus the back of a half-round beading for a deck or coachroof edge is planed to a slight hollow curve, and beadings which fit into internal angles are planed to a more obtuse angle. Fitting the half-round beadings is easy enough, but with angled beadings care must be taken to see that some gap is left below each face right in the corner and that neither face is actually bearing against the wood it is sealing other than at its outer edge. Fitted with a generous quantity of soft bedding to ensure that the hollow is totally filled and screwed very hard home – with all screws well into solid wood and not near the edge of one piece – such beadings will remain watertight for years. The author always used a builder's material, Secomastic, to bed down such beadings, and up to eight years (which was the oldest such beadings he ever had occasion to remove) the Secomastic remained flexible and very sticky.

Beadings look nice if all the screw heads are dowelled over. But the author preferred to leave the screw heads flush with or just below the surface of the beading, so that if it ever became necessary the screws could be hardened down by half a turn. However, this was never found to be necessary when well-seasoned iroko or mahogany was used for the beadings.

Chapter 14

Caulking, stopping and painting

Caulking

In some ways, caulking seams can be likened to the choosing, storing and drinking of wines. In both there is an element of mysticism, and 'experts' have pronounced at length on the 'right' way the job should be done. In both, many people go against the advice of the 'experts' with apparently satisfactory results; and in both one hears of or observes instances where disregard of 'expert' principles has led to some form of disaster.

The first thing to be borne in mind is that circumstances alter cases. The *vin du pays* which goes so nicely with the illegally caught trout of a scratch picnic lunch would certainly not be the drink to accompany the *truite aux amandes* at the Lord Mayor's Banquet. Similarly, seams can be seen caulked with quite a variety of materials and tools, from old coir rope put in with a large bricklayer's chisel to a torn-up shirt inserted with a screwdriver.

The essential element of caulking is to get into the seam a line of fibrous material which will swell when it gets wet, and which will not spew out of the seam when the hull starts to work in a seaway. Very few, if any, would disagree that proper caulking cotton, put in with the aid of a full set of caulking irons hit by a split-head caulking mallet is the best way of dealing with the seams of any reasonable sized cruising boat; but it must be remembered it is not the only way. The author was shown how to put in caulking cotton by three different shipwrights, and it was interesting to note that, whilst the broad principles used by the three were similar, each had his own individual differences in method. Since seams caulked by all three remained leak-free for many years, it must be acknowledged that variations in the process are quite acceptable.

Caulking is, apart from the noise, one of the nicer jobs on a boat. It is not a dirty job, and it cannot be rushed. Probably the biggest disadvantage is that on a boat of any size there is rather a lot of it. Whilst caulking, the worker can profitably be mentally assessing the rest of the work to be done, because once a good rhythm of work has been established it does not demand a great deal of mental effort, though some concentration is needed if sore fingers are to be avoided. The best way of learning is to watch a skilled shipwright at work, and then to practise on some off-cut planks nailed to a couple of suitable uprights.

Basically, the drill is to pull out from the ball of caulking cotton a suitable length of the very lightly laid rope. A ball with six strands to the rope is handy since three strands are what is generally needed for seams on the average small or medium sized cruising boat. 'Suitable length' is about 30 per cent greater than the length of seam to be caulked. The strands are separated out, and the required number are twisted up to make a loose rope. The twisting is most easily done by folding back the ends of the strands, twisting the folds tightly together and gripping them in the chuck of a wheelbrace. The easiest way to get a uniform twist down the whole length of the rope is for the worker to stand as high up as is reasonably practicable, either on a high trestle or on the deck of a boat hauled up ashore, with the rope to be twisted spread out straight in front. The wheelbrace is then turned at moderate speed, and waved up and down so that as the rope is twisted the wave travels along its length – just as one could shake a kink into a skipping rope. The far end of the length being twisted can be left attached to the ball, or can be held down by a ballast pig or heavy stone.

Enlarging the accommodation on the ninety-year-old cutter, Sea Breeze:

(upper left) *Metal strap floors fitted over a low centreplate case with metal mast step welded into floor structure. Raising the deck:* (upper right) *frames cut, stem cut back and entire deck assembly raised on chain hoists;* (lower left) *new* top scarphed on stem, and frames extended, larch planks lying in foreground ready to fit; (lower right) *quarter view of hull of* Sea Breeze *with the whole deck raised and hull ready for launching* (S. Lindsey-Wood)

This beautiful, unidentified half-decked cutter is of c1880 vintage (so is photograph). One or two examples of this design (inspired by West Coast of Scotland fishing boats) are still to be seen in the Crinan area (courtesy of Graham E. Langmuir)

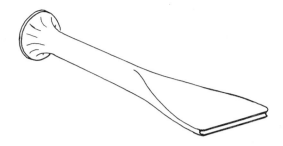

Fig 171   *Caulking iron*

Twisting must be stopped before the rope is at all 'hard'; usually it will start to form secondary twists on itself when it is about right. If the twists do not run reasonably uniformly from end to end, they may have to be helped along by giving the middle of the rope a few twists between the palms of the hands.

The rope is then hammered into the seam in a series of small loops. Some workers run straight along the seam in one go, catching up successive short lengths of the cotton with the end of the iron and knocking them in; others prefer to make larger bights at 51–76 mm (2–3 in) intervals and then go a second time down the seam closing in these bights. Care must be taken not to cut the rope with the iron, and not to hammer the cotton right through, especially on light hulls with thin planks. A narrow-bladed, blunt-ended iron is usually used, held against the lay of the cotton so that it drives in the loops but cannot cut them. The cotton is then hardened down into the seams to a uniform depth with a broader grooved-ended iron (Fig 171).

The garboard seam is left until last. On transom-sterned boats the work is started at the transom on the uppermost seam, driving the cotton well into the seam leaving an end which can be cut off flush. When the stem is reached the rope is split, and (on a three-strand rope) two strands are taken up past the end of the plank above, and one strand is taken down. The ends are cut off after they have passed the end of the next plank up (or down), and are driven well into the seam. Finally the garboard seam is caulked, continuing up the stem over the end-strands of all the other seams. The caulking can then be hammered well

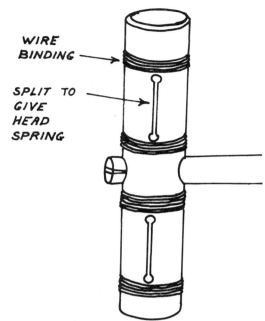

Fig 172   *Sprung-head caulking mallet*

into the garboard seam and up the stem because, as these seams are in rebates, it is impossible to drive the cotton right through the seam.

If only a portion of a seam is to be re-caulked, the old caulking should be withdrawn for a length of 0.6–1 m (2–3 ft). The individual strands are separated and cut to different lengths, and the twisted end of the new cotton is married in. Anybody who is genuinely ambidextrous is always at a great advantage when working on a boat – a job which is easily done right-handed on one side of the hull will be equally easy left-handed on the other side. However caulking is one job for which any worker must learn to work either-handed, or must learn to work both 'forwards' and 'backwards'.

Although proper caulking irons are indisputably the right tools for the job, if none are available a reasonable substitute can be made by grinding a groove into a blunted metalworker's or builder's chisel with about a 51 mm (2 in) edge and radiusing off all sharp corners (Fig 171). A proper caulking mallet (Fig 172) makes the work easier, as the splits in the head give a noticeable spring, and prevent the worker's arm from

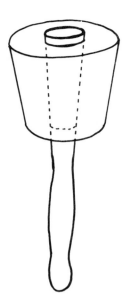

Fig 173 *Simple 'dead headed' mallet which can be used for caulking*

pitch, melted and run in hot from a ladle with a narrow spout. The seams were slightly overfilled, then when the pitch had cooled the surplus was cleaned off to leave neat black lines between the planks. Paying with hot pitch requires considerable patience and a steady hand, and unfortunately it often leaves small air bubbles in the pitch at which leaks can start. Natural movement of the deck planks also helps to generate leaks in the pitch. One rather neat way of curing minor leaks in seams on a laid deck is to melt the pitch locally with a soldering iron, running in a little more either by holding a small block of pitch against the iron or by chipping flakes off a block and laying them over the seam before the iron is run along. A 60 or 100W electric iron is the ideal tool for the job, but a tinsmith's iron heated by a blowlamp or primus stove can be used provided it is not too hot. Some owners prefer to use marine glue for deck seams instead of pitch, but it is considerably dearer and no easier to run in.

tiring nearly so quickly. However, for anybody accustomed to using a 'dead headed' mallet or an ordinary hammer, the much greater head length of a caulking mallet can prove an embarrassment and can result in a lot of mis-strikes. The author was given a very nice 'dead headed' small maul (Fig 173) with a conical-section head which proved to be very good indeed for caulking provided it was held loosely so that the impact shock was not transferred to the hand or wrist. Having a circular head, it did not matter which way on the maul was held, and it was the inertia of the swinging head which did the work, the wrist muscles merely initiating the swing and the loose grip allowing the handle to swing free for the last few degrees before it hit. Anybody who has access to a wood-turning lathe could make one in an evening. The shipwright who made the author's said that the head was made from the root-end of an old apple tree, on a beech handle.

Stopping

Stopping can be almost as contentious a subject as caulking, and most experienced workers have their own special recipes. Deck seams were traditionally payed with

Since the last war, efforts have been made to find better ways of stopping deck seams with compounds which will remain flexible enough to allow for natural movement of the deck, which will not harden and crack, and yet will not move out of the seams or stick to people's feet. Synthetic rubbery compounds seemed to offer excellent possibilities, and in the 1960s one compound appeared to offer the final answer. On a trial deck panel, it was possible to remove the planks from the beams once the compound had set, leaving the teak planks glued together by the stopping compound, which was flexible enough to act as a hinge. This sample remained in excellent condition for many years, stored in a garage, but on boats' decks left out in the sun, irradiation with ultra-violet rays altered the structure to a hard, brittle type of rubber and cracks up to 6 mm ($\frac{1}{4}$ in) wide across the seams opened up in the second year. However, a very much more expensive synthetic rubber compound produced by the International Paint Company appeared to retain its flexibility and adhesion to the wood over an eight-year trial period. The only problem with such modern synthetic compounds is that it may not be possible to clean out the seams of an old boat to the point at which a good chemical bond can be guaranteed. An owner who lays a new deck must resolve for himself whether to gamble on using new technology, which might be expensive and which might fail in a way that might not permit of easy and cheap repair, or whether to use well tried and tested techniques and put up with their known disadvantages.

It is in topside seams that one finds the greatest variety of compounds, and most chandlers stock tubes of 'goo' with names which suggest suitability for such stopping. Some set hard, and some are so flexible as to make it difficult to get a decent paint finish over them. Most such proprietary stoppings tend to be expensive, and little if at all better than many of the traditional recipes, which may be based on beeswax, rosin or linseed-oil putty. The author was always very satisfied with the mixture made up in his local boatyard, which was largely linseed-oil putty and red-lead powder, with a bit of grease and possibly other additives. This was easy to work with, firm enough to paint over, but retained enough softness to 'give' as the wood swelled. When old seams were raked out, the stopping was not nearly as brittle as that in seams stopped with some proprietary stoppings or with plain putty.

The action of putting stopping into topside or bottom seams is difficult to describe, but easily learnt. Roughly it can be summed up as 'Roll the stopping in, then smooth it off'. This, on a complete hull, is another somewhat long task which demands little thought or physical effort.

Painting

Those who require advice on painting should read the literature published by the major paint manufacturers. All the details of which paints to use and how best to apply them have been written up by experts; in particular the International Paint Company have published some very comprehensive booklets. In most boatyards, owners argue over the relative merits of the old-fashioned oil-based paints and the newer

polyurethanes or epoxy-based paints, but world circumnavigator Peter Tangvald claimed that the best approach to paint and varnish was not to use them at all, but to dose the boat regularly with an animal or vegetable oil. He advocated whale oil, but after some correspondence with him, the author decided that linseed oil would smell better. It was tried on several areas that would normally have been varnished, and found to be a most satisfactory finish in that it can be applied while out sailing; but it does lack the lovely gloss of newly varnished wood.

Although others may well disagree, the author has always felt that the older oil-based paints are best for wooden boats, as they more readily allow the moisture-content of the timber to change and hence are less likely to allow the timber to retain a high moisture-content which could encourage rot. As a test, some squares of well-seasoned 13 mm ($\frac{1}{2}$ in) cedar were stored in a desiccating chamber for about a month, then covered with ordinary marine paint (metallic pink priming, undercoat, then enamel), epoxy based paint, polyurethane, and a good-quality yacht varnish, all carefully applied to the makers' instructions. The samples were all weighed on a laboratory balance, then plasticine dams were built on the upper surface of each sample and filled with water. After about another month the samples were cleaned and weighed. The epoxy paint appeared impervious, but the other samples had all absorbed moisture. Another weighing a week later showed that the moisture-content of the enamelled and varnished samples had fallen, but the polyurethane-coated sample had lost little if any moisture. Since boats have a nasty habit of damaging their paintwork, and any damage will let in moisture, it seems wise to use a finish which will let it out again.

For underwater finish, the usual choices are tar (or black varnish), antifouling, or a metallic paint such as 'hard racing copper'. The easiest way to choose is to observe other boats as they are hauled out for the winter, and to adopt the finish which appears to show the best results in the area where the boat is to be kept. On cruising yachts which are being fitted out for ocean voyaging, the expense of copper sheathing is probably justifiable. The process of sheathing a hull with copper is not described here, because it is a job which must be done properly and the amateur who can cope with sheathing will not be seeking advice from this book.

Over years of trying new finishes in the hopes of finding one that really will give a good result with little effort, the author has come to the conclusion that there is no substitute for hard work in the preparation of the surface, and that many coats carefully rubbed down yield the best results. Rubbing down is most easily done with wet and dry emery paper, and the work is greatly facilitated if the area being rubbed down is kept continuously wet with a hose dribbling water over it. The hose can be held in the hand holding the emery paper on its block, and large areas can be rubbed down without the paper getting clogged up as happens if it is just dipped in a bucket of water every so often.

Bedding compounds and preservatives

Most of the older school of shipwrights seem to have their own recipes for bedding and stopping compounds, the commonest of which usually start with a basis of either raw linseed oil and red or white lead, or pitch or gasworks' tar. Beeswax and grease tend to feature prominently among the advised additives. The essentials for a good bedding are that it should be soft enough for any surplus to squeeze out of a joint but not so soft that it will run, fall or creep out on its own. It should dry out slightly, so that it can be painted over, but it should never set hard. Also it must have no adverse effects on wood or any of the commonly used metals, and for anything other than work down in the bilges it must not bleed through or discolour any paint put over it.

Stopping has similar requirements, but must have enough 'body' to stay put in a seam or over a screw head. Obviously, it is essential that beddings and stoppings are not affected by water.

For amateur use, which often means very occasional use, it is useful to have a bedding or stopping compound which will not harden if it is stored for a long time before use. This is the main failing of the various linseed-oil based putty compounds; they do dry out if not used when they are fairly freshly mixed. The products of Messrs Secomastic Ltd of Bracknell, Berkshire, are excellent for use as bedding compounds, but are a trifle too soft to use for stopping. As they are normally supplied in cartridges for use in proper dispensers, air cannot get to the main mass of the compound, and cartridges can be stored for years.

The requirements for good bedding and stopping materials can be met by a wide variety of compounds, and it is most unwise to suggest that any of the traditional recipes are wrong. Many of them have withstood the test of time, and if an old shipwright swears that it is the scales of fresh caught mackerel that make his 'patent' bedding so effective, it is not worth arguing. Who knows, one day some chemist may find out that there is some trace element present in these odd additives which acts as a catalyst and gives the compound its special properties.

Wood preservatives offer the novice another bewildering field. Here there can be no doubt that fresh, dry air, salt water, and linseed oil are major ingredients. Oil and paraffin appear to help. One hears stories of old hulls decaying away to leave the engine bearers, a few frames and the planking below the engine still relatively sound. There can be little doubt that a coal or coke stove aboard a boat, used regularly in cold, damp weather, does help to ensure good ventilation and keeps the boat dry below. Fresh water is bad for boats, and the old dodge of strategically placed blocks of rock salt is probably effective in that they would convert any condensation or rain water to brine.

The salts of copper and other non-ferrous metals are alleged to be good for wooden boats. Since they tend to be highly poisonous, especially if compounds of mercury, they probably are very effective in killing off fungi and other forms of life which regard wood as a valuable addition to their diet. There are various proprietary wood preservatives available, of which the author always used Cuprinol (clear), but any owner who feels he has a problem which needs curing by the correct application of a good preservative or rot inhibitor should consult an expert such as John Perryman of Lowestoft.

Part four
Spars and rigging

Chapter 15

Spars

Masts, booms, gaffs, bowsprits, topsail yards etc, all have to withstand bending and compressive stresses. Many boats have hollow masts, some have hollow booms, and a few have hollow gaffs and topsail yards. Some boats of up to about 10 tonnes (tons) have hollow upper spars of bamboo, which may suffer from long splits extending along several sections. If the bamboo is not distorted and the fibres are not broken, a split bamboo yard can be 'repaired' by binding it with a roll of electrical insulation tape, but otherwise damaged bamboo spars are best replaced. Other repairs to booms, gaffs and bowsprits can be handled in the same way as those to masts. Solid spars can be made from a full tree-trunk, cut from a solid baulk which does not include the centre of the tree, or laminated from two or more pieces of wood. Hollow spars may be made from very thin veneer rolled into a tube, may be built up in simple box fashion from four planks, made from two carved halves glued together, or may be built up from shaped segments.

Masts are sometimes circular in cross-section, but hollow masts or built-up masts are more usually pear-shaped or oval, though square sections with rounded-off corners, rectangular sections, and even basically triangular sections can all be found. Other spars tend to be more circular, but rectangular- or oval-section booms are not uncommon. The first rule in any repair work on spars should be to try and keep to the original shape, unless the boat was badly rigged.

The design of new masts and rigs is beyond the scope of this book, and it is assumed that the work to be done will be repairing or copying an existing spar. One thing all spars have in common is that they must be made from good quality, clean, straight-grained timber, usually pine or spruce.

Solid masts

Broadly these can be divided into two distinct classes: those for gaff rig, and those for more modern Bermudian rig. On gaff masts, the upper ends of the shrouds usually loop round the mast, resting on hound cheeks and bolsters bolted on either side of the spar, and on a grommet laid on a shoulder at the masthead, whereas on Bermudian masts the shrouds are usually shackled or pinned onto metal tangs which either form part of a mastband or are bolted onto the side of the mast. A Bermudian mast will also have either a track for the mainsail slides, often fitted on a wooden 'bone' running up the back of the mast, or a luff groove.

There are exceptions. Some gaff masts have their rigging shackled to metal tangs, and one Bermudian-rigged boat owned by the author had its lower shrouds resting on chocks, with a cut-out in the bone behind the track through which the eyes passed. A 1 m (3 ft) section of the mast track was removable so that the shrouds could be put on and taken off. Generally the gaff mast is likely to be a grown tree whilst a Bermudian mast is more likely to be cut from a baulk of spruce or made up from two or more pieces glued together. Many older solid masts have a hole in the top, closed by a wooden plug. These holes were put in so that the mast could be 'fed' with linseed oil or some other wood preservative at regular intervals.

A solid mast may be in need of repair through damaged or loose fittings, through being broken, or because of rot – often started at a loose fitting. If rot is the cause of the trouble, the best course of action will probably be to make a new mast, especially on 'grown tree' masts, along which rot seems to travel at an alarming rate. All

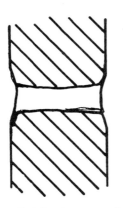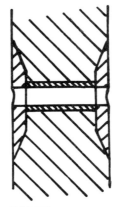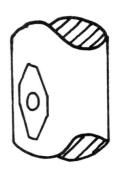

Fig 174   *Reinforcing a worn hole in a solid mast*

too often by the time it is realised that there is rot in a solid mast, the centre of the spar will be too far gone for any simple repair to be effective. If a grown spar is to be replaced, John Leather's book *Gaff Rig* should be consulted.

Shakes (longitudinal cracks) in grown masts can be a source of worry, but provided they are clean, do not extend right in to the centre of the spar, and do not run behind any fittings where they could form water-traps, they are not harmful. Shakes should never be filled with putty or stopping, but should be thoroughly dosed with linseed oil or wood preservative.

Fittings on grown spars, especially large eyebolts to which halliard blocks are shackled, can work loose in the wood by compressing the wood fibres. Any such oversize holes make grand starting places for rot, so they should be attended to promptly. The hole should be bored out slightly oversize and an oak plug glued in. Then oak graving pieces should be fitted on each side of the mast and a new hole bored, running through the oak plug so that the bolt will bear on oak at all points instead of the softer pine of the mast (Fig 174). Some owners set metal plates into the mast to take eyebolts etc, and the more weight-conscious use reinforced plastics such as Tufnol. Any such non-wooden pieces set in a mast must be very well bedded in to ensure that there can be no chance of a water-trap behind the fitting. The author has used Tufnol pieces set into Araldite epoxy resin with great success.

The hounds, where the shrouds pass round the mast, may need attention. Sometimes the chocks which support the shrouds are abysmally crude, comprising plain rectangular blocks bolted to the round mast, leaving dangerous water-traps, and allowing the loops of the shrouds to bite well into the pine of the mast (Fig 175). Such crude chocks are best removed and replaced with a pair of carved oak blocks set into the mast and through-bolted. The oak pieces should be carved to give full support for the rigging, and should extend far enough down to prevent any part of the loop in the wire from touching the pine of the mast. Bruising of the front and back of the mast by the eyes can be prevented by gluing on two or three half-round strips of oak (Fig 176). All the oak pieces must be shaped to eliminate any possibility of water-traps. Oak reinforcing strips or plates can also be set into a mast to spread the load of a gooseneck band, and also to toughen the spar where it passes through the deck. Any such oak pieces should not be set in so deeply as to weaken the spar significantly at that point; they are there solely as a surface protection.

One sometimes finds copper tingles on a mast to prevent the gaff jaws from chewing into it. These tingles are usually simply two or three sheets of thin copper bent right round the mast and nailed on. It is not unknown for the mast above such patches to fall off in a decent blow because, if not very well bedded on, the copper forms a first-class rot-trap. Attention to the

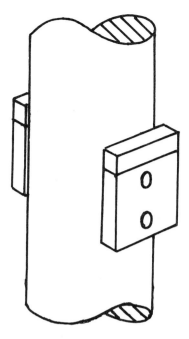

Fig 175 *Simple rigging chocks which form ideal rot-traps*

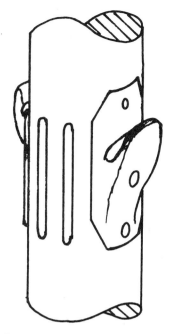

Fig 176 *Shaped oak chocks and rubbing strips*

gaff jaws possibly adding rawhide bindings, or long oak beadings on the mast, form a better cure; but great care must be taken in shaping and positioning any such beadings to ensure that while they will take any chafe of the gaff jaws they will not impede the jaws from turning freely round the mast.

The most obvious repair likely to be needed on a mast is when the latter has been broken. The standard repair for a broken solid mast is to scarph a new end onto whichever is the longer piece of the original or, if the break is in the middle, to scarph in a new section. Very long stopped scarph joints should be used. With modern

glues the strength of the joint will be more than adequate, but – and it is a big but – the rigidity of the spar will be altered, and it is not unknown for masts which have been scarphed to fail near to the scarph under bending loads. The new portion of the mast should be shaped with a draw-knife, but more timid amateurs may feel happier if they use a large spokeshave set to a coarse cut.

Glued-up solid masts can have graving pieces and pressure-pads set in exactly as on a grown spar, but a broken glued-up mast should not be repaired by simply scarphing on a new piece. Such a mast, if

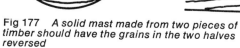

Fig 177 *A solid mast made from two pieces of timber should have the grains in the two halves reversed*

properly made, should have been constructed from two pieces of wood (probably
Sitka spruce) cut from the same baulk, but
with one piece reversed to the other so
that all irregularities in the grain cancel
one another out (Fig 177). On Bermudian
rigged dinghies and small craft, a luff
groove for the sail may be cut in each half
before they are glued up (Fig 178). When

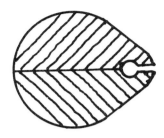

Fig 178   *Luff groove in a solid mast for a dinghy*

a new portion of such a mast is being made,
it should be made in the same way as the
original, ie from a cut and reversed baulk.
The joint to the old portion should be cut
as a veed stopped scarph, with the 'internal'
joint faces on the new portion being cut
and finished before the two halves are glued
together (Fig 179). Great care must be
taken to ensure that all joint faces are a
perfect fit.

Some racing boats have solid masts which
are laminated up out of a number of strips
of timber, with each piece selected specially
and cut and glued so that the completed
mast will have the maximum strength
coupled with controlled flexibility possible
within the racing-class rules governing size
and weight. In effect the mast is a very
carefully laminated spring, and clearly a
plain scarph joint will ruin this overall
springiness. To make a reasonable repair,
each separate lamination will have to be
cut back to its glue-line, and a new piece

scarphed onto it making the best possible
match for the timber type, density, and
run of grain. The new portion of the mast
will be built up gradually from the centre
out, keeping the joints in adjacent laminates as well separated as possible.

One side of the luff groove on a solid
spar may break away at the lower end. If
the spar is a good one, with straight-
grained timber, the split may run quite a
way up. If the break is clean, the broken
piece can be glued back in place with a
urea-formaldehyde adhesive. Strips of polythene tape can be bound round the mast
to hold the strip down until the glue sets.
When repairing a broken side to a luff
groove, it is most important to have a
length of line fed along the groove, in order
to pull small pieces of wood through to
wipe away all runs of glue from the inside
of the groove.

If the break in the side of the luff groove
is an old one and the faces of the wood are
dirty, it is best to plane off the side of the
mast at an angle and to glue on a new piece
with the largest possible joint area. The
portion of the groove must be shaped on
the new piece before it is glued in place,
but the outside is better shaped after the
glue has set.

Hollow masts

Hollow masts of whatever form are usually
plugged wherever any rigging attachments
have to be fitted, so repairs to these points
can be made in the same way as for solid
masts. The differences in repair techniques
come when a hollow mast is broken. Masts
made up from four planks glued into a box
form can be mended by scarphing on new
planks, keeping the joints on the four sides
as well separated as possible. Built-up masts
over about 9 m (30 ft) long can be repaired
by scarphing on new sections, but this work
can be tricky because quite long lengths

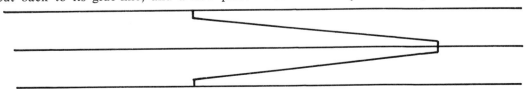

Fig 179   *Veed scarph joint in glued-up solid spar*

of sound wood will have to be carefully cut back to the original joint-lines in order to keep the scarph joints between old and new sections well staggered. Smaller built-up or hollowed-out masts are hardly worth repairing, as the work in making up a new section and in cutting the scarph joints is not far short of the work in making a new mast. Depending on the shape of the broken mast, it may be possible to use the larger portion of it as a boom or gaff.

The lightest of all hollow masts, which are those rolled up from veneer such as used to be made by McGruers, are virtually unrepairable, other than by cleaning off the broken ends, fitting in a long solid plug, then rebuilding the mast over the plug with narrow strips of veneer of varying length. The result will look much as the mast did before, and it should be strong enough for sailing, but the extreme lightness and whip of the original will be lost.

There is nothing to be scared of in making a new hollow mast – except perhaps the cost of a long baulk of straight-grained Sitka spruce. It does require careful work, and it also requires planning and preparation, but the work itself is all basically simple. Provided all tools are kept sharp, spruce is a lovely wood to handle and, when the satisfaction of balancing some 9 m (30 ft) of finished mast on one's shoulder and seeing how wonderfully flexible it is, is compared with the actual effort involved, the making of hollow spars becomes one of the most rewarding tasks to be met with in working on boats. Also, there is the thought of how much one would have had to pay for a professionally made spar!

A square-section box-form mast made from four planks needs no detailed instruction – a glance at the broken mast will make the method of construction quite clear. Carved or built-up masts are not quite so obvious.

The first requirement is to set up a working surface. There is little likelihood of the average amateur having access to a full flat-topped bench some 9–12 m (30–40 ft) long, but all the work can be done on piles of blocks or on frames or trestles as shown in Fig 20. It is most important that all blocks or trestles be set with their tops in

line. The top need not be horizontal; if the ground slopes it is better to arrange for the working height above ground to be as constant as possible. The top surfaces can be set level by sighting over them. Those whose eyesight is not too brilliant can make sighting-jigs which consist of pieces of tin with flanges bent so that they will stand upright, and long, thin horizontal slits about 1 mm ($\frac{1}{32}$ in) wide cut parallel to the base and at a constant height. All the plates are painted matt black, two plates being needed for each trestle and four plates for wide blocks.

Plates are stood at each end of the two end-trestles of the set, and lights are placed behind the slits at one end. Simple dark cardboard masks are placed round the lights so that from the far end the only light which can be seen passes through the slits in the masks. Pairs of masks can then be placed on the intermediate trestles, the height of which is adjusted until the light can be seen through all the slits. Trestles are easier to set up than blocks, because their tops can be taken as being level along the axis of the mast, whereas blocks must be adjusted to be flat and level in two axes. Such levelling with slits and lights is best done late in the evening.

For a mast carved out of two halves, a few clamps should be made to hold these whilst the glue sets. These clamps can be very easily made up from two flat pieces of wood, a wedge, and a nut and bolt. The jaws should be deep enough to span the whole of the mast to be glued, and the wedges should be cut to match the thickness of the mast after gluing, which will be done before the mast is trimmed to its fore and aft profile. The 'few' clamps needed is one for every 150–200 mm (6–8 in) of the length of the mast (Fig 180).

A new mast carved in two halves

Making a hollow mast in two halves begins by planning how the hollow will be roughed out. If the worker has access to a powerful bench circular saw, the easiest way is to run the two halves of the mast over a 13 mm ($\frac{1}{2}$ in) thick radiused edge-cutter. If such a facility is not available,

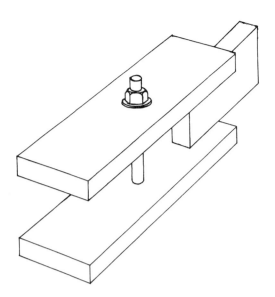

Fig 180 *Simple 'wedged clothes peg' clamp*

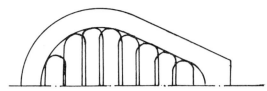

Fig 181 *Determining the cuts needed to rough out a hollow mast*

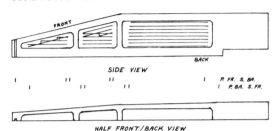

SIDE VIEW

HALF FRONT/BACK VIEW

Fig 182 *Side and front elevations of the mast with all lengths shortened relative to the widths and start and finish points for cuts noted. Start and finish points (adjusted for offset distance) are shown between the two views. The upper set is used for cutting the port side from the front and the starboard side from the back; the lower set vice versa*

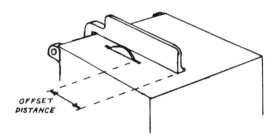

OFFSET DISTANCE

Fig 183 *Measuring the offset on a circular saw*

then possibly a hand-held circular saw, perhaps with a 6 mm ($\frac{1}{4}$ in) wide cutter can be used. Failing that, the hollows can be cut with a chisel and a grooving plane.

Once the method and size of cutter to be used have been determined, the settings for every cut can be worked out. This is most easily done by drawing full-sized sections of the mast at the upper end of each section of the hollow, and then drawing in the profile of the cutter to be used to establish the number of cuts necessary, the depth of each cut, and the distance in from the edge of the mast (Fig 181). Front and side views of the mast are drawn with all cross-sectional dimensions the correct size, but the length reduced on a scale of perhaps 20 to 1. The outlines of the required hollows are drawn in, and then the lines taken by each cut can be added. If the mast has a reasonable taper, it will usually be found that extra cuts will be needed in the lower portions of the hollow sections (Fig 182).

Measurements of the circular saw to be used are taken, and a scale drawing made to determine the distances from the end of the mast to a fixed point on the saw (usually the end of the fence) which must be used to ensure that the cutter will start and stop in the right place (Fig 183). When this is being worked out, it must be borne

in mind that one half of the mast will be cut the opposite way to the other. That is, if a given cut working in from the front is being cut upwards on one side, the corresponding cut will be downwards on the other side, so start and finish offsets will have to be added for one side and subtracted for the other. It is essential that all cuts be made against the rotation of the sawblade, never into it, which would allow the blade to roll the wood over itself, with fairly disastrous consequences (Fig 184). This involves some mental gymnastics visualising which way the two halves of the mast will have to sit on the saw for each cut, and if there is any doubt it is worth splitting an old pencil and laying the halves over a block of wood to simulate the saw

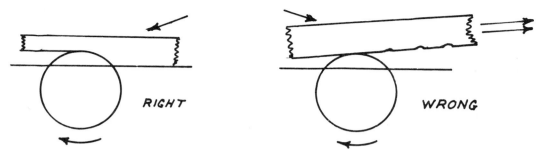

Fig 184 *Always cut against the run of the saw (left), never with it (right)*

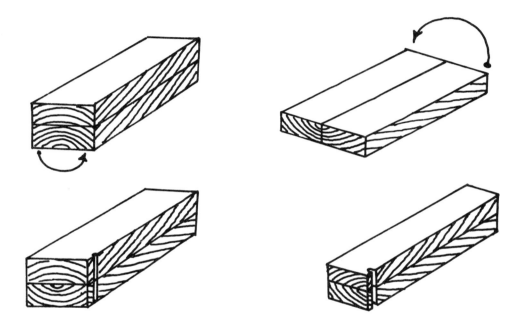

Fig 185 *Two ways in which a baulk of spruce can be cut and reversed for mast making*

so as to be absolutely certain. The use of red and green pencils for the cutting lists for the two halves of the mast helps to reduce the possibility of confusion.

To achieve nice rounded ends to the hollow sections, the deeper cuts nearer the centre of the spar should be made longer than those near the front and back; but it will be found that with a reasonable-sized saw the deeper cuts will automatically be longer if all cuts are finished at the same point relative to the fixed mark on the saw.

When all the depths and start and finish

points for all cuts have been listed and double-checked, actual work on the mast can be started. A baulk of spruce about 300 mm (1 ft) longer than the finished mast is split and one half reversed relative to the other to balance out any slight irregularities in the grain. Fig 185 shows two ways in which this can be done, with the angle of the grain greatly exaggerated for clarity. The two halves should be clearly marked to ensure that, as they are worked on, their correct relationship cannot be upset. One easy way of making an indelible mark is to

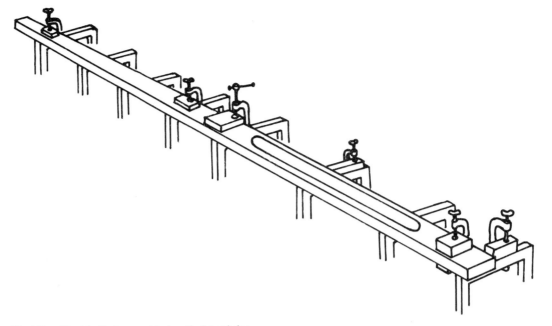

Fig 186 *Mast-half clamped to trestle bench for cutting out hollows*

run a single saw cut across both pieces about 25 mm (1 in) in from one end.

After marking, the joint faces are planed flat and smooth, and the back face is planed. The profile is marked, and the front face cut and planed to size. Some workers like to leave an extra 0.8 mm ($\frac{1}{32}$ in) or so on each face to be cleaned off after the mast has been glued up. If the faces are left oversize, the amount of the surplus must be constant, and it must be added to the fence settings for the hollows.

If a fixed power-saw is to be used to rough out the hollows the limit marks for the length of each cut can be painted on the outer (side) faces of the two halves. It is best to paint bands about 25 mm (1 in) wide, placed so that the actual limit of each cut is the outer edge of the band, to give 25 mm (1 in) 'warning zone'. To avoid any chance of confusion, the bands should extend only one-third of the way across from the edge to which they apply. If a hand-held saw is being used, the marks will have to be made on the front and back faces, running up to the joint faces so that they can be seen whilst the saw is run over the wood. Alternatively, it may be found

easier and safer to clamp clean flat pieces of wood over the joint faces of the halves to limit the travel of a hand-held saw. Care must be taken when clamping not to bruise the timber.

When a hand-held saw is being used it is best to clamp one half of the mast on the 'workbench' with its edge overhanging the front of the supports or blocks, so that the fence on the saw cannot foul the 'bench'. The clamps holding the mast down must be placed clear of the hollows being cut. On a long mast, chocks should be clamped to the tops of intermediate supports to hold the timber forward against the pressure of the fence of the saw (Fig 186). If the timber tends to bend too much between the supports, the half of the mast not being cut can be used as a support beam, again taking great care not to damage the joint faces.

If the hollows are being roughed out with a hand-held saw (or by other hand tools) it is easier to make all cuts required from one face in each hollow in turn, resetting the tool between each cut; whereas with a fixed bench-saw it is easier to make all necessary cuts on both pieces of the mast at each setting of the saw, working from both front and back faces. This means the pieces will have to be turned end for end between cuts. The saw must have clear space greater than the length of the mast beyond each end of the saw, but it is unlikely there will be space to turn the halves keeping them flat, so they may have to be turned end over end – which can be fun with a very whippy length of spruce! Codline guys tied on the end of the piece are a help, but it needs three or four people to turn them end for end. It makes the work easier if there are some trestle-type roller supports to take the weight of the ends of the baulks as the hollows are cut.

With any form of power-saw, making the first cut in each section of hollow is always the worst, as all the swarf has to follow the saw round, and the process is accompanied by a disturbing smell of burning. With care and a steady pressure on the wood, overheating of the saw blade can be avoided. It is important to keep the saw cutting, as it will rub and overheat if it is allowed to 'idle' in the cut. On all subsequent cuts, most of the material removed can escape into the growing hollow. Note that for roughing out a hollow a power-saw must be used with no guard over the cutter, so great care must be taken and any would-be watchers, especially children, must be kept well away.

If no power-saws are available and the hollows are being cut with a grooving plane, the set-up will be similar to that for a hand-held saw. The ends of the grooves will have to be chiselled out to allow access for the nose of a grooving plane unless an 'old woman's tooth' type is used. Having tried both an 'old woman's tooth' and a Stanley 55, the author would far rather put up with having to hand-chisel groove ends for the nose of the Stanley 55 and work each groove 'middle to end' than put up with the risk of tearing the wood which is ever present with the naked cutter on the router plane.

Roughing out with plane, chisel and gouge is not a very quick job, but with power-saws it takes only a few hours if all the settings have been worked out in advance and all necessary limit marks are properly made. Converting the somewhat ragged roughed-out hollows to smooth,

glass-papered recesses of correct profile takes a little longer! It is as well to make up two sets of stout card templates to check the hollows. One set should be just marginally undersize, and one set about 1.6 mm ($\frac{1}{16}$ in) undersize to give a warning that the hollow is nearly to size and shape. Templates should be made for every 0.6–1 m (2–3 ft) of the length of the hollows when there is any taper on the spar. The accuracy required in shaping the hollows will depend on the size of the mast and on the finished wall thickness. If the hollows are shaped to a tolerance of 5 per cent of the wall thickness, and later the outside of the mast is also shaped to 5 per cent, then opposite walls of the finished mast could differ in thickness by 20 per cent (one side under thickness both inside and outside, and the other side over thickness). It is worth being as accurate as possible and getting a really good finish in the hollows – the only extra cost is a bit more time and patience, and one might as well have a mast to be proud of, even though no one will see the hollows after it is glued up. If the hollows are left rough and ragged, the strength of the finished mast will be less uniform, and a broken mast – which will reveal the slovenly workmanship – is more likely.

When all the hollows are finished smooth, the slots for the masthead sheave are cut. Do not forget to cut only half the required width of slot in each half of the mast. One sometimes sees glued-up masts with double-width slots. Any slots for internal halliards are cut and, if a masthead light is to be fitted, the wires can be run up in one half. If internal halliards are to be fitted, a length of string should be laid in place and its ends brought out through the slots and taped up to the side of the baulk. Finally, the joint faces of each half should be sanded with a large sheet of sandpaper held over a very flat block, taking great care not to round off any edges. This sanding is essential, as the rubbing of the joint faces when sawing or planing out the hollows will burnish over the wood fibres so that a weak joint will result if fresh fibres are not exposed by sanding.

The halves of the mast can then be glued together. A two-part urea formaldehyde adhesive such as Aerolite is the easiest to use for this job. Everything should be set out ready: the two halves of the mast, joint faces up; any sheave boxes; clamps; polythene sheeting; and a good supply of helpers. Alignment of the two halves lengthwise can be ensured by gluing the sheave box into its slot in one half first; and fore and aft alignment can be eased by clamping short pieces of wood (masked with polythene sheet) to the front and back faces of one half about a quarter of the length in from each end. The use of slightly curved pieces of wood such as offcuts of steamed ribs will make it easier to drop the second half onto the first.

The glue should be spread on one half first, in the words of a well known advertisement, 'Not too little, not too much'. The acid hardener is then spread on the second half, using as many helpers as possible so that the whole length can be spread uniformly before the first-spread glue can soak right into the wood. This second half is then lowered onto the glue-coated half, checked for alignment, and clamped.

The quicker the clamps can be put on the better. The first should be put on about a quarter the length in from the ends, then those at the middle and ends, with successive clamps midway between those already on. The more helpers available for this job the better. When all the clamps are firmly secured, the glued baulk should be turned upside down to let any glue which has run down from the joints inside the hollows run back over the joints.

When the glue has fully cured, the clamps are taken off, the sides of the mast are sawn to their profile, and the outside is trimmed to final shape, using templates to ensure accuracy. The shaping of the outside of a hollow mast is far more critical than that for a solid spar. Finally, the excess length at each end is cut off and the mast is ready to have any metalwork fitted.

When making a hollow mast it is important that the wood is dry when it is glued; so unless one has the benefit of a heated covered workshop, it is as well to get all the work from first cutting the baulk to gluing up done as quickly as possible when a fine spell of weather comes along.

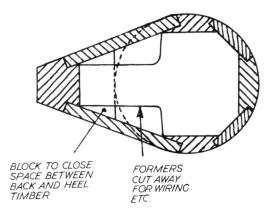

BLOCK TO CLOSE
SPACE BETWEEN
BACK AND HEEL
TIMBER

FORMERS
CUT AWAY
FOR WIRING
ETC.

Fig 187   *Section through built-up mast, looking downwards from just above the first former*

A new built-up mast

Masts over about 9–10 m (30–35 ft) long can be built up from planks. Eight planks give the best pear section for an amateur to tackle. The construction comprises a roughly square block on the aft edge to carry the sail-track, moderately thick side and front members, and four thin 'filler' planks (Fig 187). Formers or plugs are inserted wherever fittings are to be through-bolted, and on a tall thin mast light intermediate formers may be put in to help during its building. The masthead and heel up to the start of the sail-track are usually solid plugs with the timbers of the mast run over them. Built-up masts of this type must be carefully planned to get the joint angles right, and the cutting of the joint faces in the four main members must be done accurately. It should be noted that if there is any taper on the mast, the side timbers and filler panels will have to be cut to a slight curve. For a really first-class mast the inner faces of the sides and front member should be radiused, but this will not make a great deal of difference to the finished weight or strength, whereas it will add considerably to the amount of work involved.

Any (or all) of the timbers of the mast can be built up from lengths of wood scarph-jointed together. Scarphs in a pair of timbers (such as the sides or the filler panels) can be set at the same height, but the heights of different pairs of scarphs should be well staggered. All joints should

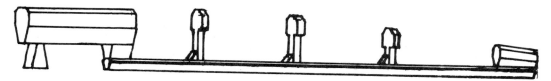

Fig 188 *A built-up mast being constructed.*
Head and heel timbers and formers are all glued
to the back. The sides will be glued on next

run so that the upper piece lies on the outside of the joint. Front, side and back
timbers should all be prepared with the
joints cut to finished size; but the four filler
panels are best left sawn but not planed to
finished size until their widths can be
checked as the mast is built. All necessary
formers and internal plugs must be cut to
size, and the slot for the masthead sheave
should be cut in the front and back timbers
and in the upper filler block.

The mast is built up on its back. The
back timber to which the sail-track will be
screwed is clamped to the building trestles
after checking that the trestle tops are
exactly in line, and after a centre-line has
been marked on the trestles by twanging a
tightly stretched chalked thread over them.
If the mast has a curve aft at the top, the
trestles at that end will have to be set low
to accommodate the curve. A filler block
is glued on the lower end of the back to
close the space between the back and the
heel timber. The solid heel timber is then
glued onto this filler block with the lower
end of the heel resting on a block to keep
it in line with the back timber. The masthead block is glued onto the back, checking
that the slots for the masthead sheave line
up. These joints can all be clamped or
weighted until the glue has cured. The
internal formers are glued in place on the
back, usually with a small triangular block
to reinforce the joints (Fig 188). All the
formers must be checked very carefully to
see that they are square to the back and
are all in line.

When all the joints to the back have set,
the main side timbers are glued on. These
must be put on as a pair. The sides of the
heel block are coated with glue, and the
side timbers put on and clamped lightly,
after which they are held in to each former
and to the masthead block to ensure that

they are correctly aligned, then the clamps
holding them to the heel block are tightened. The edges of each former in turn are
coated with glue, and the side members
clamped over them, up to the masthead
block. Any runs of glue over the formers
or the blocks must be cleaned off immediately. When the glue holding the sides has
set, the clamps can be taken off and the
front member glued on. Since all these
joints will be hidden on the finished mast,
resorcinol glue can be used. Urea formaldehyde is normally used to glue spruce
masts where the joints are visible because
the dark purple of resorcinol does not look
very nice on a clean, varnished spar.

When the joints on the front have set,
the joint faces to take the filler panels are
checked over and any necessary minor
adjustments of the faces on the heel- or
masthead-block faces are made. All formers
must be checked to ensure that they are not
proud of the joint faces for the filler panels.
The latter can then be checked in place and
planed to make the most perfect fit possible.
The front panels are put on first, starting
at the heel, and 'rolling' them down, gluing
successive formers in turn, and spreading
the glue along the joint faces to side and
front members. This job is easier if there
are three or four helpers. One helper holds
the upper end of the very flexible filler
panel; one holds the panel just ahead of the
area being glued; one spreads the glue up
the mast, and one presses the panel down
into the recesses in the side and front members. This happy arrangement of helpers
leaves the owner free to supervise the work.
If all the joints are well cut, and the filler
panels are a good fit, no clamping should
be necessary; but if a panel does not lie
right home, it can be pulled in with a
tourniquet of polythene tape wrapped round
the whole mast.

After the glue holding the front filler panels has set, a final check-over is made of all joints inside the mast, wires for masthead lights etc are inserted, and the rear filler panels are glued in. A mast glued up in this way does not require much in the way of final shaping, and the result of a few weeks' spare-time work should be a very light, graceful spar which would have been extremely expensive if made professionally.

Chapter 16

Mast fittings

Gaff jaws and mast hoops

Gaff jaws are found in almost infinite variety, from a pair of slightly shaped pieces of oak bolted each side of the end of the gaff, to elaborate metal fittings which look like exhibits from a Great Age of Engineering display. Some of these chew the mast about unmercifully; some jam on hoisting or lowering the sail; some are too flimsy and need constant repair; some scare their owners by their great weight; but there are many more which work reliably and efficiently and never cause any worries at all. There is no 'best' type of gaff jaw. What is suitable on one boat may be quite unsuitable on another with a mainsail of different shape or size.

If gaff jaws are in need of repair the first question to be asked is, 'Were they satisfactory?' If the answer is 'yes' and the breakage is clearly a non-recurrent accident or general old age, the best course is to replace them exactly as they were. If the original jaws were not satisfactory, then advice should be sought from an owner of a similar type of vessel.

When wooden jaws need to be repaired, the whole jaw should be unbolted or unriveted from the spar and replaced. If the jaws have any significant curvature, the replacement should be made from timber with a suitable curved grain. All faces of gaff jaws need to be well smoothed and rounded so that they cannot chafe the mast or any of the halliard falls which run up the mast past them.

Broken metal saddle-and-eye fittings are quite straightforward to remake, copying the original or another fitting known to be satisfactory. It ought to be possible to make a lightweight copy of a typical metal saddle out of a plastic material which would be much less likely to chafe the mast, would be corrosion-resistant, and would have quite adequate strength, but to the best of the author's knowledge, this idea remains untried.

Mast hoops seem to cause rather more problems than their size and complexity (or rather lack thereof) would suggest. Damaged ones may be repairable, but given a supply of fresh-cut timber and steaming facilities they are so simple to make that it does not seem worth repairing them. Some hoops are bolted up instead of the more usual rivets so that (in theory) they can be sprung open and slipped round the mast like a giant key-ring instead of having to be fed over the top of the mast before it is rigged. Unfortunately, old hoops are usually somewhat brittle, and attempts to open them up may break them. Also, it is said that the bolts can chafe the mast badly. When one considers the problems of getting replacement hoops on to a rigged mast, it is surprising how few boats one sees with a couple of spares on the mast, lashed down to the gooseneck and ready for use in emergency.

Some owners have found good hoops so difficult to buy that they have changed to a lacing for the luff of the mainsail. On small boats this may be a good alternative, but on bigger craft hoops make it so much easier to climb the mast when sailing that they are well worth making.

Some owners experience problems with the hoops canting and jamming on the mast as the sail is hoisted or lowered. Any such canting is easily eliminated by fitting a light line from the gaff jaws down the foreside of the mast, tied to each hoop in turn so that the hoops sit level round the mast.

Steaming mast hoops is a simple operation, as is riveting them up, but great care must be taken when riveting to ensure that the inner face of the hoop is left perfectly smooth. Any rough edges, or the edge of a nail head, will soon start scratching and scoring the mast.

Crosstrees and spreaders

Crosstrees and spreaders are fairly simple pieces of wood, but especially on Bermudian-rigged boats they play a crucial role in keeping the mast up. In two instances known to the author, failure of a spreader has resulted in the immediate breaking of the mast. In one case the cause of failure was unknown; in the other the spreader split lengthwise because the shroud which passed through a slot in the end of the spreader was driven into the wood by being under tension (Fig 189). Another spreader failure (which luckily did not result in failure of the mast, but did result in bruises to the crew as the alert helmsman tacked in record time) happened because a swept-back spreader was cut with its curved end slightly cross-grain, and the end simply sheared off (Fig 190).

All spreaders should be made from the best quality wood, with the grain running straight from the end which carries the shroud to the heel, which should be shaped to bear against the mast. Large spreaders can be built up from two relatively thin main struts spaced apart with blocks glued and riveted in place (Fig 191). The end fitting which takes the shroud must bear onto the main struts, and usually at least one of the main struts will bear against the mast.

In all types of spreaders, the slot in which the rigging fits should be cut into a block of lignum vitae or Tufnol set into the end of the spreader with a small-angle dovetail, and glued with an epoxide resin. This inset block should be square-ended so as to spread its load over the largest possible area of the softer wood (Fig 192).

The commonest way of ensuring that the shroud stays safely in its slot is a split pin put through the end of the spreader horizontally. If not protected, this can be a perfect device for mangling the leach of an overlapping headsail and for chafing a well squared-off mainsail – commonly applied protections vary from a few yards of sticky tape to old tennis balls cut and

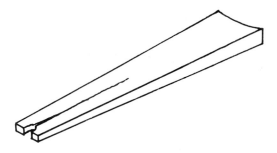

Fig 189 *A spreader with an unreinforced slot for the wire, can be split by the wire*

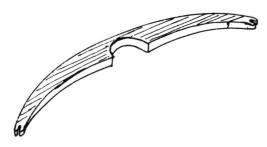

Fig 190 *Swept-back crosstrees. These may be dangerous as the wood is short-grained at the end. If a sweep back is considered essential, laminated or steam-bent timber should be used*

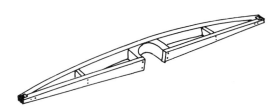

Fig 191 *Built-up crosstrees for larger boat*

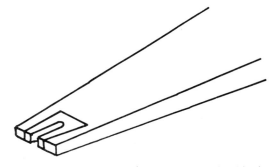

Fig 192 *Spreader tip with inset reinforcing block*

fitted over the ends of the spreaders. One very neat way of holding the shroud in its slot is to make plastic end-caps for the spreaders. This can be done by shaping a piece of hardwood to match the end of the spreader, then taking a length of PVC piping of appropriate diameter and softening it in boiling water – or by judicious heating in an oven – until the hardwood plug can be forced in, and the PVC shaped down to it. (Wear heavy, watertight gauntlets for this job.) When the plug fits nicely to the required depth, the piping is cut off about 13 mm ($\frac{1}{4}$ in) beyond the end of the plug, softened, and moulded in to a curve. All ragged corners and edges can be pressed out with a warmed, stout, knife blade. When the shape is satisfactory, slots are cut in the top and bottom to take the shroud, and holes are drilled each side of the slot to take countersunk-head screws into the block in the end of the spreader (Fig 193).

If a spreader fails while out sailing – and the mast survives – a usable temporary

Fig 193   Moulded plastic end-cap and shroud retainer

repair can be made by screwing, nailing, riveting or lashing a suitable length of straight-grained wood below the broken spreader; or by concocting a wire lashing to hold the shroud out to the end of a split spreader. But apart from such emergency 'get you home' measures, spreaders should be regarded as unrepairable and new ones should be made out of good sound timber. If swept-back spreaders are essential, they should either be cut from curved-grain timber, or be steamed to the curve.

Chapter 17

Blocks and fittings

On gaff masts, the fittings usually consist of assorted eyebolts to which are shackled the various necessary blocks, and a mastband for the gooseneck. Some older working boats dispense with a gooseneck and use flat jaws on the boom-end which turn against a wooden ridge set in the mast – admirably simple and easy to repair. Some gaff masts have a masthead sheave set in, and large masts may carry fittings for a topmast. All the woodwork involved in repairs to these fittings is usually simple and obvious. Broken metal fittings are best replaced. Wrought or forged fittings are generally to be preferred to castings or welded fittings, unless the worker knows exactly the purpose of the fitting and also has enough metallurgical knowledge to decide where welding or casting can be used safely. Any iron or steel fittings should be hot-dip galvanised.

Sail-tracks

Bermudian masts will almost always have an inset masthead sheave and metal sail-track, with tangs for all other fittings. Mast-tracks can get broken or dented, and it may be necessary to replace part of one. The fitting of the track is obvious, but what is often not so obvious is how alignment between the replacement portion and the original can be guaranteed. Any misalignment can leave a step, and if even the smallest step is left one can be certain that a sail-slide will wedge itself against it – but not until one is in the situation of needing to get a reef down really quickly or face losing the mast! The easiest way of ensuring alignment is to use a small hand-file to cut what are in effect short scarph joints on the ends of both the old and new portions of the track. The plain metal-strip track for slides which clip round the edges

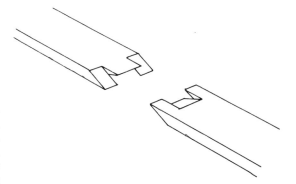

Fig 194   *Joint in plain strip track for external slides*

of the track is joined by three scarphs; two small ones facing one way, and a larger one in the centre facing the other way (Fig 194). It is important to cut the faces between the scarphs cleanly, as it is these faces which align the edges of the strips.

Incidentally, when buying metal to replace a track of this type, always try to buy strip rolled to size. The author was once sold strips which had been guillotine-cut from large sheets, and the cutting had forced a sideways bend into the strips which took a long time to work out of the metal so that it could be used.

Jointing an external track is not quite so simple. Positive locations in both planes can be ensured in a variety of ways, of which that shown in Fig 195 is the easiest to cut. A tongue with well-defined sides, narrower than the opening in the track, is filed in the base, and reverse angles are filed in the outer lips of the track. Sideways location is by the edges of the central tongue, but if one is prepared to do a bit more complex marking out, the slopes on the lips can be filed at a compound angle which will give further sideways location.

On both types of track, when the joints

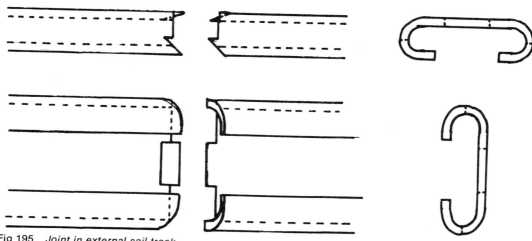

Fig 195   *Joint in external sail-track*

have been cut and checked together, all
sharp edges should be taken off with a fine
file. A lightly greased slide should now be
run over the joint, holding the slide angled
to the track so that if there are any pro-
jections, it will catch. If it shows any hesita-
tion at the joint, find what was catching it
and eliminate it. The next time a slide
catches, it might be 6 m (20 ft) above deck
on a wild and stormy night.

Tracks are best bedded onto the mast
with wet varnish.

Masthead sheave

Masthead-sheave slots often need repair.
Many masts have a plain slot of suitable
size cut in the mast with a hole cross-drilled
for the pin on which the sheave rotates.
Over the years the wood around the slot
can get bruised by the halliard, and the
slot gets gradually wider until there is just
enough space for the halliard to jump off
the sheave and wedge itself immovably
between this and the side of the slot. If
there is anything more than a working
clearance between the sheave and its slot,
the mast should be repaired at the earliest
possible moment, before major repairs are
necessary. Refacing a slot is much simpler
than mending a broken mast.

The simplest method of repair is to remove the sheave and pin, chisel the sides
of the slot flat and clean, and glue in oak
facings (Fig 196). These facings must allow

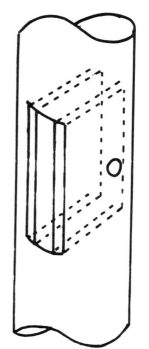

Fig 196   *Slot for masthead sheave fitted with
oak facings*

sufficient clearance for the wood to swell
in wet weather and still leave a working
clearance for the sheave to rotate, but they
should not allow for any more than this
essential clearance.

Some slots are cut overheight and overwidth so that the splice on the end of a
wire halliard can be passed over the sheave.

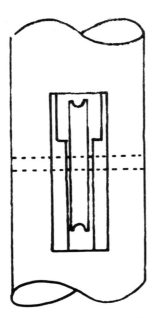

Fig 197 *Oak facing with groove to allow the splice to pass*

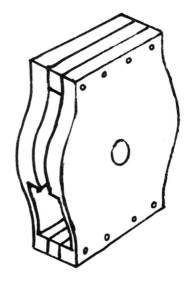

Fig 198 *Plastic case for masthead sheave*

This is very bad practice, and is asking for a jammed halliard. If the sheave is narrower than the splice on the halliard, then the lower end of the slot should be widened to allow the splice to pass through when the pin and sheave have been removed (Fig 197).

A much better arrangement for a masthead sheave is to make a proper sheave-box in a reinforced plastic material such as Carp brand Tufnol. Such a box can be made with quite a close clearance, and can be provided with lips which project beyond the face of the mast and prevent the wire halliard from bearing against the wood as it leaves the sheave. The completed box can be glued in the mast with Araldite epoxy resin.

If the sheave used fits the wire nicely, the sides of the box may have to be quite thick to allow a groove to be cut to pass the splice (Fig 198). Excessive weight can be avoided either by milling or turning recesses in the sides, leaving them at full width only at the centre and by the rim of the sheave. If no mill or lathe are available, the sides can be lightened by drilling large holes.

On racing boats a surprising amount of weight can be saved high up the mast by drilling holes in fittings, and thinning down various parts. Metal spindles on all blocks can be drilled out, the sheaves themselves can often be drilled, and so can the shells of all blocks. With care in the design, corrosion-resistant fittings can be made from bronze to be lighter than commercially available aluminium equivalents. (That is than some of the cheaper aluminium fittings – some of those available for the larger and more expensive ocean racers are excellent in their strength-to-weight ratios.)

Any owner who is contemplating lightening fittings is well advised to make up perspex models, and test them under polarised light so that redundant material can be removed without significant effect on the strength. As an extra precaution, it is useful to make up at least one extra fitting and test it either to destruction or to a stress so far beyond the greatest snatch-loading likely that further testing becomes obviously pointless.

Mastbands and tangs

Replacement mastbands and tangs for rigging attachments can be made from stainless-steel sheet, or from bronze – never use brass for any working fitting on a seagoing boat. If bronze is used, it is essential that the steel rigging be electrically insulated from the bronze fittings. This can be done very simply by having the rigging spliced round a solid eye made from nylon or Tufnol; such eyes being very easy to file to shape from a piece of sheet plastic. Before making any such eyes, a splice made round an ordinary bent-metal thimble should be examined critically; usually it will be seen that the wire does not lie in contact with the thimble's flats. The exact shape taken by the outside of the wire should be drawn on a piece of card, then by drawing a line parallel at the appropriate distance in, the required shape for a perfectly fitting eye can be found.

In fitting mastbands or tangs, some owners like to use tangs secured to the mast in pairs with a through-bolt. This offers a very secure anchorage for the rigging, especially if the hole in the mast which takes the bolt is oak reinforced, but the author has always preferred to use a mast-band with tangs riveted and brazed or welded to it. The band can sit on a slight step in the surface of the mast, and can be held with a multiplicity of small screws which ensures that the load of the rigging is spread as evenly as possible over the whole of the spar instead of being concentrated in one bolt.

Some builders set bands on Bermudian masts into a groove around the mast so that the outer surface is flush and there can be no step at the top of the band against which water can lodge. This is excellent in theory, but it can have one practical snag. With the usual one-piece band which is open at the back to clear the sail-track, either the band must be forced down the mast until it snaps into place in its groove, or it will have to be opened out to get it in place. In most cases, this opening out of the band will distort the metal beyond its elastic limit. The band is easily bent back again, but as anybody who has ever bent a piece of metal knows, it must be bent beyond its final required position. There is always a certain amount of 'spring-back'. Because of this, it is impossible to make a band which has been opened out fit properly into its groove. Because of this, it is better to sit the pre-shaped bands on a single step in the mast, bedding them into Araldite 103, and providing a fairing of sawdust-loaded resin over the band's upper edge. This allows the band to make the best possible contact with the wood without becoming distorted, and the resin both seals the band to eliminate a water-trap and bonds it to the mast. If the band has been drilled with weight-reducing holes, a sealing fillet of resin round each hole will add to the strength of the assembly.

Chainplates and other metal fittings

Although they are structurally part of the hull, chainplates can best be considered as part of the rigging. An owner who is restoring or repairing an old boat should not need to concern himself with chainplates; it should be possible simply to refit the originals when all woodwork on the hull has been completed (possibly after re-galvanising). Unfortunately this is not always the case. Some boats have been (and still are) built with inadequate or badly fitted chainplates, and many boats have been altered over the years to leave them in an unacceptable condition. As an example of what can be seen, one Essex oyster smack had distinctly heavy shrouds secured with large turnbuckles and shackles to massive chainplates, each of which was fastened to the shear strake with three short No. 12 woodscrews! Luckily, her keel-stepped mast was sound and of such proportions that, with her cut-down triangular mainsail, the shrouds were not called on to do much real work.

One of the dangers of converting from gaff to Bermudian rig, so popular today, is that the loading of the mast and rigging may be totally different. Many gaff masts are designed to take the forces from the sails and transmit them to the hull via the mast step in the keel and the main beams and mast partners. The loading on the shrouds may be negligible and indeed some types of gaff-rigged craft, such as the North American 'cat boats', have no shrouds. If attempts are made to convert such boats to Bermudian rig, either the rig must be of low efficiency, really little more than a storm-trysail rig, or the shrouds will have to start doing some real work in holding up the rig and carrying the sailing forces.

Attempts to hold the top of a keel-stepped mast in one place relative to the hull can result in the mast trying to bend between the deck and the shroud attachment-points, giving rise to complex S bends in the mast, which may fail because of the compressive forces it has to carry. This failure can be avoided either by converting to a deck-stepped mast, or leaving out the wedges so that the mast is no longer acting partly as a strut cantilevered out from keel and deck, but is free to bend in a simple curve from its heel to the shrouds. Clearly, in either case the shrouds must take both the heeling and driving loads generated by the sail plan.

The loading on the shrouds (and hence the chainplates) can be guestimated very easily. If the boat is a beamy, shoal-draft type (other than a dinghy in which the crew sit out), it may be assumed that, as the boat heels over, the centre of buoyancy will move outboard (to leeward) about a quarter of the beam of the boat. Thus the overturning force heeling the boat must be the weight of the boat multiplied by a quarter of the beam. This force is applied at the chainplates which are roughly half the beam from the centre line, so the average direct loading on the chainplates must equal half the weight of the boat.

On a deep-keeled boat a different approach can be adopted. The chainplates can be assumed to be at one end of a bell-crank lever system, with the ballast keel at the other end and the lever system pivoting about the centre of the hull. Some very wild approximations of angles of heel, ballast ratio (the percentage of the total weight of the hull represented by the ballast) and the ratio of half beam to depth of the hull, give an impression that the direct steady-state loading on the chainplates will again approximate to half the weight of the boat.

Such crude exercises in load calculating are of interest in that they reveal the terrible inadequacies all too often found in chainplates, but they give no idea of the actual strength required, which must be

adequate to withstand the shock-loading imparted to the rigging under real sailing conditions. As anyone who has watched a modern ocean racer in rough going will realise, these shock loads can be very much greater than the mean direct load.

Being far too lazy to get involved with reams of calculations of moments of inertia and wind forces, the author merely assumes that the combined strength of the chainplates on one side of the hull must be greater than that necessary to support the total sea-going weight of the hull, and if the design can ensure that the entire boat can safely be hoisted on a crane by any one chainplate, all should be well and the rig should remain attached to the hull in rough weather.

Whatever the rights and wrongs of such approximations, it is evident that chainplates need to be very securely fastened to the hull. Bolts through the planking and a frame provide the best fastening, and the more planks which can be spanned by the chainplates the better. External chainplates which run well down the topsides can look unsightly, and can also increase the drag when the boat heels, so there is a tendency to restrict their length or to fit them inside the planking. Fairly short external chainplates can have their fastenings to the hull reinforced by fitting three or four bolts through the planks and frame to an internal plate which continues down the frame to distribute the loading over a greater area of the hull. Internal chainplates cause problems where they pass through the deck, but if the slot in the deck is well caulked and stopped, then a hardwood pad with a suitable slot is well bedded down and screwed to the deck, and this slotted pad is then caulked very hard to the chainplate, leaking can be eliminated. The block is prevented from splitting by a pair of stout transverse rivets beyond each end of the slot.

The chainplates and their securing bolts should be of a metal which matches the hull fastenings, ie bronze or gunmetal on copper-fastened boats, and galvanised-iron plates with steel bolts on iron-fastened hulls.

All other metal fittings on the boat should

be examined to see if there are any mixed metals involved which have been causing hidden corrosion. Any fittings which it is suspected might have been made of brass should also be checked. A fairly hefty clout with a hammer on a part which will not be hurt by being slightly bent or dented, will distinguish between gunmetal or good quality bronze and brass which has become de-zincified over the years.

In some yachting circles there is a tendency to look down on galvanised-iron fittings, but if the iron is of good quality, was properly hot-dip galvanised, and is further protected with oil, varnish, or even the somewhat garish looking 'silver' paint, such fittings will last for years, even outlasting the rest of the boat. Personally, the author would restrict the use of ordinary cast iron to ballast, using spheroidal graphite iron for any 'working' fittings which are to be cast. Wrought iron is an excellent material, but really good quality Swedish wrought iron is rare these days, which is a good reason for keeping any old iron fittings well galvanised and protected – they may be irreplaceable!

Mild steel is stronger than iron, but is much more susceptible to corrosion. Welded fittings can vary enormously in strength, depending on the skill of the welder and the care taken in making the welds. Some welded fittings such as mastbands, cranse irons, and boom-end fittings which have eyes welded to bands, can be extremely weak, with only a partial fillet of weld round the outside of what looks to be a large area of joint. Any such hollow welds can be corroding internally from the residues of chemicals used in the galvanising process, and it is only when the fitting fails that the extent of the corrosion is revealed. If the pedigree of any such fittings is not known, periodic shock-load testing with a hammer of appropriate weight may reveal a fitting which might be likely to fail in the near future.

It is a sound policy to remove metal fittings from a wooden hull periodically to examine both the back of the fitting and the wood beneath it. It is not unknown for an apparently sound fitting on a newly painted boat to be hiding a substantial amount of rust and wood decay.

Never be gentle with chainplates, jib-sheet fairleads, tracks for moving fairleads and other such fittings when working on a boat. If they will not stand a clout with a hammer or a good pull, they should be refitted. It is much better to find the weak spots when the boat is ashore than when she is out at sea.

Part five

Miscellaneous

Chapter 18

Rudders

Rudders and their mountings vary widely, as does the amount of repair likely to be needed. Luckily, the possibility of work being needed on a rudder varies more or less inversely with the difficulty of getting at it. The somewhat massive rudders fitted to older deep-draft, counter-stern boats generally escape damage; but transom-hung rudders, especially the broader, shallower variety, are a fruitful field for minor – and major – repairs. Lift-off, drop-blade rudders sometimes seem to have been invented to guarantee continuity of employment for boat repairers.

Fixed-blade rudders

The main-post of a deep, heavy rudder might be a candidate for attack by rot or worm where it passes up through the rudder trunking, but this is very rare. Usually any damage is to the blade or the lower bearings.

If decay of the upper rudder-post is suspected, the rudder will have to be dropped out and inspected, and unless it was known that this was going to be done when the boat was brought ashore, there is an even chance of a good session with spade and pickaxe being necessary to allow the head of the rudder-post to clear the underside of the counter.

These old-style rudders are usually made from three hefty pieces of wood, one for the post and two for the blade. The pieces are usually fitted together with long iron dumps and bound with iron straps. Separating the pieces can prove difficult as the dumps may be well rusted into the wood and, unless there are very good reasons for retaining part of the original, the best course is usually to make a copy of the old rudder. If the original had a brass band round the head with the boat's name engraved on it, this band should be transferred to the new replacement.

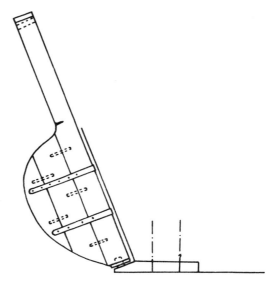

Fig 199   *Rudder fitting through trunking in the counter, and resting on pin in end of false keel*

Some rudders of this type are held up merely by an extended false keel to which is fitted a pivot pin which engages in a bearing plate fitted on the lower end of the rudder-post (Fig 199). The portion of the false keel which carries the pin may have to be unbolted to release the rudder. On other boats the rudder is held in place by one or more metal straps bolted to the sides of the keel and deadwood, and which pass through a slot or slots between the rudder-post and the first timber of the blade, the post being rounded off into the slots to allow free rotation in the strap (Fig 200). When such a rudder is being replaced, it may be possible to re-use the original metal straps. Iron straps which are normally permanently below water do not corrode rapidly in the absence of any galvanic action, and often a good clean and re-galvanising is all that is needed.

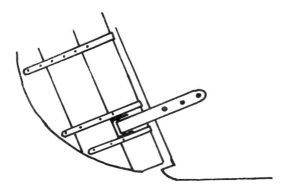

Fig 200 *Strap bearing around rudder-post*

One possible reason why a rudder may have to be remade is because the original has been modified so that it can no longer perform its function properly. It is not unknown for an old sailing boat to have been converted to a motor-sailor at some stage in its history. Such conversions often involved the fitting of a large, slow-turning screw on the centre-line of the hull, so a large aperture had to be cut out of the rudder to clear this screw. Possibly later a newer, faster engine swinging a much smaller propeller may have been fitted, leaving the large gaping hole in the rudder doing nothing. Or rather, the hole does nothing until the boat begins to heel in a bit of a blow, and to develop weather helm. Then the hole acts as a pressure release, and the sideways force developed by the rudder, instead of holding the stern up into wind, is dissipated through the hole, and the boat becomes totally unmanageable.

More-modern deep rudders may be built up on a metal tube or solid rod which runs up through the counter in a flanged metal tube. Their blades are usually built up between straps brazed or welded to the metal post. The wooden parts of such a rudder are easily replaced, the work being done with the rudder still in place on the hull. There can be problems if the metal post has got bent. In this event, the best solution is to find an engineering company who can offer the services of a large hydraulic press, and hope the bill will not be too large. Unskilled efforts to remove one bend often result only in making more bends.

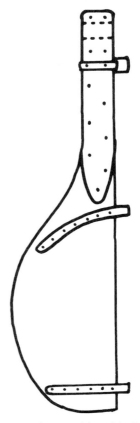

Fig 201 *Transom-hung rudder with single-plank blade and reinforcing side-cheeks*

Transom-hung rudders usually present no problems in repairs, once the discovery has been made that they are often distinctly heavier than they look and feel when they are hanging in place. Older boats and boats with broad rudders may use the same build as the older deep-draft rudders, with a wooden post and two or more planks in the blade; but many boats of around 10 tonnes (tons) have the blade and post cut from a single stout plank of elm or mahogany with side-cheeks which reinforce the upper part of the rudder and continue up to form a socket for the tiller (Fig 201). On such rudders a broken aft-edge of the blade can be repaired by cleaning off the edge and fitting a large graving piece with suitable metal reinforcing pins. Broken side-cheeks are best replaced completely, as they have to convey all the steering forces from the tiller to the blade. The side-

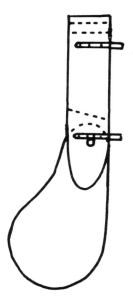

Fig 202 *Drop-blade rudder with pivot bolt at top of blade*

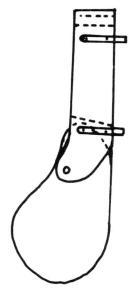

Fig 203 *Drop-blade rudder with pivot bolt at bottom of stock*

cheeks should be riveted on, with alternate rivets put in from opposite sides. If a replacement rudder is being made, the side-cheeks should be glued to the blade with resorcinol resin.

Drop-blade rudders

Drop-blade rudders may develop excessive side play in the blade as the stresses of sailing gradually force open the lower end of the rudder stock. There is little that can be done to improve an old rudder with this defect; the only really effective remedy is to make a new one. If the blade is metal, it can usually be used again if it is not badly pitted with rust. The pivot hole might need to be cleaned up, in which case a larger diameter bolt will have to be used. Some drop-blade rudders are designed with the bolt fairly high up in the blade, relying on the side of the stock below the bolt to take the side forces on the blade (Fig 202). For maximum durability, the bolt-hole should be re-positioned as low and as far aft in the stock as possible, relying on the portion of the blade above the bolt, and the stiffness of the blade, to transmit the side thrusts to the stock which is then prevented from opening out by the pivot bolt (Fig 203).

When a new stock for a drop-blade rudder is being made, the two side-pieces should be cut from radially sawn timber, that is, cut from a plank which passes through the centre of the tree. Do not try and use the middle of such a plank, as the very centre of the tree may be dead and brittle, and avoid using any sapwood. If the cheeks are cut from slash-sawn timber (timber from a plank cut near the edge of the tree), the cheeks will warp and either jam against the blade or leave wider edges to the slot, which will allow the blade to slop about. Timber will always try to warp in a direction which will straighten the annual growth rings, and the use of radially sawn timber ensures that the sides of the slot between the cheeks will remain parallel.

The socket for the tiller should be cut into the inner faces of each cheek; the cheeks are then glued and riveted together with a filler piece slightly thicker than the blade. The holes for the pivot bolt should be drilled oversize, and the bolt fitted with large washers with a thin-walled tube between them. The tube is carefully cut to length so that when the bolt is tightened hard down, the washers are in contact with the side-cheeks and prevent the slot from opening, but the tube prevents the bolt from being tightened until the slot is closed up to bind on the plate. A castellated nut should be used, and the bolt should be cross-drilled to take a split pin. The loss of a pivot bolt when out at sea can be most embarrassing, and it is unlikely to happen just after one has been practising sailing the boat without a rudder and steering only by the set of the sails! Owners of seagoing boats with drop-blade rudders are well advised to practise this art of rudderless sailing, and also to check the rudder cheeks and pivot bolt at frequent intervals.

Chapter 19

Changing the size of the boat

When an old boat needs major repair work on the hull, an owner might think about altering the size of the boat whilst making the repairs. Many counter-sterned boats have their size altered in the course of repair work, when it is decided to cut off the tip of the counter rather than to rebuild the whole end of the boat. Any such shortening of a hull is obviously a relatively simple job, but it is not widely appreciated that increasing the size of a hull is not always as difficult as it might seem. A not inconsiderable number of working boats were lengthened as their owners decided they needed something larger.

Changing the size of a boat requires very careful consideration on two scores. First there is the effect on the sailing qualities of the boat; secondly there is the actual amount of work to be done, and the return that can be expected from that work. It could well prove that it would take less effort to build a new hull than to make radical changes to an old one. There are several advantages to building a new hull, chief of which are that the old boat is available for sailing while the new one is being built, and that once the new one is finished the old one can be sold. However, if the old hull needs to be repaired anyway, the balance changes.

There are four basic ways in which a boat can be enlarged: by widening the hull; by lengthening amidships; by lengthening the ends; and by raising the top. The beam can be increased by cutting the boat in half lengthwise, opening out the stern and fitting new tapering garboards and new floors across the hull at every frame. Usually the stern would need to be extended to achieve a reasonable shape to the modified hull. The author has not heard · of this being done on what might be called a serious sailing boat, but only on small dinghies.

Lengthening amidships was often described as having the hull sawn in half, the ends dragged apart, and a new section built in. The actual process is slightly more complex, because to maintain strength, the joints in the keel, planks and stringers need to be well staggered and, if the hull is to maintain reasonably sweet lines with no bad flats, the frames, at least over the midships third of the hull, need to be re-spaced.

The ends can be lengthened by replacing an upright stem with a raked or curved clipper-stem, and a transom stern can be extended into a counter. Both of these extensions give more deck space, and usually result in a drier hull in rough water, but they both involve considerable re-planking, extra frames and new decking.

Most enlargements to old boats are made by increasing the height. One neat way of doing this is to replace all deck beams with new beams with more camber, and a more cambered cabin top. New bulkheads, cabin front, and cockpit back will have to be made, but the original cabin and cockpit sides can be re-used, as can most of the deck planking. Such re-decking can make a surprising difference to the comfort below without significantly altering external appearance.

Many small cruisers of 5 tonnes (tons) and under were built with conventional side-decks and a fairly narrow coachroof. The comfort aboard such boats can be greatly increased by extending the cabin top out to the sides of the hull and forward beyond the mast step. The topsides can be raised from the aft-cabin bulkhead right to the stem, but the work involved is considerably easier if the original foredeck is left in place possibly to the deck beam forward of the mast beam. From this beam aft to the cabin bulkhead, the old decking is stripped off; the sockets in the beam shelves are plugged, and extension frames are fitted beside the original frames. Usually the extensions are run down as far as the bilge stringer. New beam shelves are fitted over the length of the extension, and the new full-width deck fitted. The opportunity can be taken to increase slightly the deck camber, and to fit higher slides for the main hatch. If a beading is run round the hull at the level of the old deck edge, and the added planks are varnished instead of being painted the same colour as the topsides, again the change in the appearance of the boat is not too great, but the gain in space below will be considerable.

One of the most interesting extensions known to the author was done in the early 1960s by a member of the Old Gaffers Association. Stan Wood (now Lindsey-Wood) took his 24 foot cutter *Sea Breeze* ashore to enlarge the accommodation. *Sea Breeze* had started life in 1873 as a copy of a US Lakes 'cat boat', and had been progressively converted to a pretty little low-freeboard cutter, with a new deck and coachroof fitted in 1950. Stan's enlargement, which is believed to be unique, was done by cutting through the hull horizontally; raising the entire deck and cabin top 254 mm (10 in) on chain hoists; fitting extension frames and stem, and filling in the gap with a couple of extra larch planks each side. Stan also altered the shape of the centreboard, cutting down the height of the case, and fitting iron strap floors. The increase in freeboard improved rather than detracted from the appearance of the hull, and it certainly did not spoil her sailing performance as *Sea Breeze* continued to win prizes in the hard-fought Old Gaffers races in the Solent. It is worth noting that at the time of writing, she is being fitted out for her 108th year, which shows the sort of life which can be had from a wooden hull. She is not the oldest boat which takes part in Old Gaffers races. One wonders how many of the GRP 'replicas' launched in 1973 will be around in the year 2080.

Acknowledgements

Writing this book has brought back memories of many friends who have helped me to acquire knowledge of boats and their construction. There are so many of these friends that it is not possible to name them all. I hope that all those not named here will accept my heartfelt thanks for their part in making this book possible, and will not feel offended that I have selected only a few for special mention.

For continued help and encouragement over the years, I must record my debt of gratitude to the late Jack Feesey, of Dan Webb and Feesey, Maldon, and to his yard staff, Jim Barbrooke, Frank Parke, Peter Wright, Roy Pitt, John Yardley, and 'Tubby' Wright, all of whom taught me so much. There were also many owners in the yard who gave help, encouragement, advice and instruction; owners like Frank Ducker, Reg Hopkins, Roy Clark, the late Len Clarke, and Sam Poulton of the Maldon Little Ship Club.

More recently, many members of the Old Gaffers Association have helped with stimulating correspondence and discussions. For their help with the actual preparation of this book, I must thank O.G.A. President Michael Millar, and founder member Stan Lindsey-Wood for the loan of photographs of their work; my wife for typing the manuscript and help with correspondence; Ted Pearce and his colleagues of the Island Cruising Club for their most helpful and encouraging comments on the draft, and last but by no means least James Mac-Gibbon and the staff of David and Charles Ltd for making the transition from typescript to finished book such a pleasant process.

JOHN A. SCARLETT
Galashiels, 1980

Index

Numbers in *italics* refer to photographs